His Loving Touch

Miracles and Healings

Elaine Balestrini Vizard

Copyright © 2023 Elaine Balestrini Vizard

All Rights Reserved

ISBN: 978-1-962108-00-3

Cover Design by Elaine Balestrini Vizard and Son Joseph Vizard

This publication is a Memoir focused on my family of four generations. Some names have been changed to protect the privacy of those who have died. Most names have not changed, though I expect some wish they had a more interesting, name. Any resemblance to actual persons living or dead is intended.

This is a work of love that took many years in the making, filled with true stories, no fabrications. It is written to inform, warn, and hopefully entertain you the reader.

HIS LOVING TOUCH

Healings, Miracles

Elaine Balestrini Vizard

Beatrice Frenette Balestrini

Dedication

-I lovingly dedicate this book to God who patiently waited for me to fulfill His request.

-To my mother who was steadfast in believing that the Holy Spirit was our guide, our thoughts, our hands, our words as we wrote.

-To my husband, Dave and our children who believed when all too often I wanted to quit, and did after my mother died.

-To my sister, MaryAnn who encouraged me every step of the way, babysat, and paid a scamming agent to help find a publisher.

-To my good friend, Roni who gifted me with my first typewriter to begin my work because she believed in me.

Acknowledgement

I am grateful to God for asking me to write this book, and for His faith in me to see it to completion. There are no words to describe the amount of work and research that went in to writing a book, but what God asks, you do. I am thankful for all those whose stories built this beautiful memoir. I am eternally awed and thankful.

About the Author

Elaine Balestrini Vizard was a Charge Nurse for 36 years, caring for the elderly and their relating diseases, especially Alzheimer's, until she was injured, which ended her nursing career. She is married, mother of five, grandmother to ten; five boys and five girls. She started writing in high school where she received many accolades. Elaine became a freelance writer published in newspapers and magazines. She was also a book review editor for The Bread of Life Magazine for eight years. Eventually she dedicated her free time to writing this book, and is currently working on another book about her daughter, Mary who was diagnosed with a rare heart defect at age four, so rare she was one of five in the world.

Preface

I wrote this book from its beginning to tell the true stories of a supernatural God, a God who loves His people, a God who shows his softer side through His son Jesus. God desires a personal relationship with us and through His son Jesus we are offered that opportunity.

I am not a teacher, a preacher, or a minister, I am you, an average person, a daughter, sister, Nurse, wife, mother grandmother Aunt, and friend.

I have come to know the God who called me by name, the God who gave me life and placed me in a Catholic/Christian family. There are many reasons for my growth in Christ and as you read this book you will come to know the many reasons why I have a heart for Jesus.

This book tells the many true stories of God's supernatural power in the ordinary lives of my family and friends. Some are extremely personal but necessary to understand the depth of the many gifts God gave, and continues to give us.

I pray and hope you reach out to the God I have come to know. A God who makes the impossible, possible.

Introduction

How this book came about was a miracle, to say the least, and is the first story within this collection of many miracles and healings.

It began as a simple car ride to Sick Kids Hospital in London, Ontario, Canada. It was a two-hour drive and as per usual on these visits for my daughter Mary's checkups, we listened to the radio, played games, or just sat in quiet reflection.

All the way to the hospital I had an uneasy feeling which wasn't new as I often worried if the doctor would find some new, rare condition that seemed to plague my daughter's life. Although I was, and continue to be a strong Christian, my belief's in putting my worries into God's very capable hands became like a football game. I would visualize in my thoughts handing it over to God then ran as fast as I could but then I would look back and run toward God grabbing the football-worry was back in my arms. I would then run with it ignoring the voice in my heart asking me to stop and trust Him.

Trusting takes growth in every relationship, but in my relationship with God my failures became stepping stones to trust. Failure is maybe too strong a word, they were more moments of answered prayer, moments of spending time with God, and like Martha and Mary in the Bible Jesus tells Martha what is more important.

Luke 10:38-42

"As Jesus and his disciples were on their way, he came to a village where a woman named Martha opened her home to him.39 She had a sister called Mary, who sat at the Lord's feet listening to what he said.40 But Martha was distracted by all the preparations that had to be made. She came to him and asked, "Lord, don't you care that my sister has left me to do the work by myself? Tell her to help me!"

41"Martha, Martha," the Lord answered, "you are worried and upset about many things, 42 but few things are needed—or indeed only one. Mary has chosen what is better, and it will not be taken away from her."

I often found myself lacking, being Martha, instead of Mary. It takes time to grow that relationship, and it is often sporadic. The more time I listened and sat quietly in His presence the more His voice became familiar to me.

Sometimes it is a whisper, sometimes it sounds like thunder, but most often it is a quiet still voice within my spirit.

After our daughter's appointment I walked to the car breathing easier knowing her condition had stayed the same. Would I ever be able to breathe normal again? We had a custom of stopping at a quaint restaurant before we left London to go home. It was a time to gather our thoughts, relieve our stress while enjoying each other and eat some delicious food. It was always the same restaurant with a fireplace, and depending on the weather we usually chose the table in front of the fireplace. Dave and I always wondered if we were doing the right thing by eating at a restaurant as our finances were not the best. It might not have been the right thing financially but it was good for our bodies and souls.

Mary fell asleep on our way home, while Dave and I sat quietly, both of us in our own personal thoughts. That's when it happened, that small still voice of God spoke to my spirit.

"Elaine, your mother is in the hospital for her heart but she is fine. I want you to write a book with her telling of the healings and miracles within your family."

Did I just hear that correctly? Of course, my thoughts went to my mother but was this a growing time? I have learned through the years if what I hear is from God then it will come to pass. I immediately told Dave who believed as I did, he took a quick side glance and nodded saying "okay," both of us knowing if it was from God, we would know on our return home. I sat thinking and praying about it for the rest of the drive home.

Entering our driveway my sister Mary Ann who was babysitting, flew out the front door clearly distraught over the news of our mother. I hugged her shaking body and immediately told her what I had heard in the car, even though I was unsure myself

She pulled away to look at me with a shocked expression saying with a shaky voice "that's true, mom is in the hospital! Suddenly realizing my complete sentence, she grabbed my shoulders while her tears fell on to her arms, "You said mom was going to be okay, right?"

"I hope so," let's talk more in the car."

By the time we arrived at the hospital, some thirty minutes away, I quickly drove into the parking lot grabbing the ticket that would tell how long we stayed. As I finally found a parking spot and pulled in, I realized I didn't have any money. I must have said it aloud, as MaryAnn frantically told me not to worry about it as she opened the car door, slammed it shut and quickly walked to the emergency room entrance. I have never seen my sister move so fast, by the time I caught up with her she had already found out mom had been admitted to a room and the number.

We literally ran to the elevators, and I was so thankful one opened immediately, or I think my sister would have become super woman prying the elevator doors apart.

We reached mom's room, both of us trying to get through the doorway together. I heard my dad's laugh suggesting we come in one at a time. It was comical looking back, as my sister and I were not slender in any means of that word.

We found mom sitting comfortably in her hospital bed, with a smile on her face, amused at our antics of trying to get through the doorway together.

Dad sat at her side visibly struggling to pull himself together, as my brothers stood quietly fighting to keep their laughter from escaping their smiling faces. I am sure they were all very worried, but it seems the doorway incident broke the tension.

"How are you mom?" my sister and I asked at the same time.

Again laughter, "you're eleven months apart, you're not twins. You don't have to do everything together," my oldest brother said with a lopsided smile.

I laughed but quickly put all my attention on mom.

Before I said anything I looked at my sister who said "you first."

I looked at my mom who was smiling, "how are you mom?"

"I feel good now," she responded, "but first tell us how Mary's appointment went."

I explained that everything was the same, no changes. The family was relieved that Mary was stable. I was more than relieved that mom was fine, just as God had said

I was anxious, I needed to talk with my mom about what had happened. She must have felt my need and after thirty minutes she asked the family to leave us alone as we needed to talk.

"Why don't you go to the cafeteria and get something to eat," she suggested. Dad, knowing what mom needed to talk about encouraged everyone to leave, "my treat." he added, and everyone left closing the door behind them.

As soon as the door was shut mom quickly said, "Elaine, I have something unbelievable and so amazing to tell you."

"I do too mom," and I started to speak as I sat on her bed holding her hand. "No Elaine," mom said, "let me talk first."

I stopped talking so mom could begin.

"My heart was racing and beating irregularly, so your dad rushed me to the hospital. I was taken into emergency quickly and hooked up to many machines. I was so afraid and felt horrible, there were doctors and nurses working on me all at once. The monitors beeped loudly and there was much talking and activity and then something amazing, actually miraculous happened. The machines and conversations seemed to fade away, I thought I was dying, then I began to hear another voice talking to me.

I smiled knowing where her conversation was going.

"This is so hard to explain," mom continued, "if it didn't happen to me, I would find it hard to believe. As I was saying, all the noises faded away and I heard God talking to me in my spirit. I knew it was His voice I had heard that small still voice before.

He said, "Beatrice, I want you to write a book with Elaine, about all the healings and miracles within your lives." After that all the voices and machines came back to life but God had given me peace knowing my heart would be fine. It seems just after I became aware of all the noises returning my heart started beating regularly and I looked at the big clock on the wall, it was 3:15 p.m."

With that she looked at me asking why I was smiling.

"I'm smiling because your story is my story."

Mom's eyes grew wide as she looked at me, I could almost see those wheels turning in her mind, she wasn't confused, she was startled and amazed at the same time.

I then continued to tell her everything that God said to me, even to the point where I too looked at the clock, 3:15 p.m.

As we sat there in quiet each with our own deep thoughts. We knew that this was a miracle, yet the gravity of what God was asking became an unimaginable, work I was not ready for.

"Mom," I said, "I believe this is from God, but you're not a writer and although I write I am not a professional. How is this going to work? How am I going to write a book, I work almost full time, I am married, mother of four, and with Mary so ill, when am I going to find the time to do all that He has asked of us. We need to write all the stories down, yours and mine, and where are we going to find the time to do this?"

I sat looking at my mother with tears streaming down my cheek. I could not grasp the reasoning of why God would ask us to do this.

"Elaine," mom took my hands, "God has asked us in an undeniable way to do this. He will see us through this, with the power of the Holy Spirit, He will guide us in this. I don't know why He has asked us, but we will do it. There is no questioning His request, and we must obey."

I knew mom was right, but so many questions were now filling my mind. Questions that could not be answered. I know mom was overcome with the immensity of this unquestionable project too, but she was right, there was no denying His request.

Looking at each other, yet not seeing we sat silent until we realized God had said one more thing and we spoke it aloud at the same time. "Psalm 96:1-4," okay that was a little spooky. God had given us the proof of what He was asking us to do. Mom had her Bible and we looked up this passage.

Psalm 96:1-4

1) Sing a new song to the Lord!

Sing to the Lord, all the earth!

2) Sing to the Lord!

Bless His name!

Proclaim His deliverance every day!

3) Declare His glory among the nations

and his awesome deeds among all the peoples!

4) For the Lord is great,

and greatly to be praised;

He is awesome above all gods.

And so it began, in the face of all difficulties, all blocks and detours, His Loving Touch was born.

Photos With Mom

Contents

Dedication i

Acknowledgement ii

About the Author iii

Preface iv

Introduction vi

Chapter One

Socks vs Covid 19 1

Chapter Two

The Piano 5

Chapter Three

Aunt Nellie 15

Chapter Four

Home Again 30

Chapter Five

Two White Rosaries 57

Chapter Six

After The Honeymoon 67

Chapter Seven

A Touch of Hell 77

Chapter Eight

I Was Blind but Now I See 120

Chapter Nine

Grandpa and the Madonna 151

Chapter Ten

Unexpected Healing: And was that An Angel 165

Chapter Eleven

Heavenly Visit...189

Chapter Twelve

Jesus and Mae..211

Chapter Thirteen

Aunt Gert 246

Chapter Fourteen

Wedding, Sex and Pregnancy..257

Chapter Fifteen

A Common Miracle? 302

Chapter Sixteen

Weight, and Wait!..359

Chapter Seventeen

Daddy, You Forgot Me 391

Chapter Eighteen

I Will Pay the Price 428

Chapter Nineteen

Choices Made..464

Am I Christian or Catholic? or Both..485

Epilogue..498

Chapter One
Socks vs Covid 19

Healings and Miracles come in all sizes, from what we feel is a small answered prayer, or a large one. I don't believe that God puts them in that category. For instance, I had prayed for some socks to come in the mail for my grandson's birthday. He was into Star Wars and since it was during the current Pandemic of 2020/21/22 known as Covid-19 and all its variants I often shopped on Amazon. This Pandemic was difficult on every family all over the world as we were all under restrictions. No socializing, stay at home orders, no visiting family members. We couldn't see our children, grandchildren and all family members unless we used the internet to Skype or Facetime on Facebook. This was difficult because you couldn't hug them, kiss their cheeks, talk face to face. Because of this it became more important to me to make sure my gifts were personal and always loving. I have always made personal cards for each birthday, but now it became extremely important to up my game, so to speak.

Gabe my grandson loved the dark side of Star Wars, the side I was not a fan of. As I searched Amazon I found Star Wars socks, ones with the words written on the bottom of the feet, 'If you are reading this I have gone to the dark side. I hesitated to buy them with another Star War themed pair of socks. I called my son Joe to ask him if this gift would be appropriate to give to Gabe. Joe didn't think there was anything wrong in getting them so I ordered them.

Covid-19 had played a big part in delaying deliveries as everyone was shopping online. As Gabe's twelfth birthday approached the socks had not yet arrived. Amazon had sent me an email stating the socks were delayed. the evening before Gabe's birthday. I knew what this meant, they were probably lost. As I lay in bed that night, I spoke to God as I often do throughout the day.

Lord, I know it isn't important in the grand theme of things, but it is important to me. Lord, please bring the socks tomorrow Thank you, Jesus." When I woke the next morning, Dave was already up and pointed to a package that had arrived from Amazon. Did I dare believe God would answer my very unimportant prayer? Yes, I knew God cared for everything, but socks? As I opened the package there, they were, two pairs of Star Wars socks. Although I have been the recipient of many an answered prayer but this took my breath away. I had known in reality that this was almost impossible, especially during the Pandemic where everything was stopped and or slowed. But there they were Gabe's gift, and my spirit soared at this simple but great little miracle God had given me, restoring joy to my heart at knowing He heard and He answered. I guess God had a sense of humor, I mean He was God and I am sure the dark side didn't fit into His realm of holiness, but my prayer was answered and Gabe loved his gift. My husband had to bring the gift and card to his house leaving it on the front porch so the protocols to stay six feet away and have no personal contact was obeyed. So, this wasn't easy, but in the face of this dark menacing virus which was killing thousands, had to be obeyed to protect all our loved ones. The prayers of many for God to end this crippling pandemic of Covid-19 and all its variants has not been answered miraculously. But it is being answered through the wisdom He gives to scientists, researchers, and the daunting task to find a vaccine. They did and currently many people are receiving them. A miracle? Yes, God and Science, God and Doctors are not in competition with each other. I believe God gives us wisdom and the talents to also answer prayers. Sure, God could eradicate a virus but often He uses us to answer prayers. I hope by the time you read this Covid-19 will have fallen off the earth, written in history, never to

To God Be The Glory

Chapter Two
The Piano

Healings and Miracles come in many different forms. When I was overcome with the medical problems of two of my children, I needed an outlet, that's where the piano became a melodic symphony of God's grace.

The piano comforted my fearful mind, my unsettled body, my restless spirit. The Piano comforted my soul and flowed gently to the ears of my children as they fell asleep. in their beds. This was my harbor in the storm. Having two children with heart defects I was in need of a comforting instrument and the Lord opened that door.

I vaguely remember the details of how the piano came to be. But there it was, and having just received our Income Tax refund it was at the right price we could afford, Knowing the burden of our finances I struggled to allow myself this selfish pleasure. What kind of wife and mother was I to desire buying such a frivolous object? I felt shallow, irresponsible and impractical. I had always desired to learn how to play the piano, but when this opportunity came to buy it, I hesitated. Dave's words changed my mind, "Elaine, we have been praying for you to have a piano, and I believe our refund and the piano at the price they are asking is not a coincidence, it is God's timing, and we're buying it". That day Dave made the call to the small music store owned by a church friend. He offered to deliver it free, and that was that, two days later the piano sat perfectly in our front room. I now had to learn to play it.

Not far from where I lived was a rather boring, rectangle, medium sized, plain reddish-brown brick building, situated beside the school and church hall. Our church and all the buildings were built of the same brick and were easy to be found as they were all located on the main street of our small town. Our town was like any other town in Ontario Canada. We celebrated all holidays with decorations and parades, where the excitement of candy being thrown into the crowds lining the street were caught and quickly picked up by the many children, and yes adults too. You couldn't walk down main street without being met by many a friendly face, where conversations were had as if time was no issue. I loved that small town, and I loved that rectangle building. In that building housed offices for meetings and other small functions but most of all it was the home for three Catholic Nuns who were very active in my Church. As you walked in the front door to the right was a small chapel with an altar. It was always open but could be closed off with a folding divider. This little chapel seemed to fill the whole building with a sense of holiness, a feeling you were standing on Holy ground, and the smell that greeted you was from soft flowing scented candles that seemed to penetrate your very soul.

This building was a place of comforting peace, where the only noise that could be heard was the creaking on the upstairs floor as somebody walked.

Sister Agnes lived there, a person I rarely saw but that changed one night as I sat in a church pew waiting for my parents and a friend after attending a Healing Mass. Many people had left but there were others who remained to pray or talk to members of the healing team.

As I sat quietly reading my Bible, I became aware of someone entering the pew in which I sat.

"Mrs. Vizard, would you mind if I sat beside you?"

Looking up I was surprised to see Sister Agnes.

"Of course, Sister, please do." I had little contact with Sister Agnes, she always seemed aloof, not in a rude way, just more quiet and possibly shy. I had become good friends with another nun living in the small convent, Sister Rosalie was the complete opposite of Sister Agnes.

Sister Agnes was a pleasantly plump woman, while Sister Rosalie was a very thin almost fragile woman. Both were strong in faith but Sister Rosalie was more verbal about it, and more active in the community. Although Catholic they were more ecumenical, meaning open to all Christian churches, not just Catholics. We were/are all one in Christ.

Sister Agnes sat quietly beside me, and I being also shy, well, conversation didn't flow easily between us.

"How are you, Sister Agnes?" I said trying to break the silence.

"I am well Mrs. Vizard, and you?"

"Oh, please Sister, call me Elaine. Mrs. Vizard is too formal between friends," I smiled.

That was all it took and conversation flowed freely.

"Sister Rosalie has told me about your situation with your sick children. I hope you don't mind my saying?"

"Oh Sister, I am an open book, and Sister Rosalie has asked permission to tell others. I have no problem with that more prayers are always welcomed."

Sister Agnes continued, "She also told me about your piano and how you were using self-teaching books to learn to play."

I repositioned myself to look more clearly into her face, "I am Sister, but I find it difficult, although it says easy lessons on the cover," I laughed.

"Although you can self-teach, it isn't as easy as they profess it to be. I imagine it must be difficult to find the time with four young children to care for."

"It is Sister, but I somehow manage when they are otherwise occupied, like sleeping."

Sister Agnes smiled that shy radiant smile that brightened her face. When talking about the piano her whole demeanor changed. She became more animated, enthusiastic and excited, it was clearly a topic she loved.

"Mrs. Vizard, sorry, Elaine, you seem very interested in learning the piano, and I believe you know I give lessons at the Convent."

I nodded yes, "I was recently told this by Sister Rosalie, when I mentioned we bought a piano."

"I am so happy that we have been able to have this chat, and I hope you aren't offended with my asking you if you would like me to teach you to tickle those ivories?" as she said this her fingers moved as if playing a piano.

"Oh Sister, I would love that, but I honestly can't afford lessons and I don't want to become a burden as I can't promise I would be able to make time for them."

I didn't realize that my mom was sitting behind us, hearing everything that was said until she excitedly sat forward startling me as she spoke.

"Sister Agnes, I am Elaine's mother, Beatrice, and I know her dad and I would love to pay for the lessons."

I turned to look at my mother, "Mom, have you been behind me all this time? The last time I saw you, you were talking with Father Sam and praying over someone."

"Yes, I quietly sat behind you while you were praying, and I'm glad I did. I hope you don't mind my overhearing your conversation Sister Agnes?"

"Not at all, in fact I was aware someone was behind us. I am so happy to meet you Beatrice; I believe you were meant to hear the conversation."

I had to stop my mom, my parents couldn't afford piano lessons and I let Sister Agnes know this. "My parents are loving, generous people, but like my husband and I, they too struggle with finances. I am sorry Sister Agnes, but I have to decline your loving offer." I gave my mother a look in hopes she would not continue with this discussion.

"How much do you charge Sister Agnes?"

"Mom. Stop. Please!" I pleaded.

Sister Agnes softly touched my hands, "Elaine, why don't you go get some refreshments, and let your mother and I talk" I felt as if I was a student being dismissed, no longer part of the conversation, no longer in control. Reluctantly I left, feeling embarrassed at my mother's request, mom usually wasn't so bold.

But talk they did, working out a payment for the lessons. Mom later told me Sister Agnes had volunteered lessons for free, but mom insisted on paying something, and at a price that made them both very happy and in spite of my doubts, my piano lessons became a reality.

I didn't know how to feel, but before Sister Agnes left the church, she came to me saying she would work a schedule with me that would be flexible. I was so grateful and hugged this precious woman who gave me a most beautiful dream come true.

After Sister Agnes had left, mom and dad came to my side, I turned to hug them and dad whispered into my ear,

"Not a word." I understood dad's meaning and let the topic of the lessons go They drove me home and as Dave had stayed home to take care of our children, I quickly entered our home telling him about the evening's events, and he was somewhat less excited about it as I was, I guess he had to be there. However, he was happy that I was now able to have piano lessons.

Sister Agnes called me two days later and, it was arranged that once a week on a Saturday when my parents could babysit that I would sit with Sister Agnes learning the basics of piano playing. This was a slow process; one I would grow impatient with. I wanted to play beautiful music, symphonies that would suddenly come to life under my short, chubby stubby fingers. Sister Agnes disagreed with my assessment of my fingers, "You have fine fingers for playing Elaine, so don't use them as a means for not playing well. You just get frustrated too easy, but you will overcome that.

Eventually as I continued to practice, I graduated from the simple childhood songs like 'Happy Birthday', 'Old MacDonald' and others, to more pleasing melodies that challenged me, taking me to a place of comforting peace. It was a time when my doctor told me I needed a soothing outlet to help bring my blood pressure down, to replace the fearful pressures of the day with something I enjoyed. He suggested meditation, but God knew what I needed most: The Piano!

When I sat on the piano bench at home I was transported to a soothing, comforting world inside my spirit and mind. My physical situation didn't change, but my spirit soared like soft musical notes drifting toward heaven in praise.

Was the piano a miracle for me? Yes, and Sister Agnes was an added gift of love from God. I will always cherish those lessons, the moments where God took me to heavenly moments of pure enjoyment when I sat on my piano bench positioned my fingers and became a symphonic pianist. Well not symphonic, and not a true pianist, but in my world, at that moment that is exactly who I was.

A miracle? A healing? Yes, because God knew what I needed most, a place within my spirit that would soar to the heavens in melodic symphonies of Praise to the God whose Grace was forever present.

To God Be The Glory

Not me, but me in my mind.

Daughter Mary at recital

Our son Joey, making sweet noise

The Piano became a part of our home life. Celebrations, a place for decorations, and recitals, always in the background but always a peaceful harmony of love.

Mary teaching brother Adam

Our four children we had a fifth soon after.

Chapter Three
Aunt Nellie

Some miracles are not seen as miracles, sometimes it is how the person perceives it. How the miracle plays out in one's life, as in the story of my Great Aunt Nellie.

My mom Beatrice was born on June 18, 1917, the year before the Pandemic of 1918 -1920 struck Canada, killing fifty-five thousand Canadians.

Mom was the seventh child born to an average family at that time. Her mother stayed home while her dad worked as a metal worker building many high-rise buildings, until he fell four floors breaking his back. Luckily or miraculously, he wasn't paralyzed, but he was never the same again.

This began the years of hardship for her family, and at the tender age of 12 in 1929 the stock markets crashed on what was called Black Tuesday, leading to pandemonium. The rich became middle class, middle class became poor, and the poor became destitute in what was called the Great Depression. It was the worst economic downturn in history, at that time lasting a decade.

During this time my grandmother became pregnant with her 10th child, her first baby a ten-pound girl died at birth and sadly her tenth ended in the same way

Eugenie, Meme as I called her spent many a day and night looking out the window crying. Mom said she just stood there, didn't clean, didn't make meals, didn't tend to her family as was her daily routine. Meme went to her doctor but he was unable to help her pull out of this deep dark hole.

Eventually Meme was sent to a Psychiatric Hospital many miles away, where she would get the help she so desperately needed. Today we know this to be Postpartum Depression and can be very devastating as it was for Meme. We now know more on how to treat postpartum, which usually lasts four to six weeks, severe cases up to a year. Today, she probably would have been treated without being put in a hospital. The sad part about this was she was away from her children for five years. Why? Because during the era of the Great Depression hospitals were subsidized by the government with each patient they had, so she stayed much longer than she should have.

With Meme hospitalized eight children became too much for my grandfather to care for. The five boys were older and felt they could care for themselves, but the three girls were younger and were separated taken in by family members.

My mom went to stay with Meme's sister Nellie who lived on a farm with her large family. Mom calls this the greatest blessing of her life. Her mom and dad although Catholic were not strong in their faith, but her Aunt Nellie was a different story. Aunt Nellie's belief in God shone in every part of her life, and she remembers seeing this small, slightly chubby, blue-eyed woman get out of bed in the middle of the night, kneel, stretch her arms out and up and pray. It was there, in the presence of Aunt Nellie where mom learned the wonders of God's love.

An example of the bell mom rang for meals, and emergencies on the farm.

A family dinner on the farm

Aunt Nellie

My meme on left
Aunt Nellie on right

Mom, Where?
Age?
Young and Beautiful!

Mom age 17

approximately
age 25

During World War II Aunt Nellie's youngest son was sent overseas to fight the evil forces of hatred. Back then it was the German regime under Hitler.

Every night Aunt Nellie would kneel, praying to the Lord to bring her son safely home. Every day she dreaded that Official black car which she had seen drive up to neighbor's houses to inform them of the death of their loved one.

"Killed in action," they would say. One day would that happen to her? to the family? One day would that black car drive up in her dirt roadway?

Thankfully that car never appeared, and her son James came home, back into the embrace of his family.

And in the style of the prodigal son's return, the family celebrated his home coming by inviting friends and neighbors to share in their joy. As the days passed James joined in once again helping to care for the farm, but this didn't last very long.

Mom by then had left Aunt Nellie's home having a much different life as an adult. She however did go to visit Aunt Nellie and the family she had lived with for at least five years. Aunt Nellie had called mom to tell her of James' home coming, and asked her if she would like to visit and see James. Aunt Nellie always paid the train fare for mom to visit, and after two weeks' mom was able to take the time to go.

By then joy of James' return turned to worry and mom found in James a very different man, a man that she didn't recognize.

Aunt Nellie told mom that when James came home, he seemed fine and happy; but now just two weeks later he had become a stranger pulling away from the family.

Mom witnessed this for herself, when she greeted James with a big hug and smile. She was saddened by his response at seeing her, "he hugged me back, but there was no smile, he seemed distant and depressed, eager to get away from her. I knew what Aunt Nellie was worried about, and I too became quite concerned. This was not the cousin I had come to know. The cousin who welcomed me when I first arrived at Aunt Nellie's, the cousin who teased me as he taught me how to do some of the chores on the farm. One day he taught me to milk a cow, and when I finally became successful at getting the milk it didn't go into the pail, it squirted into James' face. I was worried that James would be angry, instead he laughed saying, "okay Bea, next time aim for the pail;" then faster than I could react he grabbed me, picking me up and threw me into a large loose pile of hay. By then we were both laughing so hard it caught the attention of Robert Aunt Nellie's oldest son who came over to us telling us to get back to work. I knew Robert wasn't angry because he always had this twinkle in his eyes and smirk on his face when amused.

James had also taught me how to ring the heavy cast iron triangle bell that stood just outside of the kitchen door to announce that the meals were ready. On the old bell was a rod with a hook on it and hung on the bell so it wouldn't be lost. It became my job not just to help make the meals but to ring the bell, and I always made sure that rod was hung back up where I found it. I also became aware of the second job the bell had, which was to announce an emergency, and I had to learn the specific ring so that the family and other farms knew help was needed."

Mom continued reminiscing but now her smile, her facial expression, became sad and her shoulders slumped in the memory she was about to share. I wanted to stop mom to tell me another day, as the sadness she expressed brought tears to my eyes.

Mom visited with Aunt Nellie and the family for two weeks, and every day James withdrew more, to the point where he stayed in his room most of the time. Aunt Nellie had the family doctor come to the house and talk with him, but the doctor just told the family to be patient, and gradually he would improve. One positive blessing was that 'James would sometimes eat with the family at dinner time.

Mom said the meals were "hearty and plenty. I am sure my brothers at home didn't have near the food I had living with Aunt Nellie. I often wondered back then how I could send them some of the food, but there was no way to do that, the farm was hundreds of miles away. Aunt Nellie sometimes sent some money to help them, and I hoped they would spend it in making sure they too had food to eat. During the depression food was scarce in facet many farmers lost everything, but somehow Aunt Nellie's farm flourished, and they always thanked God for their bounty, sharing their plenty throughout their community.

Three weeks after James came home, one week after I arrived, we all sat waiting to see if James would join us for breakfast. Aunt Nellie lived in hope that James would once again join them for all the meals. That morning Aunt Nellie asked her oldest daughter Anne to go ask James to come eat breakfast with the family. I remember so clearly when Anne climbed the stairs that were connected to the kitchen, James' room was at the top of the stairs. They always knew if James was awake by the sounds of activity coming from his upstairs bedroom. Aunt Nellie, closed her eyes, biting her lower lip, and I'm sure she was praying James would come. We heard Anne knock on his door and call his name repeatedly until we heard the creaking of a door opening. Did we dare hope that James was coming, or was he once again refusing to come? The silence was pierced with an ear shattering scream of horror, and with lightning speed everyone jumped up, overturning their chairs as they ran up the stairs. I stayed with Aunt Nellie as she continued to sit in silence. Robert called down to her to come to James' room. She knew without anyone saying a word what must have happened. As she slowly stood up, I ran to her side and we climbed the stairs, one at a time. Reaching James' room, the family had to step aside to let Aunt Nellie pass where Robert took hold of her arm and guided her to the chair beside James' bed. Aunt Nellie slowly placed her hand on James' chest, he was still, "he is gone," Aunt Nellie whispered. Everyone was crying but now their sobs became louder James was just twenty-five years old.

The family doctor was called and came immediately to their home. After examining James, he informed them that James likely died from shell shock (known today as post-traumatic stress disorder, PTSD.) James was deployed to fight on the Rock of Gibraltar and due to the constant bombing the doctor stated, "His heart just gave out."

"Beatrice, "Aunt Nellie asked," would you please go ring the bell to announce something serious has happened." I remembered the ring to do this, the very ring James had taught me, and his words "now don't get them wrong Bea, we don't want the neighbors rushing thinking it's an emergency, there isn't enough food to feed them dinner." That was the moment I began to cry. I heard someone open the kitchen door, and then I felt Robert's hands strong and comforting turn me around and I wept as he held me close, and was vaguely aware of the neighbors as they rushed into the house.

I made sure I stayed to help the family with all the preparations, and to support Aunt Nellie in her grief. She was amazingly strong and calm. and I knew Jesus was her source of strength during this horrible time.

James' funeral service was held at the Catholic Church in the community. I remember thinking how wonderful and loving this community was. The priest was a close friend of the family's, in fact when I lived with Aunt Nellie, he often came for the evening meal and stayed to play the game planned for that night. I can still hear James' laughter, he always seemed to enjoy game night more than the rest of the family.

After the service there would be a reception at the farm. Neighbors and friends were bringing large amounts of food so Aunt Nellie wouldn't feel she had to cook. But most knew that wouldn't happen, and I remember her cooking for the funeral reception. As I helped, I asked her several times to go sit and let the rest of us take care of the food, she would just softly touch my cheek softly saying "Bea, I need to stay busy."

At the reception I helped to set the food out on long tables made of barn wood, everyone attending the reception helped, so many hands made light work.

I looked around and saw Aunt Nellie talking with her neighbor Margaret, and decided to join them. It upset me when I heard Margaret ask her if she was angry with God? I flinched at the question; Aunt Nellie remained calm. Margaret gave me a stern look but continued talking, repeating her question.

"Nellie, you prayed for so long that your James would come home safely and when he does, he dies. You must be so angry with God; it must shake your faith."

Aunt Nellie's unshaken reply was simply this, "I was given a miracle and I thank God that my son came home and that I was able to hold him once again, more than what most mothers had. Now I can lay him beside his father and know where my son's body is. Most mothers don't have that, Margaret; it is written in" …

Job 1:21

'Naked I came from my mother's womb, and naked I will depart. The Lord gave and the Lord has taken away. May the name of the Lord be praised,"

and with a touch of her hand on Margaret's shoulder, Aunt Nellie walked away to talk to someone else. Aunt

Nellie held no anger toward God, and trusted in Him unwavering in her beliefs."

All the years mom lived with Aunt Nellie she had the best example of God's love. His love was beyond the grave, beyond the pain, beyond any situation life would bring, good or bad.

Mom learned what God's grace and mercy was and could do. By the time mom was able to go home, she was prepared for another life, another beginning, she was ready because she was taught by a short, slightly chubby, blue-eyed woman, and this woman showed by example the true meaning of a loving God, His son Jesus and the truth in the power of the Holy Spirit. She knew the true meaning of having Jesus as her Savior. This was her strength, and she thanked Aunt Nellie for all she had given her.

Even though mom had left Aunt Nellie's side in her late teens, and had visited the farm, in her twenty's eventually the visits stopped as life for mom became busier. Mom however stayed in close contact with her through the phone. They would continue to talk about all that was happening in their lives, and mom would continue to learn about God's love.

Aunt Nellie believed in the power of prayer so much that when people became ill, she would lay her hands on the person and pray for a healing.

My mom remembers on one of her visits that her cousin Anne had a large ulcer on her leg which caused her much pain. Anne had gone to many different doctors to rid her of this sore, but it wouldn't heal. Aunt Nellie seeing her daughter's suffering laid hands on her daughter's leg, simply asking the Lord to heal it. This became an open testimony of God's power, a miracle of love as the ulcer disappeared by the next day. The doctors couldn't explain it, no one could, but Aunt Nellie could and she gave God all the glory, as did the family. Mom was a witness to this miracle.

Aunt Nellie showed mom a God who loved her, a living God who cared for her. With her aunt as an example, it seems my mother had a rare teacher, a precious gift. Aunt Nellie lived to share her life, her living faith with many until the age of ninety-nine when she was called home to share in her Savior's glory.

God's grace is so beautiful to see in action. So often we forget that He is there to help and guide us in our sorrow, and our day-to-day living. Even if we forget, He is there in the abundance of His grace, a miraculous love that fills our being and our very souls through the outpouring of His Holy Spirit. This is His comfort, His peace that passes all understanding, and blessed is the person who calls out to Him and recognizes His presence, His voice.

I don't remember meeting Great Aunt Nellie more than a few times, but when I did, I knew there was something different about her. I know now it was the presence of God.

Aunt Nellie was a miracle of love and faith, she was the healing miracle that embraced my mother as a young teen who by her example taught my mom the meaning of the ever-continuing miracle of life, and passed it on.

To God Be The Glory

Chapter Four
Home Again

Some miracles are personal where only the person receiving it knows it happened. When that person tells the story, it is then up to the listener or reader to believe it or not. It all comes down to believing the story teller. Are they honest? Does that person often tell stories that are beyond belief? Well, that's up to you to decide. My mom was a woman of integrity, her life was an example of love and truth. Like Aunt Nellie, she lived her faith. Mom was not judgmental; she wore her heart on her sleeve as some would say. Mostly her inner light shone in and through her eyes, her actions, her unconditional love.

This is another story of faith, a miracle of God's unique love.

"I was afraid to leave my aunt's home and her side", mom told me. "I didn't know what was next for me, I know I only felt secure and safe in the embrace of her unconditional love. I wondered who was going to teach me more about God, Jesus and the Holy Spirit. I was like a sponge needing to absorb the knowledge I continued to thirst for.

As we said our goodbyes at the train station Aunt Nellie placed a wrapped gift in my hands. She told me to "...hold on to this Bea, this will bring you to where you need and want to be. Remember our times together held in our Savior's presence. God Bless you, my child." And with that my slightly older cousin James who I felt closest to said "whenever you need me just ring that triangle bell you rang to call us all for our meals, and I will come running. On the off chance I don't hear it, call me on the phone. I will be there for you." I was about to climb the steps to board the train when he picked me up and placed me gently on the first step of the train. Kissing me on the cheek with a mischievous smile he said "go home pest," and placed a small replica of the triangle bell in my hand. I wish I knew where I put that bell, I really treasured it," she said absently starting at her hands as if seeing them. She looked at me teary eyed, and I knew she was remembering James, the fun they had, and the way he died.

"Okay, back to my story. The train started moving and I found a seat, waiting patiently until the man came around to collect my ticket, I gave it to him quickly and eagerly opened the gift my aunt gave me. I held my breath as I brought her gift to rest over my heart. It was her Bible, the one we used daily when studying it. My hands were shaking; I was so touched by her generosity. I had hoped to have a Bible of my own one day; but Aunt Nellie's? This was her precious Bible the one she turned to for comfort, and knowledge. I became emotional and wondered what I was I going to do without her in my thoughts. I didn't realize I had said my thought out loud until a woman sitting next to me touched my shoulder and said, "I don't think you have to worry about that, it seems she gave you the best part of who she is," as she looked at the Bible. The woman was right, Aunt Nellie gave me the best part of what made her who she is. Her Bible was an example of God living in her. I wanted that too, every day of my life."

"I was reading the Gospel of John when the train came to a slow stop. I was home and I wondered if anyone would be there to greet me. I wondered if my brothers and sisters would recognize me or I them. I was now eighteen, teetering on nineteen, a woman, not an awkward thirteen-year-old. I was different I knew that for sure. I knew I was blessed living with Aunt Nellie, I stayed in a much-loved home. I had hoped my sisters had the same experience. My brothers stayed home under the not so much watchful eye of my dad. Would we be okay as a family?"

I knew my oldest brother had moved away to find work and was completely across the country. Would I ever see him again?"

The Great Depression was still a factor most people were experiencing, she had forgotten, living on a farm most of their food was home grown, and plenty; of course, Aunt Nellie shared what she had with others in need.

As mom stepped off the train a whole new life and world came rushing in, many of her family were there to welcome her, even her mom who had been discharged from the hospital, the reason she was able to go back home. She looked for her dad, he wasn't there, she wondered why he didn't make it.

As she arrived into the old, but clean home she knew she wasn't over the rainbow anymore. He mother had tried to make it look so nice, but what could you do in the middle of a depression where food and repairs were desperately needed. Clothes were old and worn, some threadbare, the shoes her mother demanded they take off so they wouldn't dirty the old wood floor she had just washed, were missing soles, and many had holes. No, she was not over that rainbow.

"I then went to see my dad when my brother Wilfred told me he was in bed. I looked at my brother, he just said, "go see him Bea, he will tell you." As far as I knew my dad had gotten back on his feet, but now my brother's words were scaring me. I looked around at the family, their eyes told the story. My mom held my hand and led me to their darkened bedroom. I gasped when I saw my dad's wasted body. I looked at my mom with questioning eyes, but my dad's weak voice called to me. "Beatrice, come closer my girl, I need to see you up close and talk to you."

I didn't want to talk; I didn't want to hear what he had to say.

As I came to his side, I could clearly see something was horribly wrong "Beatrice you look so beautiful, you have grown into a young woman, I have missed too many years of your growing up. Lay beside me like you did as a child." I did as he asked and tucked myself under his opened arm laying my head on his chest, a chest that seemed to cave in. I listened to his heart, it didn't beat like a normal heart and his breathing was shallow and heavy. I thought my head was too heavy and decided to move. "No Beatrice, stay where you are." He seemed to forget his struggles and suffering and began to talk. "While you were away, I did recover from my broken back and was up on my feet again, but only for a little while. I couldn't go back to work; I just wasn't strong enough and then the doctor's thought that maybe something else was wrong with me. They put me through a lot of tests and after a few months they told me I had bowel cancer and there was nothing they could do for me. I am sorry my girl that you had to come home to see me so ill, but you need to know I am dying and don't have much longer to live." Mom quietly cried as the enormity of the situation dug into her heart.

Mom wanted to leave and go back to Aunt Nellie. But thought again when she remembered what her aunt had told her. "Beatrice, Jesus is your rock, always go to Him in prayer." And that's just what she did, she did what Aunt Nellie did, she read her Bible and prayed, prayed harder than she ever prayed before.

As days passed mom gradually adjusted to a whole new way of living. Her siblings were so happy to have their mother back, she made meals, good meals out of what little they had. Mom being the oldest of the girls helped her mother, she cleaned, mended socks and some of the older boys tried to fix their shoes. The rainbow vanished into a haze of attending to her dad, watching him draw closer to his end. Oh, how she longed to go to the old tree on the farm, where she so often took comfort in, but she was a woman now and her family needed her. The weather was growing cold and they needed to keep their house warm for their dad. Everyone went out every day to look for coal along the train tracks, mom didn't think they would find much as most families in the neighborhood was doing the same. One day while they were all out searching for the diamond of black heat, they returned home with so little it wasn't worth putting into the stove. About thirty minutes after arriving home there was a knock on the door. It was the neighbors with outstretched hands holding the precious black diamond. One of the kids looking quite shy said, "We talked about it and thought we should give you all the coal we found today, you know, to keep your dad warm."

Wilfred ran to get a sackcloth and the coal was placed inside. Once the coal was emptied into the bag the neighbors rushed away barely giving the family time to say thank you. Mom said this was God's miracle of love at the hands of His children.

Mom remembers the last time she lay beside her dad. Her menstrual cycle was so painful that month she could hardly walk, and as she brought some soup to her dad he said,

"Bea, I know pain and I can see it on your face. What's wrong my girl?"

Mom slightly embarrassed answered, "it's just my monthly visitor dad."

"I understand; I have a pain pill that you can take to help you."

"No dad, you need your pain pills."

"Let me help you," her father said, and at that he placed a pill in the palm of her hand, gave her his water so she could take it, and she did.

"Lay down by my side as you wait for the pill to work."

Mom did just that and snuggled by his side, and with his one arm around her mom eventually fell asleep, feeling like a little girl again in her daddy's arms.

"It felt so natural," mom said, "I remember the feelings of love and protection in his arms. Even though he was dying, and the world was falling apart that all went away as he held me as I fell asleep. Did God feel this way? Would His spirit hold me in His care? But God was different, I couldn't feel His presence like I did my dad's."

Those moments held a special place in my mom's heart. She would always have the memory of her dad caring for her.

That was the last memory mom had as her dad went into a coma, and as she and the family watched his chest rise and fall, his breathing became less and less until he slipped from this world. All mom could think of was that her dad was now living on the other side of the rainbow. She wasn't sure he went to heaven because he rarely spoke about the Lord, but she had prayed for him and had to believe that one day she would see her dad again and they would both dance on streets paved with gold.

After her dad's funeral mom was brought back to the dark reality of needing to find a job, which in itself would take a miracle. With so many people unemployed during the Great

Depression, a miracle was all she could hope and pray for.

Mom having learned at Aunt Nellie's side continued to grow in the Lord, studying her Bible daily, but as her prayers went unanswered for finding work her faith began to weaken. She needed to help the family keep their home with food to eat and warmth during the long winter months.

Why wasn't God answering her pleas? Mom was so distraught she quit going to church and attending mass. Every day was consumed in looking for work. She didn't dare call Aunt Nellie as she didn't have the strength or desire to hear her aunt's encouraging words. Mom just wanted to live in her self-pity depressed reality. She was still young in her faith, and other than her dad dying, this was the deepest valley that threatened to devour her.

Mom's despair was so great she was tempted to quit fighting and allow herself to fall into that deep, dark valley of mental anguish, metaphorically speaking. Even though some of her brothers had found small temporary jobs, it wasn't enough to keep them going month to month.

Every day mom would put on her coat to hide the well-worn clothes she wore, but the coat was in no better shape than her clothes. Her stockings had holes and runs in them, and her shoes were ready for the garbage, yet each night she would mend and repair her tattered clothing for the next day's excursion of searching for a job.

Mom had given her resume to many companies, large and small without any phone calls for an interview.

Mom told me, "I was desperate Elaine, any hope I had was fading like my faith. I lost all hope in God, and prayer became a chore, an empty verbal repeat of the hour before, "Please God help me find a job?" and again my prayer hit a brick wall."

"I always walked the alleys and dirt roads so no one would see me in my worn-out clothes and shoes. I would often readjust the cardboard in my shoes to cover the holes where my feet and toes would stick through." Mom laughed, "Even the cardboard had holes in it."

"One day I passed the side door of the church I had attended so often in the past. The door was slightly open and I needed to sit down as my feet were killing me. I peeked in, there was no one in the church so I went in and sat in a pew close to the back. Sitting there I took off my shoes and rubbed my cold dirty feet, I looked up at the large crucifix on the wall above the altar wondering why He had left me? Forsaken me? I was too depressed to remember that Jesus felt forsaken by His father, that we somehow had that in common. But Jesus was God made man, and He knew His father had a plan which was greater than His suffering. Jesus knew He was the Savior taking on the sins of all. Jesus is our pathway to the Father. God is so Holy that sin separated us, but through His son Jesus' death and resurrection that was removed, and we are free to go to God. When you are depressed and lose hope you forget that God's will is greater than ours. He knows what's best for us, even though we may disagree with that. Sometimes giving into His will is the very source of setting ourselves free. But I didn't want to wait for His will, I needed it, wanted it now, my family depended on my getting a job. Eventually I had to remember the hope of His will.

At that moment questions entered my thoughts, what would Aunt Nellie do? Would she curl up in a ball and give in to hopelessness? Or would she continue to trust in her Savior?

No matter what! In good times and bad Aunt Nellie would not falter, her faith would stand in the face of all her trials, and each trial grew her faith.

As I sat in the pew," mom continued "I decided to be honest with God and spoke to him from my heart, from my desperation."

"God, I feel like you have forsaken me, and my family. I know I should be thankful for all that you have given me, instead of complaining but I'm finding that hard to do. Jesus, please help me find a job. I am sorry for not thanking you enough, I just feel empty inside and lost. Find me again Lord, please find me again. Lord, are you listening to me? I then laid my head on the railing of the pew and cried."

"I didn't cry for very long because a deep peace came over me. I looked up and over the altar I saw a beautiful fluffy white cloud like presence come toward me. I closed my eyes and shook my head thinking I was hallucinating. Then suddenly, without doubt it became all so clear to me, this was God. The fluffy translucent glowing cloud came over me wrapping me in its heavenly calmness, the oasis of God's love, comfort and peace. A thought within my mind whispered as if it was a voice speaking aloud."

"Beatrice I am with you. All will be well." The presence of His comforting grace continued to embrace me for another minute then I felt His presence leave. I felt rejuvenated, joyful, positive and so blessed. Whatever happens I know He is there with me, and He was all I needed."

"When I left the church, my path did not change I still stepped into the alley and started to walk home, only this time with a spring in my step, and an unexplained hope in my heart.

I heard a voice calling out to me. "Beatrice stop!"

"Was this God calling me to stop? No, I was sure that wasn't God's voice. I kept walking not wanting anyone to see me in my clothes. "Beatrice stop!" The voice was louder and I finally recognized my brother Wilfred's voice. I turned around and saw him running toward me.

"Bea, why did you walk faster when I called you?"

"I didn't recognize your voice at first Wilf. What is it?

I waited while Wilf caught his breath.

"You're out of shape Wilf." I teased him poking his tummy."

"Ha ha ha," Wilf sarcastically laughed.

"Bea this is important, the big Pharmaceutical Company you gave your resume to called and asked for you. They told me to find you and tell you to get there as soon as you could for a job interview.?"

I shrieked with joy and grabbed my brother in a big bear hug. Then I suddenly realized my appearance was not suitable for a job interview

"Oh Wilf, how can I go looking like this?"

"Bea, are you kidding me, go now, everyone looks like you, they aren't going to care: Just go. NOW!"

Feeling somewhat deflated, thinking they wouldn't hire someone looking like me, but then I remembered the peace that covered me in a fluffy cloud of grace embracing me just minutes before, and I ran toward my future."

"When I arrived for the job interview there were many others waiting for their turn. I was naive to think I was the only one they called. I sat by a woman named Shirley, both of us similar in our dress; poverty has a way of keeping you humble and ready for friendships with common ground. Shirley went into the interview first, and when she came out, she was smiling. She got the job. I was so happy for her, and prayed I would have the same outcome. Coming out of my interview Shirley was there waiting for me, and ran to me when she saw the smile on my face."

"Oh, Beatrice I can feel we are going to be good friends, isn't this wonderful, God has blessed us, giving us what we needed most. Our hero coming to the rescue in the final moments of our need and answering our prayers."

By then I was crying as I listened to her words. I hugged her back, both of us crying. How could I have ever doubted my Savior?

When I went home to tell everyone the good news my brother Wilfred grabbed me and twirled me around.

"When do you start Bea?" the whole family asked in one voice.

"Tomorrow morning," I smiled, "and I was told not to worry about what clothes to wear as they would give me a uniform and shoes. Imagine that, shoes with no holes," Everyone laughed, and then Wilf announced another miracle.

"Hey everyone," he yelled to get our attention over the loud celebration of my news. "I got a job too."

Everyone grew silent. "What did you say Wilf?" I asked.

To be overdramatic Wilf enunciated each word he said.

"I…Said…I…Got…A…Job…Too," With Wilf's announcement the family burst into an almost frantic, chaotic celebration. We held each other jumping, dancing, singing 'Happy Days Are Here Again' (1930, music by Milton Ager, lyrics by Jack Yellen) at the top of our lungs with tears of joy streaming down our cheeks.

Once we all calmed down, I ran to the phone, and as told by Aunt Nellie reversed the charges. Aunt Nellie was such an amazing blessing when I returned home. Every month she would send a care package via the train for the whole family. A couple of times she would come to visit and help my mom cook with the added groceries she brought with her.

I excitedly told Aunt Nellie everything in great detail and she rejoiced in Praising God by saying a beautiful prayer of thankfulness. "Amen Aunt Nellie, Amen!" mom replied.

When mom returned to the family, she asked them to join hands with her to thank God for His amazing blessings. How could they forget their Hero who swept in answering their many prayers?

Not only did mom receive many miracles that day she also became good friends with Shirley, and they in turn became friends with many other Christian women who were hired. They did not share the same Catholic faith as mom but Aunt Nellie had told her, "Beatrice, you don't have to be Catholic to be a Christian."

God calls us from different faiths, quoting the scripture of Mark 9:39-40, Jesus said, ***"...for no one who does a miracle in My name can in the next moment say anything bad about me. For whoever is not against us is for us."***

To God Be The Glory

Mom's Dad Joseph, and mother Eugenie, on their wedding day. August 26 1911

Mom with brothers Wilfred and Edgar. Also picture of Uncle Wilfred

Mom with Shirley best life long friend she met at job interview.

Chapter Five
Two White Rosaries

There are times a miracle comes in ways that were least expected. God answers prayer sometimes delayed, but always at the right time

Eventually all her siblings found jobs, some closer to the end of the Depression. Because of their needs being answered they reached out to their community to help other people in need. The devastating Depression ended officially in 1939 with the beginning of World War II. but for many it continued beyond the official end.

However, my country of Canada was hit hard, so it is told and, the Depression came to an end: eventually. But I am sure many other countries could say the same thing.

Mom continued to work at the Pharmaceutical Company for many years. She was embraced by many good friends, some of them becoming inseparable. They lunched together every day at work, and as finances grew, they vacationed together, renting a cottage in which they all shared. It was a strong, loving, caring sisterhood, until they all fell in love and married where of course married life took precedence.

Mom dated a good loving, very handsome gentle man named Bruce. She liked him very much and remembers on their first date spilling her meal of spaghetti and meatballs on her beautiful white dress. "Bruce was so kind, he took me to emergency after a waitress gave me an extra uniform she had, and I was told I had first degree burns. I really was not in horrible pain but Bruce took me home only to return later that night with a takeout order of Spaghetti and meatballs for the whole family. Bruce insisted on taking my dress to have it professionally cleaned, I was about to refuse when my mother handed him the paper bag in which the waitress had put it in. The lesson I took from that was to never order Spaghetti on a first date again, especially while wearing white," she laughed.

"Bruce offered to buy me a new dress but I refused, that was just too much to expect from him, making me feel very uncomfortable, after all it was only our first date."

"We dated for a few years and Bruce proposed to me but I eventually broke up with him as there was no spark, no deep connection. I was heartbroken for him, for me, but I didn't love him enough to marry him. He was a good friend, but not the man I wanted to spend the rest of my life with. Bruce understood and eventually he did meet the right woman. I don't know if they lived happily ever after, but I do know he married her."

Mom said she dated other men but no one grew that spark in her heart like the man she eventually married: my dad.

Even though her work friends were now having babies they continued to meet together. They decided to make it their mission to pray for mom daily to meet the right man; eventually.

Mom called Aunt Nellie to tell her about Bruce.

"Well Beatrice it wasn't meant to be; you would have been very unhappy. God will bless you with the right man." Aunt Nellie then paused to pray with her.

A week later, mom was invited to go to a charity dance to help support the many wives and families who lost their loved ones during the war. She would be going with her married friends, along with their husbands, feeling somewhat displaced she agreed to go, but deep within her heart she didn't want to be the only single woman in her group.

When mom reluctantly dressed for the dance having put on her makeup and brushed her hair to the desired look she wanted, she went to the front door and waited for her friend Shirley and her husband to pick her up.

While she waited her mom met her at the door holding the White Rosary Aunt Nellie had given her while she lived with her.

"Beatrice I was talking to Nellie and she mentioned giving you the white Rosary to hold in your hand at the dance."

"Why? Mom asked.

Her mom shrugged, "She said when she was in prayer the thought came to her for you to hold the Rosary in your hands during the dance." Mom was uncertain about doing that, but her mother placed it in her hand saying, "just do what Nellie said."

Mom trusted her aunt completely, but a rosary at the dance didn't make sense. She took the rosary from her mother and put it in her small hand bag and walked out the door to her future.

At the same time the same thing was happening at my dad's house. My dad was also invited to the same charity dance. His mom Anna met him at the door before he left, she touched her son's face, "Joseph, you smell so nice, you look so handsome, you take after your mother; yes?" "Si mamma," he answered. My dad being the oldest in the family of his four siblings smiled at his mother. He was so much like her, a man of integrity, a man who was active in his community, one of the few who organized the charity dance.

"You're a good man Joseph, your papa (dad) and I are so proud of you.

Dad took hold of his mother's hand while it was still laying softly on his face and brought it to his lips and kissed it, "Voglio bene alla tua mamma." (I love you mom)

His mother smiled as she looked into her son's eyes. "Joseph, I have something I want you to have while you're at the dance, placing a White Rosary.in his hand, then folding his hand over it.

"Joseph, I want you to keep this with you, and hold it in your hand the whole time."

"Why," her son asked.

"Because God might bless you with a good Italian Catholic girl who will see it and go up to you and talk."

Dad learned many years ago that dismissing his mother's words were not a good thing, and put the white rosary in his pocket. His mother tapped his hand saying, "Joseph, you need to keep that rosary in your hand all night, not in your pocket."

"Don't worry mom I will take it out of my pocket when I get there."

He didn't, at first, but there came a time when that white Rosary was taken out of his pocket and prominently displayed in his hand.

Why? Did a certain woman catch his eye?

My mom arrived with her friends and because it was so crowded stood on the left side of the church hall with her friends.

My dad and his friends did the same going to the right side of the hall.

The music was loud and many were dancing including their friends.

Both not having partners stayed put just watching the crowd. Mom at age 28, Dad at age 29 had both thought they would never find that right person to share their lives with. Although dad had been engaged but the woman, he thought would be the love of his life cheated on him, with his cousin and best friend; and that is a whole other story.

As they watched the couples dancing the crowd seemed to shift and that is when the miracle happened.

As mom continued to look around, she noticed a dark, handsome man on the other side who was looking at her. At this point mom took the White Rosary out of her purse and held it loosely in her hand to be seen clearly. She knew the rosary might discourage the wrong man from approaching her. But she was shocked when this very handsome man reached into his pocket and pulled out a White Rosary, holding it up so she could see.

Mom's heart started to beat hard and fast as she realized what was happening. Did Aunt Nellie have inside information that she would find someone to love, or was it just a coincidence?

She pushed away the coincidence thought. What kind of man would hold a White Rosary at a dance? Her kind.

Then it happened Joseph and Beatrice began walking toward each other. It seemed God had parted the crowd like the Red Sea when Moses led the Israelites as they escaped the Egyptians who had held them hostage for so many years.

"That was definitely not the Red Sea," mom said, "but to me it was a miracle of epic proportions."

As they walked toward each other, White Rosaries easily displayed, the orchestra was playing the song At Last. (Written by Mack Gordon and Harry Warren.) I was not familiar with this song until I heard it on a television commercial., sung by Etta James. So, I knew the song my mom was talking about, and I truly love that song.

Getting back to my mom and dad, With the orchestra playing At Last mom was familiar with the song, knew it was being played, but it wasn't until later when one of her friends commented on the song and its appropriate timing when meeting her beloved Joseph.

As they walked toward each other eyes fixed on one another and the White Rosaries, man and woman lost sight of everyone

Finally meeting in the middle, Joseph touched the White Rosary in Beatrice's hand, "Hello, my name is Joe."

"Hello Joe my name is Beatrice."

From that moment Joseph and Beatrice, were always together at every function, every meal at each other's parents' home.

Nine months later with Aunt Nellie in the front pew, mom walked up the aisle with her White Rosary intertwined within her bouquet, and as dad reached out for her hand, while holding his White Rosary the two became one.

My version of when they met

Engagement picture

The engagement is announced of Miss Beatrice Frenette, daughter of Mrs. J. E. Frenette of Wellington avenue and the late Mr. Frenette, to Mr. Joseph Balestrini, son of Mrs. and Mrs. Louis Balestrini of Betts avenue, the marriage to take place February 15 at 9 a.m. at Holy Name Church. Miss Frenette was entertained at a miscellaneous shower in the hall of St. Angela Merici Church, 125 guests being present, many from out-of-town. During the evening a mock wedding was staged. Refreshments were served buffet style.

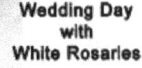

Wedding Day with White Rosaries

Holy Name of Mary Church

MR. AND MRS. JOSEPH BALESTRINI

Couple to Reside in Windsor

At a double ring ceremony at Holy Name of Mary Church, the Rev. J. A. Rooney united in marriage Miss Beatrice Frenette, daughter of Mrs. Joseph Frenette of Wellington avenue and the late Mr. Frenette, and Mr. Joseph Balestrini, son of Mr. and Mrs. Louis Balestrini of Betts avenue.

The bride, who was given in marriage by her uncle, Mr. Louis Frenette, was gowned in egg shell satin and lace, the bodice fastening down the back with tiny buttons to the waist, and featuring a sweetheart neckline and long sleeves, ending in points over the wrists. The skirt extended into a long train. Her fingertip veil was held in a wreath of orange blossoms and seed pearls, and she wore a single strand of pearls and carried calla lilies and white roses.

Miss Gertrude Frenette, sister of the bride, as maid of honour, wore pink georgette fashioned with cap sleeves and a full skirt. She wore long pink gloves and a halo of pink plumes and carried pink roses and carnations. Miss Madeline Frenette, another sister of the bride, in aquamarine georgette fashioned with cap sleeves, and Miss Kathryn Balestrini, sister of the bridegroom, in pale blue georgette, were bridesmaids. Their gowns were styled alike and they carried tea roses.

Little Sandra Frenette, niece of the bride, as flower girl wore a three-length pink taffeta gown and carried a tiny nosegay.

Mr. Albert Balestrini, brother of the bridegroom, was best man and the ushers were Mr. Ted Terry, Mr. Wilfred Frenette, Mr. Thomas Pettinato and Mr. Cyril Frenette. During the ceremony, Miss Miriam Monforton sang "Ave Maria" and "On This Day."

A wedding dinner for 180 guests and a reception for 300 followed. Mrs. Frenette chose for her daughter's wedding a rose and gray printed crepe frock with white carnations and Mrs. Balestrini, mother of the bridegroom, wore a silver gray lace-trimmed gown and pink rose.

Later Mr. and Mrs. Balestrini left on a wedding trip to Erie, Pennsylvania, the bride travelling in an olive green suit featuring gold buttons and black accessories. They will reside in Windsor.

Honeymoon in Erie Pennsylvania, but ended up in Montreal Quebec for the last part of their Honeymoon

Chapter Six
After The Honeymoon

Some miracles come to us after great sorrow, or hardships, as in the case of my parent's desire to have children.

My parents were married on February 15, 1945, it was a quiet, small wedding...NOT... Actually, mom says, "there were over five-hundred guests, many your dad and I didn't know. We were told after we returned from our honeymoon in Montreal, that many people just walked off the street and joined in the festivities. They were not removed as it was cold outside, and as long as they didn't cause trouble, they were welcomed to enjoy the wine, food and fun." Mom laughed at this memory,

It wasn't long after my parents returned from their honeymoon when they decided to try to start a family. One evening while eating at dad's parent's home, which they often did they gave them the good news. Mom was pregnant! As mom and Grandma did the dishes they talked about the new baby and the excitement of having a new family member.

"You and Joseph are very happy, yes?" Grandma asked.

"Yes, very much mamma, I love the name he calls me; I melt every time I hear him call me that."

Grandma smiled asking what the name was.

"He calls me his little chooch, (correctly spelled ciuccio in some Italian dialects) mom smiled at the loving thought of it.

Grandma gasped as laughter took over her emotions.

"What's so funny mamma?" mom asked confused at the sudden burst of laughter from her mother-in-law.

Grandma was reluctant to tell her, but her daughter-in-law needed to know why she was laughing. "Chooch is the Italian name for jackass, Beatrice," Grandma's laughter once again consumed her as she looked at my mom's shocked face.

"What's going on in here?" Joe asked as he walked into the lion's den.

My mom quickly answered, "how dare you Joseph, I can't believe you could be so cruel."

Dad was confused as he looked at his mother standing in the corner uncontrollably laughing, and then back to his wife who looked as if she could wound him in some way.

When my grandpa entered the kitchen, he went to his wife speaking in Italian, he too began to laugh and taking his wife's arm led her away to a safe place knowing his new daughter was about to give her husband a word or two about this.

"Bea, what is going on?" my dad asked somewhat carefully trying to inflect love into his voice.

"Oh, don't you mean chooch, Joseph? Call me chooch again Joseph, call me that disgusting name again."

Laughter bellowed from the front room at the hearing of the word chooch.

"Bea," dad spoke carefully, "you're my little chooch."

"I'm your jackass Joseph! When you look at me is that what you see?" mom cried.

Dad walked up to his beautiful pregnant wife, very carefully and tested the waters. As he slowly and gently put his arms around his wife, he whispered, "Bea, I wasn't calling you a jackass, I know it means that in Italian but for me it is a loving word, a cute word for my little sweet wife. In English it means to me my cute, adorable little wife."

"Joe, you do know jackass in English can mean idiot? Mom asked through her tears.

Mom stopped crying as dad took her face in his hands and kissed each tear as it fell. "I love you my little...choo...um, wife."

"Can't you call me wife Joe? How do you say that in Italian?'

"Moglie. Oh, that doesn't sound so cute either chooch sounds much cuter Bea like a cute cuddly teddy bear."

Mom knew she was being sweet talked by her handsome husband, and eventually gave in, but gave dad strict orders not to call her that in front of family or anyone else who understood the Italian language. "Only when we are alone."

With that taken care of mom gave my dad a half smile as she threw dad the dish towel to help dry dishes.

My mother was a small woman, five foot two inches, but her pregnancy did not show as a baby bump until she was six months along.

Mom said, "Your dad and I were walking on air. We would spend hours feeling his or her kicks, talking and making decisions preparing for their baby's arrival."

However, sorrow and shock struck when at six-and-a-half-months mom went into labor, giving birth to a still born son. The whole family was devastated but no one more than my parents.

The doctor told them that the baby's death did not mean that it would be a cause of alarm with other pregnancies.

"Often with a first pregnancy a miscarriage will occur, but that doesn't determine other pregnancies." He told mom to go and live her life as there was no reason to believe she couldn't have a healthy baby in the future.

The doctor's words rang empty in her heart and soul as her fourth pregnancy ended yet again in a still birth. Four still births were too much to cope with. Mom prayed, every one prayed with each new announcement of her being pregnant, and hearts broke with the news of yet another still born baby, all boys.

Mom thought she just couldn't carry a boy; however, it is thought that the Rh factor was probably the cause.

(The Rh Factor is when the blood of a Rh-positive fetus enters the bloodstream of a Rh-negative woman, her body will recognize that the fetus' blood is not hers. Her body will try to destroy it by making antibodies which will cross the placenta attacking the fetus' blood cells. This can lead to severe health problems even death for a fetus or newborn. Later, much later it was found that mom was Rh negative, while dad was Rh positive.

Life went on in in the depth of despair, feeling hopeless my parents lived in the empty thoughts that they would never be parents.

My grandmother Anna was approached by a woman in one of the charities she worked with stating adopting a baby could be an answer. Grandma approached mom and dad with this suggestion.

They felt after praying God was giving them a miracle, a unique gift, to become parents not by blood but born of the love in their hearts.

Once dad and mom told grandma they would love to adopt they received a phone call from an adoption agency connected with their church, just two days later. The woman on the other end asked them if they would consider adopting a baby boy eight months old; if so, she would bring him to their home so they could see him. Back then adoptions were easier with many young women, and teenagers becoming pregnant out of wedlock, simply being unmarried. This back then was a great embarrassment, and so many young women would go to houses that would be home to these women until after their baby was born. Most found no support in helping them keep their babies, and their only option was to give their baby up for adoption.

After the conversation with the woman from the adoption agency mom looked at dad asking, "What did she mean consider? What is there to consider? Once that baby enters this home he is here to stay. He is ours!" mom told dad, and dad one hundred percent agreed.

Two short hours later a baby boy came into their home making them a family of three.

Richard Joseph Balestrini arrived and was baptized into the large, loving Italian and French family.

Mom remembers that night vividly, when Richard became their son

"We had nothing to care for him. No diapers, food, formula, no crib. Nothing, although the woman from the adoption agency came back an hour later and gave them a box filled with diapers, food, sleepers, formula to last them until they could get to a store.

With no crib they put Richard in between them in their bed. "It was the most amazing feeling, there he was, our son," mom told me. "I didn't carry him in my womb but he grew in my heart. Richard fell asleep quickly and we were disappointed as we wanted to play with him, and we did when we woke up to our son's babbling talk, and infectious laughter while he crawled all over us. It was the best feeling of all."

"That new sun filled morning life took on new meaning, a new way to live, and in the early afternoon as Richard napped on the couch with mom guarding him, there was a knock on their door. As dad opened the door in walked gifts galore, all the necessities a baby needed, and so much more. Grandma and Grandpa presented them with a beautiful new crib filled with gifts. It was a baby shower, a very quickly put together baby shower where family and friends gathered to welcome this precious gift from God into the family."

"We are very blessed aren't we chooch?"

Mom smiled, "yes Joe, yes we are," and they held on to each other watching Richard who woke up with the commotion, as he was held in many different open arms.

Richard their beautiful, happy little miracle was home, and so were they.

< Grandpa Luigi & Grandma Anna Balestrini

Mom and Dad >
Joe & Beatrice Balestrini
(newly weds)

< Mom holding Richard, with Aunt Nellie beside her.

Mom & Dad >
enjoying their son Richard

Dad & Rick

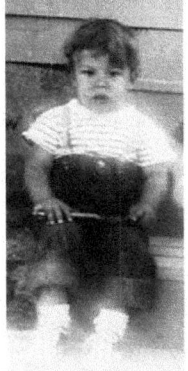
Rick age 18 months

Rick age 3

Chapter Seven
A Touch of Hell

Some healings, and miracles, have much history behind them; where the story in its fullness needs to be told to lead up to lessons learned where miracles take place. Some are even rooted in the face of evil. Whether you believe it or not there is a God who loves us all very much. Although our love for our loved ones gives us a window into God's love, we can never fully understand it, until we are home in His presence, surrounded by that love.

On the opposite side the reality of satan (when writing the name of satan I use lower case letters, he does not deserve capitals) being as present as God in our lives is in my opinion a fact not worth denying. I have been in the occult without knowing it. What? Without knowing it? Yep, it happened to my family when I was a young teenager.

Before I get into that let's go back in time. I guess we could go as far back as Adam and Eve, but we all know the details of the snake, the apple and the fall of God's plan for humanity. Poof! The garden of Eden was no longer open for business, and life took on a whole new meaning.

satan has long been the dark evil presence in our world's history. How is evil portrayed? Well, you just have to look at our world today to see how alive he is, and the destruction he leaves behind. We aren't born with hatred; we are taught it by example. There are many forms of hatred; intolerance, bigotry, racism, jealousy, genocide, judgement, superiority in one's nationality. Evil has many faces.

As a young teenager my aunt gave us a Christmas gift, a Ouija board. My mother would not let us play with it until she asked our parish priest if it was okay. "As long as you don't take it seriously it is fine," his answer wrong in so many ways. Why didn't he know the dangers of this game as people called it?

A Ouija board at the time when we used it was just a question-and-answer game. We thought the warmth of our finger tips hovering over the planchette guided it to the yes or no, or letters and numbers. The planchette is simply a pointer, but there is nothing simple about it. We were excited when we asked the Ouija questions and the pointer slid to the answer. We knew we weren't touching the pointer but was the other person playing the game moving it? When it was confirmed that no one was moving it we were more excited to watch it glide without help but at the same time, it was scary.

The main reason for using a Ouija board is to conjure up a demon to do one's bidding. We didn't know this at the time, I wish we had researched it but back then the internet did not exist.

We honestly felt we were connecting with God; however, we were calling on evil spirits, and they were right there to entice us.

The Ouija board might look harmless but believe me it is an open door to the occult.

It didn't take long before we were hooked, however the board would not answer questions without my sister MaryAnn there. We enjoyed it for a while, just asking silly questions, and getting actually correct answers.

I asked who I would marry, and it spelled out Laurence Hanna. I laughed because I would never marry someone with the name Laurence, a typical young teen reaction. However, this answer remained in my memory for all time. I did marry, but his name was David Vizard. It wasn't until many years later when Dave was united with his birth mother that we found out she was going to name him Laurence Hanna, Hanna being his birth father's name. I was stunned, shocked and believed. The spirits that guide this Ouija board know, and that is how they hook you. Of course, I didn't know this at the time, but all too soon the fun game turned into a tool of hell, and we could not escape its creepy grasp.

My mother and sister decided to quit the game and wanted to throw it away. My brother who had recently taken an interest, continued to play it. Evil pulled my sister and I in deeper as we began to do automatic handwriting. That is where you sit with pen and paper and ask who we still thought were angels about your past lives. Oh, they thrilled us with amazing stories, and as a very imaginative person, I loved the thrill of it all, but MaryAnn became frightened and had stopped.

One day when at the Ouija board I asked where they were at night when no one was playing the game. Then it spelled, "this is no game, we are always with you, sitting at the side of your bed watching you, protecting you." This scared me and comforted me at the same time. My mother watching said, "Get rid of this now! It is not a game, it is pure evil, I can sense it. Elaine, you must stop the automatic handwriting and the Ouija board, it is not from God, nor angels, it is evil." My mother was so distraught and scared I did as she said, her fearful shaky voice and words, frightened me, but the nightmare didn't end.

After my mother told us to get rid of the Ouija board my brother Rick took it saying he would take care of it. We thought he was going to throw it away, but little did we know he took it to an old dilapidated house where his friends met to play with it. Play? You don't play with the devil, he isn't there for fun and games, he's there to destroy you.

Since this house had no electricity candles were used to light the one room, they decided to be in. At night the candles painted the room with shadows, dancing flames seemed to set the mood for these sessions. With my imagination I could picture the flames shadows looking like long thin crooked fingers reaching out to take hold of their prey. But that was my imagination running wild, or was it?

Afraid yet curious Rick's friends gathered around the table each taking their turn asking this wooden board questions. At first everything was light and funny, but with time it eventually turned to a torturous den of evil, and play was not it's intent.

"Who are you?" asked one friend.

'You know who I am', the board forming the sentence by spelling it through the letters.

"No, I don't. Who are you?" the friend asked again.

'I am who you are thinking I am. You know me.'

That spooked this friend for he had often been in trouble with the police.

Every one took their turns, and each answer became darker, more intense and threatening; those thin shadowy fingers were reaching into their spirits. One of my brother's friends suggested they ask the Ouija their Social Insurance Numbers, thinking that would not be something the board could possibly know. So, one by one each person would leave the group, and the others would ask for the number on the card that person was holding. Everyone became increasingly frightened when the board answered each time with the correct numbers.

One of the friends jumped up, physically shaking, yelling frantically, "oh man, this is real, this is not right, we need to destroy this thing now! By this time everyone was standing but my brother decided he needed to ask one last question. He looked around, "someone sit down and put your fingers over the pointer with me." Only one brave friend joined Rick as he asked the powers to be, "Why was my best friend killed on my motorcycle?"

The Ouija board slowly creeped to each letter, 'It was you I wanted dead, not your friend,' and with that answer the planchette pulled away from underneath their shaky fingers and jumped off the Ouija board throwing itself into the wall breaking in half. Everyone was shocked, not able to move. How could this thing just throw itself on to the wall? Rick assured everyone that he nor his friend did that, so who did it?

Rick was the first to break from his scared stiff stance, he quickly grabbed the pieces and Ouija board and ran outside yelling, "We need to burn this thing, help me make a bonfire." His friends followed, once they realized someone was taking charge of the situation.

As Rick's friends gathered the wood and paper to build a fire, Rick ran to his car to get some lighter fluid he kept for refilling his cigarette lighter, thinking it would help quicken the board's destruction. Once the fire was in full force Rick threw the items into it. The group stood watching as it burned feeling relief until the smoke eased and they realized the board would not succumb to the hot flames. The Ouija board would not burn. Suddenly in a force stronger than itself the broken pieces of the planchette levitated out of the fire and hung over it in the air. This evil presence was strong, and fed on the fear of all those around.

One of Rick's friends decided they needed to use a stronger fluid to burn this devil's board as he called it, and ran to his car to get some gas he had stored in his trunk. Running to the fire he yelled for everyone to step back, and then threw the gas on the inferno. The gas exploded on contact yet the planchette remained hovering in the air surrounded by indescribable flames. Was this what hell consisted of? The Ouija board was not burning although engulfed in this blaze of white-hot fire. The group felt defeated and beyond scared. They knew for certain that this game was the devil's and they were the object of his evil intent, until my brother spoke a sentence that changed everything. "Burn in the name of Jesus," and with that the planchette fell deep into the fire and the Ouija board began to burn, spewing black smoke for what seemed like hours. When finally, the ashes were the only thing left, they doused it with water.

"What the hell happened here?" someone asked.

Most were still shivering, not because it was a cold summer's evening, but because of the events, the unexplainable reality of what they just witnessed.

"Rick stood silent knowing that this game was no game, it was an assault straight out of hell. "We need to remember this," Rick shakily stated when he could find his voice without quivering, "because even if some of us didn't believe before we know now: satan is real! Let's just leave and go home."

Someone had to go back into that dilapidated house of hellish reality to blow out the candles. Rick volunteered and ran into the shadowy flaming fingers that seemed to reach out to take hold of him, but Rick continued to use the name of Jesus as he doused the candles flames, then ran like a bat out of hell to join his friends.

"I don't think I can drive; I can't stop shaking. I feel like I'm going to throw up," one friend said quietly, with the others nodding to say, they too were feeling the same way.

"Well, we can't stay here, we need to get away from this place, everyone just drive slowly, but not so slow as to be pulled over by the police. This would be a hard one to explain," one friend said.

I have often wondered how Rick's friends were impacted by this intense night of demonic reality. Did some benefit from this experience, or did they eventually rationalize it as a distant memory of imagination?

As it was summer and too hot to sleep, we were all still up, except for my dad who slept soundly due to working in the heat of the day when we heard Rick's car pull into the driveway.

When he walked into the house, we all noticed how white his face was, like he saw a ghost.

"What happened Rick," mom asked as she walked toward him, "your face is as white as a sheet and your expression is scaring me."

My mom, sister MaryAnn and I stood in front of Rick, we have never seen him so scared, he was shaking and could hardly talk. Mom made him sit down and when he finally was able to speak, he told us of the night's events.

"How long have you been playing the Ouija board with your friends Rick?" mom asked.

"All week! Rick blurted out loudly. "Mom, when I was coming home and looked in the rear-view mirror, I saw eyes, they were there mom, they were real. They followed me all the way home. They were evil mom, and I am not just making it up, I am not so scared to know those eyes were real." Rick then put his shaky hands over his eyes, "How are we going to get rid of him, that fuc…g devil?"

Mom would normally say something about Rick swearing but this was not the time to reprimand him. In response to Rick's desperate plea, mom jumped up ran to her bedroom, grabbed her container of Holy Water, and started anointing every room and person in the house, even dad as he lay sleeping, oblivious to what was happening. Mom used the name of Jesus telling any evil to leave. She said it with such authority and as she did the creepy, undeniable darkness that came in with Rick disappeared, leaving in its absence the tangible presence of peace.

We now know that the name of Jesus brings deliverance from all oppression from satan, the devil. Jesus, the son of God defeated satan on the cross, and when we believe in His name, and in what He did for us as our Savior the devil has no power over that name. His name is mighty, powerful, and we have that power in His name. The devil cannot live in the presence of those who have Jesus as their personal Savior, he can scare us, and make himself known to us, but when my brother used the name of Jesus to tell the Ouija to burn, and it did along with mom telling the evil to leave, the only conclusion became very evident; there is power in the name of ***Jesus.***

As a Catholic we were always taught about Jesus, who He was, who He is, and who He will always Be, **THE SON OF GOD!** But where satan and his demons were concerned I think we always felt, although real, he was more harmless than threat.

As a little girl during one of my religion classes my first-grade teacher held up two pictures. One where there were cute little angels kneeling in prayer among the beauty of what could be considered heaven. The second picture was filled with red flames with cute little devils dancing and laughing. When my teacher asked which one, we would like to be in. Well, there was no competition in my opinion, I called out the one with the little devils, "they look like they are having fun, but the angels look bored." Of course, that was my childish view, and I hoped as I grew older my teacher chose a different way to teach the difference.

As written in the New Testament of the Bible, in **1 Peter 5:8,** Peter writes, **"Be alert and of sober mind. Your enemy the devil prowls around like a roaring lion looking for someone to devour."**

Being sober-minded means that we see with God's eyes and discernment, not allowing ourselves to be easily swayed, being fooled by wrong thinking and acting on it.

Clearly, he didn't know the dangers of such a game of reality. The Ouija board has one purpose and that is to conjure up the evil spirit world, the world of satan's domain with his demons.

Now that we were aware of the devil, we knew we needed to be of sound mind when influences presented themselves. We needed to be careful. Today there are many influences, traps one could say that the devil uses to devour those he can.

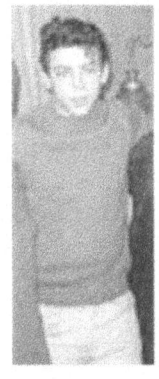
My brother Rick

Rick with his motorcycle

Aunt Gert

My sister MaryAnn and I, exact ages during the ouija board terrors

Me, MaryAnn and Mom in happier times

Rick became a fisherman of people for God's domain.

Now that my family came to the realization that the Ouija board, along with automatic handwriting and other tools of the devil were not from God, or His angels, we began to be haunted by these demons.

The devil doesn't play games; he is in it to win in any way possible. I was a mess, he had infiltrated my mind and body, but never my soul. I was haunted day and night, but especially at night when I went to bed. Evil thoughts raced through my mind as scenes and dreams played out in horrific thoughts. People being murdered, slaughtered with knives. demons dancing and screaming they would get me. Night after night I couldn't sleep, evil surrounded me in a whirlwind of terror. I thought I was going crazy. I tried sleeping with my radio on, but it too became evil as the songs took on a distorted form, calling for me to give in to the devil's grasp.

Nothing eased my mind, my body tossed and turned; I am sure my face of fear and actions were visible to my family, but no one said anything, they were consumed in their own personal hells. I'm not sure why I didn't use the name of Jesus to stop it, but sometimes fear pushes away all knowledge learned. I was not strong in the Lord back then, but I would be, eventually.

One day when my parents were out, I remembered my mom took Valium when her heart acted up with horrible palpitations, a medication our doctor prescribed for her. Would these pills help me? I went into my mother's dresser drawer and found them and took half a pill for the ritual night of horrors. I did not ask my mom for permission I just took it. The pill worked and I finally slept, but the next night hell came back to haunt me, and with each opportunity I would go into my mom's drawer and grab another half, until half a pill stopped working, then I took a whole pill. I didn't care about what I was doing, I was desperate. I knew it was wrong not telling my mom, and I thought she would know some pills were missing, however her silence told me she didn't, and I continued.

One night after I once again took a pill from my mother's little helper which now became mine, I was beyond frantic. The one pill was not working and I knew it would be impossible to grab more, I thought of taking the whole bottle and swallowing it all at once, death was the sure

way of escaping this hell I was living in. I can't explain the depth of emotional and mental pain I was in; I only knew I had to escape it.

I threw myself on my bedroom floor with my head resting on my bed. I began to cry uncontrollably. When my tears dried, I asked the air as I looked around my room, "who is going to help me?" My eyes fell on the small statue of the Blessed Virgin Mary given to me by my grandmother not long before she died. Were my eyes deceiving me? I thought I saw a drop of water glistening from the statue's eye. Did one of my tears fall on her? I stood up and took the statue to look more closely. Yes, there was a drop of water under her eye; this did not make sense. Was I losing my mind? I had been crying into my folded arms resting on my bed. tears could not have fallen on the statue as it was behind me.

I searched every inch of my room for water, was my ceiling leaking? No! Certainly, the statue was not crying: was it? But what other explanation was there? I know many Catholics who go overboard actually worshiping Mother Mary as I called her; many pray to her instead of asking her to pray to her Son for us. I am not saying you shouldn't honor her as she is the Mother of our Savior, chosen by God from all women of all times.

As I looked at the statue I heard a voice inside my spirit, my mind, my thoughts. Ok now I felt for sure that I was going crazy.

"Elaine, go to my son."

Would Satan tell me to go to Jesus? Even in my desperate state of mind I knew that wasn't the devil's voice. Was it Mother Mary telling me this?

Again, the voice echoed in my mind and spirit, "Go to my son, His name is your power."

Just in case it was true, I did go to her son. I took my dusty Bible off my dusty shelf, blew the dust off and opened it to no particular page. The first words my eyes fell on were in

Acts, Chapter 16 verses 1-5 "Once when we were going to the place of prayer, we were met by a female

slave who had a spirit by which she predicted the future. She earned a great deal of money for her owners by fortune-telling. She followed Paul and the rest of us, shouting, "These men are servants of the Highest God, who are telling you the way to be saved." She kept this up for many days. Finally, Paul became so annoyed that he turned around and said to the spirit, "In the name of Jesus Christ I command you to come out of her!" At that moment the spirit left her."

Was this my answer? Could I get rid of this satanic torture just by using the name of Jesus? I immersed myself in reading the Bible and found many more scriptures using the name of Jesus. I wasn't new to knowing about Jesus, our Priest (church) spoke about Him every week, at Mass. Had I truly listened instead of letting my mind wander to other important things like the Beatles, or whatever was capturing my young heart at the time, I would have learned more about Jesus.

I knew I was up late; summer was almost over with school starting soon, but with my sister staying at a friend's house, I wasn't worried about needing to go to bed earlier as MaryAnn tended to do. I just kept reading the Bible. Mom saw my light peeking under my door, she knocked asking if she could come in. "Elaine, are you okay?" as she opened the door. "No mom," and I started to cry. Mom rushed to my side just hugging me until the tears stopped. "Mom, I think we need to talk, I have been doing something I know was wrong, but I couldn't stop. As we sat together on my bed, I told her what I was going through after we stopped the Ouija board, and about taking her

Valium. Instead of mom being upset with me she bowed her head and cried, saying she was sorry over and over again.

"Mom, why are you sorry? I was the one taking your pills, I should be saying sorry to you."

"Elaine, I should have been more attentive but I was going through the same thing, in fact we all were to a certain degree. I did notice that my pills were depleting but I was so consumed by satan's attacks that I felt maybe I was taking more than I thought. You were wrong in taking them and should have come to me earlier. I try very hard not to take them, but these evil attacks pushed me to the brink of insanity and the pills helped. The problem is they can be addictive and their effect lessens and then you take more. I believe you about your statue of the Virgin Mary, and we now know that Jesus is the true answer to our problem. Let's pray."

After that night we prayed and read the Bible, (New Testament) together, and the satanic attacks stopped, and we now had a weapon to use against the devil...Jesus! Was the statue of Mary a miracle? Yes, I know I didn't imagine it because her message was true and freeing. Yes, that was a miracle.

The attacks on our minds stopped, but satan wasn't finished with us as he will always try. No, he wasn't finished, he just changed his tactics.

Satan changed his tactics attacking my sister MaryAnn's health which unfolded one early sultry Sunday morning. We were hot, sweaty and not in the best of moods. Five-thirty in the morning was too early to get up especially in that heat. The humidity hung in the air like a pillow threatening to suffocate, and the heat burnt your skin without the help of the sun beating down on my body. I thought Church should be canceled on days like this. But my dad had to go to work early, so we got up, struggled to put our clothes on over our sweaty bodies, which was a challenge. Back then you dressed up for church, men in suits, women in dresses, some of us wearing girdles, all wearing nylons, it was like putting a second skin over our legs. At fourteen I was pleasantly plump, so girdles were a part of my Sunday dress code when all I wanted was to let it all hang loose. Girdles and bras were torture to put on when it was cool, in the humid heat it became a sticky wrestling match as you stretched, pulled, turned, and tossed your sweaty bodies into these torturous clothes. They were made to make you feel good about yourself. A must for young and old women, we had to conform to what society demanded, and even though I wasn't what would be called fat back then, I was still heavier than most girls of fourteen. Finally dressed, we piled into the car and sat on seats so hot our legs practically stuck to the seat material. It is safe for me to say we were not a happy family going to worship God.

After the service my sister and I found our way back to the solitude of our bedrooms. Peeling the now very damp clothes from my body I went back to my hot, damp bed. My only escape from the penetrating humid heat would be sleep.

Later in the morning my sister entered my room to get the record player that was given to us on Christmas of

1964. I was angry because she woke me to take my prized possession. Although it was given to both of us, I used it often, and we would often argue over whose bedroom it should stay in.

We had different tastes in music, she enjoyed Barry Manilow and the Monkees, I was a Beatle fan all the way until their music became strange and eerie echoing what was happening in their hazy drugged minds, awakening the horrible feeling of the Ouija board experience.

The answer to the argument over the record player would have been to give us both a record player, but my parents were not well off so one would have to do, of course we could have saved our babysitting money until we could buy another one; but who would keep the old one?

As the argument escalated, I finally gave in, "take it MaryAnn, and shut my door when you leave," I yelled and turned my body toward my wall. As I tried to calm down, I heard a strange noise behind me, I turned, horrified at the sight of my sister falling to the floor with a distorted look on her face. That's when the lights I saw in my mind tricked me in to believing she was being electrocuted.

I screamed as I jumped up on my bed daring my feet not to make contact with the floor, then jumped from my bed toward my opened door.

"Mom, mom," I frantically screamed, "MaryAnn is being electrocuted!"

As I ran down the stair's mom was running up, like firemen who run into the danger while others run away from it.

When I reached the bottom of the stairs, I ran to the phone to call an ambulance. As I did this mom called out for me to call an ambulance.

"I did mom, I did, I am going outside to wait so I can tell them what unit we are in."

As I waited, crying uncontrollably I wrestled with the guilty thought of leaving my mother to be with MaryAnn alone. Meanwhile in the house when mom ran into my bedroom, she found MaryAnn convulsing on the floor, mom kicked all the wires from the record player away, believing they were the reason for the convulsion. When MaryAnn's body stopped shaking, she became very still, her lips blue and her breathing so shallow it was barely noticeable. Mom told me much later that she thought MaryAnn had died, and she looked up saying to God, "so this is it," no other words could escape her trembling body as she waited for help to arrive.

Outside I paced back and forth for what seemed like eternity. Finally, I heard the sirens, and when the two men quickly exited the ambulance, we all ran to our unit. I opened the door to let them in with all their equipment and stayed at the bottom of the stairs. I called my dad at work and informed the person answering the phone of what was happening, "Please," I cried in desperation, "Please get my dad to go to Grace Hospital to meet my mom there. I think my sister is dying," I sobbed as I spoke. As I hung up the phone, I heard one of the paramedics say, "Your daughter is not dead she wasn't electrocuted, it looks more like she had a seizure."

As they rushed back to the ambulance mom went with them, I assured her I called dad, and they were gone leaving me at the side of the road: Alone.

I slowly went back into the house, walking as if my feet were made of cement, still wearing my pajama's. Walking to the middle of our front room with tears streaming down my face; tears that would not, could not stop, I asked God to save my sister. "Please God, save MaryAnn, please," I wept aloud.

My oldest brother Rick along with his best friend Ray and my younger brother Billy who had gone to a later mass walked in. Rick quickly came to my side, "Elaine, what's wrong?"

I quickly told them what happened and Rick grabbing Billy's arm rushed out of the house with Ray who had a car, and quickly drove to the hospital without a second thought about me, leaving me alone.

I continued to kneel in the front room praying and crying for I don't know how long. As long as I stayed on my knees and prayed, I felt as if I was doing something, anything to help my sister. Lost in the depths of despair, feeling sorry for myself that I was left alone, I was startled jumping up at hearing a loud knock at the front door.

As I opened the door I was met with a sudden burst of compassion, "I wondered if you were alone as I didn't see you leave. Are you okay Elaine?"

Sally, a neighbor around 17 years of age touched my shoulder, and I turned hugging her thin bony shoulders, crying. Sally slowly walked me to the couch and as we sat, my tears spent, I told her what had happened and how frightened I was.

"Is there something I can do."

Before I could think I asked if she would kneel and pray with me.

"I am not the right person for that Elaine, I don't think God wants to hear from me, I'm not a good person."

Sally's family were deep into the occult and her older brother, we suspected, was abusing her; we felt he was forcing her into making pornographic movies while getting her high on drugs.

Sally always had a haunted look not evil but a blank, lost look, almost as if she was dead inside. There is a truth to the saying, 'the eyes are the windows of the soul,' we often forget that at times our eyes speak louder than our words. Sally's eyes spoke volumes to those who could see her hopelessness, the death of life within her.

I rarely went into her home, it felt evil and after what we experienced with satan, I stayed away from people I knew who delved into the occult. Mom was different, she walked where even 'Angels dared to tread', so the saying goes. Mom often visited that family sharing her baked goods, and unconditional love. Mom and Dad were a positive example in a neighborhood of lost souls. It is a long story as to why we were living amongst them, but that is for another time.

After Sally told me she wasn't a good person I felt the Holy Spirit guiding me, and went to get my Bible. As I left her side, I realized how calm I was, even though my sister was never far from my thoughts, through my desperation God called me to take my mind off myself, and put it on Sally.

Sally looked at me confused, but didn't question my actions. I sat back down beside her, reading to her about God's love.

"How could He love me, Elaine? I am what you would call a sinner, a big, big sinner."

"Sally, we are all sinners, I don't believe in a small or big sin, sin is sin to God, whatever it is. God loves us so much Sally that He offered us forgiveness through His son Jesus." We talked a little longer about Jesus. Sally seemed thirsty for more so I gave her my Bible and told her to read the New Testament starting with John, and if she had any questions to feel free to ask my mom or I.

Sally stood up, took my hand and I asked if we could pray, so we knelt together on the floor. It was there she began to find love and forgiveness. I prayed for my sister, then for her as tears streamed down her face.

Suddenly the phone rang and we both jumped at the sound, I answered it quickly, it was my dad.

"Elaine," dad's voice was shaky. "I am coming to pick you up to bring you to the hospital. MaryAnn is fine sitting in a hospital bed and talking like she normally does.

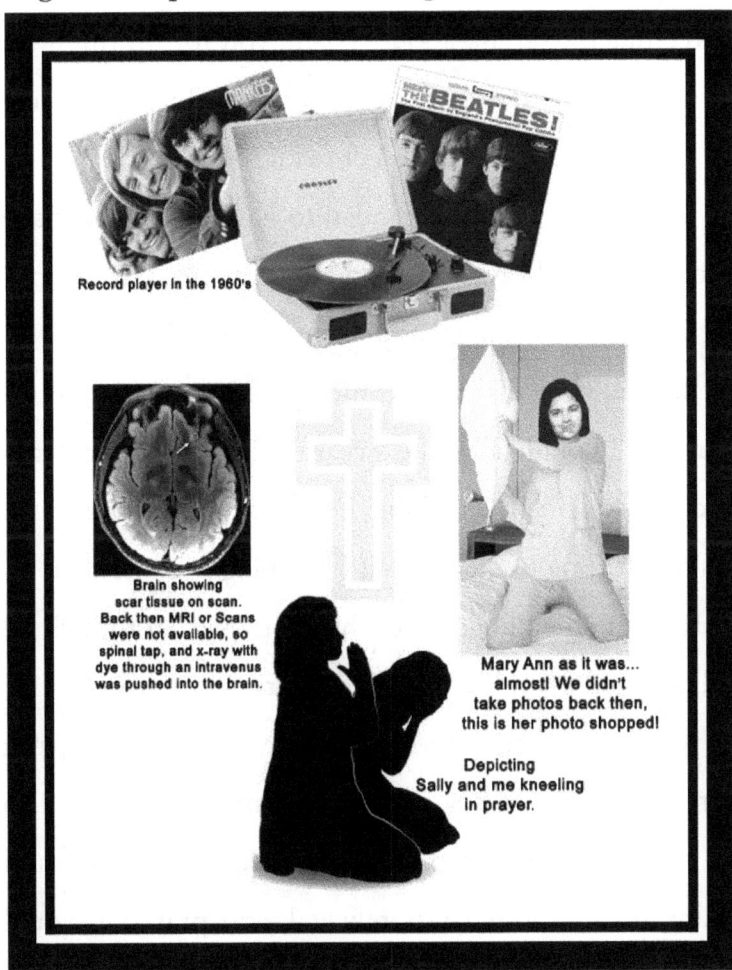

Record player in the 1960's

Brain showing scar tissue on scan. Back then MRI or Scans were not available, so spinal tap, and x-ray with dye through an intravenus was pushed into the brain.

Mary Ann as it was... almost! We didn't take photos back then, this is her photo shopped!

Depicting Sally and me kneeling in prayer.

She had a seizure but they need to do tests to determine why. I will tell you more when we're in the car. Get ready."

"I'm sorry Sally, that was my dad and he's coming to take me to the hospital, and I need to get ready." I quickly told her what my dad said and that I would keep her informed." I thanked her for coming to be with me, and hugged her, she whispered in my ear; "thank you Elaine, I have much to think about. Thank you for praying with me and giving me your Bible." With that she left through the front door, and I ran to get ready.

I have never known my dad to have a weak or shaky voice. He was always strong and courageous, but that day the fear he was feeling was present in his voice.

By the time dad picked me up his strong voice had returned, I could smell the sweat of the hot day and railroad grease as he hugged me. For some reason that smell was comforting to me, a smell I had long become used to. Today that smell lingered on his clothes even though he had changed from his overalls at work.

When I arrived at the hospital, I was met by my Aunt Gert who wrapped her arms around me as we walked to my sister's hospital room. Seeing MaryAnn sitting and talking to my mom I was relieved, and prayed I would never see her in the throes of a seizure again. Mom, Aunt Gert and my brothers decided to go to the cafeteria but I wanted to stay. As dad and I continued to talk MaryAnn made that strange noise again, and her body twisted and turned violently. Dad was quick to put her hospital bed down flat while grabbing the padded tongue depressor to put in her mouth to stop her from biting her tongue.

I ran screaming for help, which was met with nurses running to help my dad.

Aunt Gert, who decided to come back to MaryAnn's side to give my dad time to sit with my mom in the cafeteria was met with my hysterical screams. She grabbed me guiding me to the visitor's lounge. A nurse followed us to console me and explain what my sister was experiencing. My tears flowed freely, even though I had tissues to wipe them, my aunt continued to replace them as each one became soaked. Eventually my tears and nose stopped running as I grew quiet. I had heard what the nurse was saying but it didn't register in my mind. My thoughts were completely on my sister. Was she dying? Then my thoughts were only on myself, as I quietly prayed asking God to never see another seizure like that again. That fear followed me throughout my life, even as a nurse; but God was faithful in answering my prayer, and as weird as it seems, I never witnessed another Grand Mal seizure, (now known as Tonic-Clonic Seizures,) even now in writing this. I have seen many petit-mal-seizures (now known

as Absence Seizures) as my daughter suffered with these for years.

MaryAnn

After many weeks and many horrifying tests and diagnosis of a

possible brain tumor, MaryAnn was found to have scar tissue that had formed touching a part of her brain.

She was put on heavy anti-seizure medications which seemed to change her personality, but she had no further seizures.

I will always remember while she was in the hospital her neurologist came to check on her. He was followed by the Head Nurse and student nurses. As the doctor put his one foot into the room MaryAnn screamed at him, "Get Out!" with other not so nice words, while throwing a pillow at him. He quickly turned around bumping into the nurses roughly, putting his hand up saying loudly, "Med change!"

Although this doctor had a horrible bedside manner and was not kind to the nurses or his patients, he was in fact praised and honored as a Neurosurgeon and Neurologist. One of the best in Canada.

When I decided to become a nurse, I did some training on the Neurology floor, and I quickly realized why everyone was afraid of this doctor. One day I witnessed the Head Nurse locking herself in the medication room telling him she would not come out until he treated her more respectfully, and he did, for a while. Often when he was coming to do his rounds all the student nurses were told not to talk to him or approach him. In fact, there were days we were told to hide, the stairways being our choice of refuge, we could almost hear each other's hearts beating rapidly. I did not like this man, this doctor, but I did respect his position. I prayed for him from the first time I met him as my sister's doctor, and that continued until I heard of his death many years later.

And now for the miracle!

It began with the Charismatic Renewal in the Catholic Church. Most of my family eventually attended the prayer meetings that bubbled up from the Charismatic Renewal.

I had heard about the Charismatic Renewal from my Religion teacher (a movement that was far reaching in the Catholic church,) but I was reluctant to go as my experience with the occult made me question doing anything different other than going to church and reading my Bible.

That said, mom's good friend Jane from their Bible study group had invited her to a meeting, although hesitant she decided to go and called me. I listened to mom's pleas of not wanting to go alone. We were both still raw from our experiences with the occult. It just so happened I had that night off and finally gave in and went with her. I had vowed never again to be fooled and tricked into falling for any form of the occult. I had read and prepared myself in the knowledge of just what consisted of occult practices.

Although I had fears about going to this prayer meeting, all fear left as I walked in the door. My mother's friend

Jane met us with her beautiful welcoming smile, hugging us, then introducing us to many like-minded Christians. They embraced us with smiles and hugs. It soon became apparent that hugging each other was a loving welcoming gesture of friendship. Not everyone was Catholic, we were all of different faiths worshipping the same Savior, Jesus.

Jesus himself said, "Whoever is not against us is for us," in the scripture reading of **Mark 9:38-41** in the Bible, (New International Version.)

[38] "Teacher," said John, "we saw someone driving out demons in your name and we told him to stop, because he was not one of us."

[39] "Do not stop him," Jesus said. "For no one who does a miracle in my name can in the next moment say anything bad about me, [40] for whoever is not against us is for us. [41] Truly I tell you, anyone who gives you a cup of water in my name because you belong to the Messiah will certainly not lose their reward."

As time went on, I came to know what a true personal relationship with the Lord was, and my faith grew. I often thought of my Great Aunt Nellie, she was definitely a part of the Charismatic Renewal long before most people had knowledge of it.

It wasn't long before my husband of three weeks along with immediate family and relatives joined this worship group. I was happy when I saw Priests and Nuns and, other Clergy become active in this renewal.

Actually, within the Catholic Church it is known that the Second Vatican Council, famously called Vatican II (1962-1965) paved the way for the Catholic Charismatic by throwing wide open the windows of the Church to let the Spirit of God renew the Church. Pope John XIII ushered in a "springtime of faith" or a "new Pentecost."

It was during one of our meetings when a woman had a word of knowledge that someone was being healed of a seizure condition.

In Christianity a word of knowledge is a spiritual gift, listed in the Bible, in 1-Corinthians Chapter 12:4-11 (*New International Version*)

4) There are different kinds of gifts, but the same Spirit distributes them. 5) There are different kinds of service, but the same Lord. 6) There are different kinds of working, but in all of them and in everyone it is the same God at work. 7) Now to each one the

manifestation of the Spirit is given for the common good. 8) To one there is given through the Spirit a message, message of wisdom, to another a message of knowledge by means of the same Spirit, 9) to another faith by the same Spirit, to another gifts of healing by that one Spirit, 10) to another miraculous powers, to another prophecy, to another distinguishing between spirits, to another speaking in different kinds of tongues, and to still another the interpretation of tongues. 11) All these are the work of one and the same Spirit, and he distributes them to each one, just as he determines."

Some people think of the Holy Spirit as their inner voice guiding them to do the right thing, yet so much more.

MaryAnn and her best friend Truly who also had seizures, claimed the healing, as did all our family who attended that meeting. We all claimed it for them in our thoughts and hearts. One thing we were taught was to never stop taking medications until a doctor verifies that a healing is a reality. Even when one wholeheartedly believes they are healed, we need to be aware that we could be listening to our hopeful thoughts or other thoughts from the dark side, not a Star Wars saying but that of the devil and his demons.

MaryAnn called her doctor's office the next day to book an appointment. They had a cancellation for that afternoon and MaryAnn practically ran there arriving early as she was so excited in anticipating her doctor would verify it.

When her name was called, she was told which room to go into. She stood, she sat, she stood again biting her nails as she waited. As soon as the doctor opened the door MaryAnn quickly blurted out, "I had a miracle."

Her doctor hesitated for a second then walked in shutting the door behind him. He could see that plainly she was very excited. He remained calm asking her to join him in sitting in the chairs. Trying desperately to do as he asked, she finally sat, but still her doctor waited until she stopped squirming in her chair.

"Okay MaryAnn, tell me of what condition you have been healed of?"

"I had a miracle, a healing of my seizures," she answered, wiggling in her chair as she explained to him about the meeting and the word of knowledge.

"What is a word of knowledge?" he asked. "

"Well," MaryAnn prayed for the right words, "I belong to a prayer meeting with many other Christians in the Charismatic Renewal. The word of knowledge is a gift of the Holy Spirit, where a person in the meeting knows what God is currently doing or intends to do.

"I know this sounds crazy doctor, but this person said someone was being healed of a seizure condition."

"You're not crazy MaryAnn and I have heard of the Charismatic Renewal. I need to know if you stopped taking your medications?"

"No Doctor B" MaryAnn answered, "I need you to confirm it first."

"Good, that's the right thing to do. I will set up some tests to confirm your miracle."

The tests were set up quickly and it wasn't long before the results were in and MaryAnn was called for an appointment the next day.

"Well MaryAnn, all the tests came out normal and the scar tissue that caused your seizures is absolutely vanished. Our diagnostic equipment's are much more advanced now days, and I can honestly say without a doubt, that you are healed; yes, you did receive a miracle."

MaryAnn jumped up saying "Praise the Lord."

Dr. B smiled as he waited for her to sit back down and continued, "You have indeed had a miracle, a healing of your seizure condition. We can start taking you off your medications, this must be done slowly, but in the matter of a few weeks you will be off your medications.

Dr. B. was amazed, and he stood facing MaryAnn who had once again jumped up unable to contain her happiness.

"It isn't often for any doctor to witness a miracle, but I have the proof right here," as he pointed to the results. "The scar tissue could not be found," he repeated, more for his understanding than MaryAnn's. "In all the extensive tests we put you through. I must agree, you did receive a miracle."

As MaryAnn thanked him, she left the room, Dr. B stood in the doorway watching her leave, his nurse later told MaryAnn, "He just stood there, watching you, and then looked up, shaking his head and simply said, thank you. "

MaryAnn rushed home to tell everyone the wonderful news, and at the next prayer meeting she shared the confirmation of her miracle, touching the hearts of many people, those within the prayer community and those who heard of her miracle.

It is wonderful to see God in action through His son Jesus. We heard that the neighbors, Sally's family, who had lived next door to us turned away from the occult and began their journey on a new path to wholeness, in going to church and learning more about Jesus. This all happened long before MaryAnn's miracle. It seems the day Sally prayed with me was the day Jesus entered her life, and her light shone on other members of her family. We moved soon after MaryAnn's medical emergency and lost contact with them. It was about ten years later when I was attending a healing service that I saw Sally. I didn't recognize her at first as her hard makeup was now soft and clean, she was so healthy, happy, and when talking to her I found out she was married with two children.

If you don't know Jesus, give him a try, go to a good church, it doesn't have to be Catholic, just make sure the church you choose is rooted deeply in Christ. You will be embraced in the presence of His Amazing Grace, and in the knowledge of His love for you.

Miracles, healings come in many ways, physical, emotional, and spiritual, to name a few. Not everyone receives a miracle, but I am positive miracles surround us every day, you just have to be aware of the everyday moments in life. It seems in this story, we all received miracles. My family, my sister MaryAnn, Sally and her family.

To God Be The Glory

Chapter Eight
I Was Blind but Now I See

This miracle came to me all the way from France in the year 1959; I was seven years old and the baby of our family of five back then.

We lived on Labadie Road in Windsor, Ontario, just across the river from our international friendship city of Detroit, Michigan.

Labadie road was a very busy neighborhood, and to the adults who renamed it 'Incubator Road' it was a lifeline of love, caring and generosity. This road consisted of many young families, my mother said, "it felt like the news of a pregnancy, and or birth were happening almost weekly." So, it is safe to say it was a road filled with laughter, crying, little arguments, a very active road where many children of all ages met to play.

During school days' mom said, "most mothers, and some dads would sit on their front porch stoops, drinking their coffee while watching the children walk to school. This was a time for neighbors to visit each other to discuss the happenings of our community. These visits happened mostly in spring and fall; winter found us watching the children through our front screen doors."

"Summer brought a whole new dynamic to incubator road. We continued to sit on our porch stoops drinking coffee, but now it was just to watch the children play. When I look back, I realize how organized we were, two parents were always watching the children. We took turns, so each mother, or sometimes a dad could do house cleaning comfortably knowing their children were safe under the watchful eyes of trusted neighbors. It was a wonderful time, a caring time where neighbors watched out for neighbors, you don't find that too often today."

As a child it was a wonderful road to live on, I had many friends my age to play with and we always felt safe.

Today we live in a parental helicopter mode, where parents are always aware of our world filled with dangers around every corner; whether that's a misperception or not, it seems to be a reality.

Back in 1959 we walked to school, rode our bikes, played outside until dusk, depending on your age. Our play area was the middle of the street where we played kick the can, hide and seek, dodge ball, or just sitting on our door steps or backyards, playing with our toys.

One hot summer day I saw many kids crowded around my friend Vicky who had a new toy, and was the same age, although very different in size.

Me and Vicky, same age.

Vicky held what was called an action toy with a disc flyer launcher, made of hard plastic. Today it is considered a dangerous toy, but back then it was simply a toy to keep kids entertained. When searching for a photo of the toy I found an updated version, (below), I was surprised that it was still available. The stem that jutted out where the plastic flying saucer laid was the cause of my injury.

As many kids gathered around Vicky and her toy, I squeezed myself in to reach her side. Vicky was letting everyone take a turn, and every time the saucer flew into the air laughter accompanied it with oohs and ahhs. I was next to make that saucer fly; but as Vicky put it in my hand another kid who yelled, "hey, it's my turn," grabbed the toy from its tight hold in my hand, but because I didn't let go when he pulled on it the toy was pushed back into my face, and the stem jutting out pierced my left eye. I remember screaming at the pain. It all happened so quickly and as everyone stood silent in fear I ran home crying, with Vicky following close behind me.

My mother, hearing my cries rushed to my side. Every parent knows their child's cries, the cry that something was seriously wrong alarmed my mom into action.

Through my tears my mom checked my eye with Vicky explaining through her tears what happened. After mom checked there didn't seem to be too much to see except for a tiny red spot. Mom comforted Vicky saying I would be alright and sent her home. Putting a cold cloth on my eye mom brought me to her bed staying with me until I fell asleep. Rick and MaryAnn watched from the bedroom doorway; they were so frightened but mom put her arms around them so she could quietly lead them away so she could shut the door.

She told me she checked on me often but didn't worry as I was sleeping soundly. When supper was ready, she asked Rick to wake me up, but he returned saying he couldn't wake me. Rick's news caused mom to shiver in fear as she rushed to my side unable to wake me, she sat me up and her fear turned into panic as I began to vomit. When she laid me back down, she looked into my eye gasping at the blood that pooled and covered my eye. MaryAnn started to cry, but all mom could think to do was ask Rick to sit with me while she ran to the phone, knocking the lamp off her night table.

Mom immediately called our family Doctor, sobbing as she described what was happening. He was still in his office, and told her to keep me quiet, "I am coming to your house Beatrice, I am leaving right now." After he hung up mom called my dad's work, he was a Foreman on the afternoon shift at the Canadian Pacific Railroad. It just happened that dad was in the office when mom's call came, and the Supervisor handed him the phone quickly at hearing mom's shaky voice.

She told dad what happened and that the doctor was coming to check me. Mom told dad to wait by the phone, and she would call him back with the news. He was just around the corner from the hospital and could be there within minutes.

When Dr. McLister arrived, he took one look at me picked me up and told mom to get into his car so she could hold me while he rushed me to the hospital. "It was a great blessing that Vicky's mother Diane had come over to see how I was, as she was able to take control, calling your dad telling him to meet us at the emergency department at Grace Hospital. She also called your Aunt Gert to let her know what was happening. Gert told her she would be right over to take care of your brother and sister, but

Diane suggested she would be needed more at the hospital, and not to worry she would care for Rick and MaryAnn."

Mom said my dad had reached the hospital before they did, opened the door of the car gently picking me up carrying my floppy unconscious body quickly into the emergency room not waiting for Dr. McLister.

After that mom said everything happened at a feverish pace, a specialist was called in, who examined me to find that the blood pooling around my eye was actually draining behind my eye into the brain. "Your daughter is in a coma due to this bleeding, and needs to go to surgery immediately."

Mom and dad signed all the necessary papers, the ones that tell you that your child could have a stroke, or possibly die on the operating table. (Papers that echoed in my adult life when I signed papers for my daughter many times.)

Back home there was a flurry of activity as news of my condition reached each neighbor. My mom and dad's siblings, along with our parish priest came to the hospital to support them, and pray. Praying harder than they had ever prayed before.

Back then hospitals had very strict rules regarding how many visitors could be in the waiting room. But that night they made an exception in allowing my parents support system to stay.

Mom said, "when Dr. McLister and the Ophthalmologist Dr. McGraph entered the waiting room still dressed in their scrubs, everyone stood. You could hear everyone taking in a deep breath which seemed to suck the oxygen out of the air. When we were told you came through the surgery well, all that air rushed back into the room. We were told that you were in critical condition, and they would not know for hours whether you would come out of your coma."

It is hard to imagine how my parents coped with this news. I was not dying, but would I be their same little girl if and when I came out of the coma. They were also warned that I could be blind, but time would tell. Mom continued, "Dr. McLister," mom said, "told us to go home and get some rest, that he was going to stay by your side and would call us if there were any changes in your condition. Of course, your dad and I didn't want to leave, but back then, not like today, parents couldn't stay with their sick children. We weren't allowed to see you, even for a minute, so we decided to go home, but we knew rest would not be something we would get, especially when on our knees. Our parish Priest reminded everyone if they felt they needed to go to church, that it was open twenty-four hours, as was every church back then. Your dad and I decided to go home as we needed to be with Rick and MaryAnn, and to let Diane go home to her family. Your aunt Gert came home with us to babysit in case we were called to the hospital in the night."

Mom said that when they arrived home, Diane met them rather nervously, as she didn't know how we would react to the news that many neighbors came over to clean the house. On entering the house, it smelt so fresh and clean, and we were so thankful that our neighbors did this, making sure Diane knew how much we appreciated it. Not only did the house look and smell clean, but when we walked into the kitchen there on the table sat casseroles, pies, cakes and much more. I looked at Diane and smiled however, with the intensity of our ordeal we couldn't bring ourselves to eat, but I assured Diane we would later. I then tearfully told Diane what was happening while Joe went to check on Rick and MaryAnn. As Diane stood at the door to leave, she burst into tears, "I am so sorry Bea,

I wish we hadn't bought that horrible toy for Vicky, I am so, so sorry." I felt her pain and hugged her reminding her it was an accident, and no one's fault. As she left, I assured her I would call her in the morning to let her know how you were."

"That night we were told that everyone who was at the hospital had a sleepless night, some went straight to a church to continue praying."

After an agonizing two days spent in the waiting room, with only one brief visit to see me, my parents were told late that evening that I had woken from my coma and was able to tell them what had happened, in my child like way. "This means Mrs. Balestrini," Dr. McGraph told her on the phone, while my dad pressed his ear to hers in order to hear what the doctor was saying, "that there doesn't seem to be any brain damage from the bleeding. This is very good news."

Knowing I could move and talk, the doctors put me into a sedated coma, fearing I would move and risk another round of bleeding should I move my head or touch the bandages on my eye.

Since I was no longer in critical condition but still in need of twenty-four-hour supervision, many family members volunteered and a schedule was set up. Although I continued to be in a medicated coma, the worry was when I was taken off the strong sedation that I would touch or rub my eye.

Finally I was taken off the sedation and every time a family member came to watch me, which was every four hours, they would bring me a gift. I have to admit I was spoiled. Sometimes it was a set of new pajamas, often it was a new story book they could read to me. Because both my eyes were covered with shield bandages, they had to explain to me what the gift was and what it looked like.

Eventually the eye shield and bandages were taken off the uninjured eye as the doctor's felt there was nothing that could be done other than what they were doing. Because of the bleeding, both my eyes had loss of sight, and my prognosis was looking grim. My cousin Sandy who I was very close to was always a loving strong presence in my life. We had a bond, we both shared the same birthdate, Sandy being thirteen years older, and as adults we continued to grow in our admiration of each other. Sandy asked Dr. McGraph if I was able to have a doll, he nodded yes saying, "it should be fine, but someone needs to be with her when she plays with it. There is still danger of another bleed if the doll should accidentally hit her eye." That could be arranged, so Sandy brought me the most beautiful baby doll, I knew it was beautiful by the way she explained the doll's features. I was so excited. I remember Sandy laughing at my pleasure. Each family member that came would give me the doll, but would have to take it away when they left. I no longer needed twenty-four-hour supervision, but continued to have many visitors. The next time Sandy came to visit she brought me clothes to put on the doll. Sandy worked in a Nursing Home, and often did activities with some of the residents. One elderly woman loved knitting baby clothes and Sandy had asked her to make some for my doll. Receiving the clothes, I squealed with delight, and since I could now see, although not clearly from the one unpatched eye I could see to clumsily dress the doll I named Anna. As I held the doll's arm to try to button the back, I lost my grip and the hand of the doll fell on my injured eye. Although that eye had a patch and bandages on it, it didn't take much pressure to cause damage.

Sandy rushed to get Sister Martha, my nurse, who examined me, but I seemed fine, but many precautions were taken, and Sister Martha called Dr. McGraph who ordered complete monitoring. Sandy felt so horrible and stayed with me even when my parents arrived. I couldn't see Sandy's tears but I heard them in her shaky voice and the sniffing of her nose. As mom, dad and Sandy stayed at my side I slowly drifted into sleep. That small little doll's hand caused the bleeding all over again putting my life in danger. I couldn't hear the panic and desperate activity, as both Dr. McGraph and Dr. McLister arrived at my side, it didn't take long before I was rushed into surgery, leaving my parents and cousin shocked and horrified at the thought that could be the last time they saw me alive. Mom says they rushed to the pay phones to call family and friends for prayers. Our neighbors quickly went into action. Mom told me how our neighbors continued to make food and babysit Rick and MaryAnn.

When the doctors appeared to inform my parents on how this second surgery went their facial expressions alarmed them.

"Is our daughter dead?" my dad asked.

Dr. McLister quickly answered in a heartbeat, "Oh, no Joe, she came through the surgery fine. I am sorry if we look worried, I will let Dr. McGraph explain."

No Doctor likes to give bad news, but unfortunately it is part of their profession. "The reason we look worried," Dr. McGraph led them to a quiet area of the waiting room asking them to sit down. "This was another extensive bleed, and I'm not sure of the outcome. Elaine is in a coma, but we knew this going into surgery, it might take her a little longer to come out of this one. She is in critical condition and once again needs extensive monitoring and care. When she does come out of the coma, we will have to treat her as we did before, by putting her in an induced medicated coma so her eye and brain can heal. Another fear is her vision, it is highly unlikely that she will regain any vision in her injured eye, as for the right eye her vision will be impaired, almost to the point of blindness. You need to prepare yourselves for the fact that Elaine will not regain her vision. I am so sorry to give you this news."

Mom said they were numb, they knew my left eye was severely damaged, but weren't expecting that my uninjured right eye would have the same fate.

After the doctors left my parents were surrounded by a circle of family love and prayers. Sandy did not join the circle, she remained seated sobbing with her head bowed. Mom went to her and rubbed her back. Sandy just kept repeating, "I am so sorry Aunt Bea, I wish I had never given her that doll, I'm going to throw it away. Look, look what I did to Elaine, look what I did."

My mother was not a person to anger easily, or to speak loudly, but she took hold of Sandy's shoulders, "Look at me Sandy, look me in the eyes," mom said sternly.

As Sandy lifted her head to look at her, mom continued. "This is not your fault Sandy, Elaine loves that doll, and you will not throw that doll away. We are going to believe with all our hearts that she will be healed, but if God has other plans for her then we must thank Him as He will bring good out of this."

Mom was to Sandy as Aunt Nellie was to mom. I am not sure if mom truly believed in what she was saying about my eyes being healed, but, often in times of fear and worry our faith becomes stronger, and the only thing we can do is to put it in God's hands, and let Him take the wheel.

Mom held Sandy as they both cried, and as dad watched, he too slowly joined them. Dad was a man of great restraint, tears were not something he easily shed, but this was different and he allowed himself to become vulnerable, his tears joining theirs.

Because they couldn't visit me, everyone left the hospital to meet at our family's church to pray.

I recovered from that surgery, but my eyes remained heavily bandaged. I would love to say everything was good after that but I had another bleed. My mom had called the hospital to say she couldn't make it to visit me as she had a Migraine. When I was told this, I cried, causing the eye to once again bleed, and as the first two times, the third was no different. Everything was as before.

It became apparent that as time passed, the doctors' diagnosis of my going blind in both eyes was becoming a reality.

Once I came out of the coma, and induced coma, I became aware of my eye bandages being removed daily so I could be examined on how the eye was healing, and to see if I had any sensitivity to the light of the small flashlight that was shining in my eyes. My only hint of vision was a foggy dull light in what was called my good eye, but no hint of light in the injured eye.

As time passed with no further bleeding, it was decided I no longer needed the heavy eye bandages on both eyes except for an eye patch, that made me look like a pirate covering the injured eye.

My parents were encouraged to remove the patch and hold up something for me to identify. It became a daily game my dad would play with me. He would hold up a coin and would ask me what the coin was. It was mostly a guessing game as my vision in my injured eye remained sightless, while the good eye was described in terms of today as, legally blind. As I tried to see the coin I would guess as to what it was. The reward was in winning the coin. My dad with sad realization could not withhold the coin and always gave it to me even in the face of a wrong guess, which was most of the time.

It finally came to the understanding that my vision would not improve, in either eye. My nurses, especially Sister. Anne started to give me little jobs to do preparing me for the world of the blind.

My parents and family must have been devastated as anyone would. As I was so young, I didn't know the full implications of what I would be facing.

When little else could be done it was decided I could be discharged at the end of the week, but first there would be a discussion on attending a school for the blind. My parents would not be separated from me, "she's just too young," my mom cried, and in that desperation, that moment of hopelessness, that is when the miracle happened.

Sometimes Jesus swoops in at the final moment, a hero of sorts, and this is exactly what Jesus did. Through an act of faith in a divine encounter with the fruit of His mother Mary's love for Her son's children. There are some miracles that can be difficult to understand, especially when God chooses to heal through a different path.

That day, that glorious day when mom came to visit me, she said she had something special to give me. I am sure I was imagining an amazing present, but instead she took a small vial from her purse, and holding it up she said she was going to use the water inside to make the sign of the cross on my eyelids and pray.

'Elaine, inside this bottle is a drop of water from Lourdes."

"What is water from Lourdes," I asked.

She then began to tell me the story of the Virgin Mary and the young girl Bernadette.

Mom told me the story in a way a child could understand, I will now explain it in my adult version.

In 1858, from February 11 to July 16 a fourteen-year-old girl named Bernadette Soubirous had numerous visions of the Virgin Mary by a rose bush in the town of Massabielle, France, at a nearby grotto. An underground stream was revealed to Bernadette, and from that stream many people have claimed miraculous healings.

The whole story and the importance of the healing stream can be seen and researched on the internet.

As mom sat at my side, she took the patch off my eye and explained to me that my Aunt Vi's relative had gone to Lourdes and brought back a small bottle of the blessed water.

Aunt Vi asked her if she could have a drop for my mom to bless me with. Actually, it was the very last drop, and through her gracious heart she gave it to my aunt to give to my mom in a tiny vial.

Mom took that tiny last drop using half of it to anoint my eye, the other half to place on my tongue. Mom then took a piece of paper from her purse and read it aloud, weaving her own personal prayer with the prayer on the paper

Lourdes-Water Prayer
By the use of this water from Lourdes
and through the intercession of the
Immaculate Conception of the Grotto,
and our Lord Jesus Christ
I ask for healing of my daughter Elaine's
eyes to be healed miraculously.
I ask that Elaine's sight return to normal,
Bringing glory to Our Lord Jesus Christ. Amen.
And mom continued, Our Lady of Lourdes
please pray for Elaine, St. Bernadette, pray for
Elaine.

Our family never prayed to the Blessed Virgin, we honored her in prayer as the mother of Jesus, and asked her to intercede, pray for us, to her son Jesus.

As a Catholic I know many who did pray to the Virgin Mary forgetting that it was her Son who was the giver of all. I know for me, Mother Mary, as I call her, was and is important, and I often ask her to pray for a special intention, knowing she would bring it to her Son. An example of this is in the Bible, where Jesus, probably not happy that His mother asked Him for a favor at the wedding they were attending.

John 2:1-11 (New International Version)

On the third day a wedding took place at Cana in Galilee. Jesus' mother was there, 2) **and Jesus and his disciples had also been invited to the wedding.** 3) **When the wine was gone, Jesus' mother said to him, "They have no more wine."**

4) "Woman, why do you involve me?" Jesus replied. "My hour has not yet come."

5) His mother said to the servants, "Do whatever he tells you."

6) Nearby stood six stone water jars, the kind used by the Jews for ceremonial washing, each holding from twenty to thirty gallons.

7) Jesus said to the servants, "Fill the jars with water;" so they filled them to the brim.

8) Then he told them, "Now draw some out and take it to the master of the banquet."

They did so, 9) and the master of the banquet tasted the water that had been turned into wine. He did not realize where it had come from, though the servants who had drawn the water knew. Then he called the bridegroom aside **10)** and said, "Everyone brings out the choice wine first and then the cheaper wine after the guests have had too much to drink; but you have saved the best till now."

11) What Jesus did here in Cana of Galilee was the first of the signs through which he revealed his glory; and his disciples believed in him.

Mary knew her son, and she knew He would honor her in her request, although her request was in the form of a statement. The Bible verse does not say how she became aware of the lack of wine, or who brought it to her attention, but the fact remains she told her son, and when she did this, he sort of scolded her knowing what she wanted of Him. We clearly know the time for Him to do miracles was not at that time, but He honored His mother by answering her. The fact that Mary knew her son and how He would react speaks volumes as to their relationship. He honored His mother, and if Jesus honored her then why shouldn't we.

This for me is a lesson on how we should be with Mother Mary. Worshiping her and praying to her is not acceptable, but asking her to pray for us is more than acceptable; she will bring it to her son. How wonderful is that.

This is a delicate subject for many, but the important part to remember is that we can honor her as Jesus' mother, after all God chose her from all time, past, present and future to carry the Savior of the world. The Gospel of Luke says that the angel Gabriel came to Mary to tell her that she would give birth to a son, and to name him Jesus, and that He would save people from their sins. When Mary asked the angel how she could be pregnant, since she was a virgin, the angel told her that God would do this through a miracle.

I can't imagine the fear, the feelings and emotions that Mary went through. Questions probably rushed into her mind, yet this startled, scared young woman answered by saying in

Luke 1:38, "I am the servant of the Lord. Let this happen to me as you say."

Back to the story, when mom finished with the prayer of Lourdes Water, we both looked up from our bowed heads and said Amen.

Mom sat and visited me for a while until visiting hours were over. As mom left, I saw her talking to my nurse that day, Sister Martha. I didn't know what she was telling her but she did take the prayer from her purse and showed it to her.

About twenty minutes after mom left, Dr. McGraph came to examine me. He went through his usual examination, checking my eyes, shining light into them, then holding an alphabet sign asking me to read it; much like when you have your eyes checked at the Optometrist.

"Elaine, I want you to read the top letters."

Another day, another try to get them right. Every time the doctor asked me to read, he never offered me a prize, or even a penny. I was always disappointed; I remember telling him a few times I didn't want to play that game anymore. However, this time was different, instead of the serious face he usually presented, he looked at Sister Martha shocked, and asked me to read the next line, then the next line until I had read the very last line.

"Elaine, do you see these letters? Even the tiny ones at the bottom?" he asked me.

"Yes," I answered. It's funny that I didn't realize I could see, it was just another examination that I had grown use to, another I would fail.

The doctor looked at Sister Martha whose smile couldn't get any bigger if she tried. It was then, at that moment I realized I could see their faces, the colors of their hair and clothes.

"I don't understand this Sister, what has happened?"

"Jesus healed me," I answered him simply.

His head turned toward me, "What did you say Elaine?"

"Jesus healed me."

He then asked Sister to bring me to his examining room within the hospital, asking her not to use a wheelchair but to let me walk and not hold her hand.

I followed them, something I was unable to do before.

As he examined my eyes in his office, asking me many questions, he looked at Sister Martha, "what has happened?"

"Jesus healed me," I answered again.

I then told him in my child like way and faith about my mom, the water, the prayer.

Sister Martha also answered, "I believe Dr. McGraph, that Elaine has received a miracle."

Continuing to look shocked and confused at the same time, he asked that I be brought back to my bed.

I was very aware I could now see and told both Doctor and Nurse that I knew the way back, and could do it on my own.

"No Elaine," Sister Martha said, "You always need to have a nurse with you."

I took her hand and skipped back to my bed.

Dr. McGraph, had to gather his thoughts before calling my parents. He first called my family doctor, Dr. McLister, who also came every day. He was the doctor who spent the midnight hours by my side when I was in critical condition. He worked all day, then stayed with me all night. Now Dr. McLister was not in the best of condition. When I was older, he always reminded me of Alfred Hitchcock, a film maker of psychological thrillers, horror movies in the 1950's-70's, such as Psycho, The Birds and much more. It was Hitchcock's silhouette at his heaviest weight that reminded me of my doctor. Dr. McLister, was a heavy smoker, who often fell asleep during a doctor's appointment, when sitting in his office. He was one of the best diagnosticians in our province of Ontario. Most of all he was a loving, sensitive caring man of integrity, His life ended much too early from a heart attack in his late 50's.

Dr. McLister came to the hospital to see me at McGraph's urging, and was shocked at the proof of my healing, but as a Christian himself, he knew the power of his Savior, and he believed without doubt. What was there to doubt? The proof was clear and standing before him.

Dr. McLister agreed to be at Dr. McGraph's side when he finally called my parents. Still somewhat confused he picked up the rotary phone's receiver and then dialed. Remember back then a hand-held phone, a mobile phone, or cell phone were not invented yet, or at least for the general public.

As the phone rang, I am sure Dr. McGraph wrestled with what words he would say. As mom answered the phone he quickly began, maybe a little too quickly. "Hello, Mrs. Balestrini, I don't know where to begin this conversation, but I examined Elaine's vision and, well she can see, perfectly."

"Could you repeat that Dr. McGraph," mom asked as her heart quickened.

"Mrs. Balestrini, I don't understand it, but last night when I examined Elaine, she remained the same in both eyes; blind in the left and legally blind in the right. Dr. McLister is with me and he too examined your daughter, confirming what I just told you. I asked Elaine what happened and she said Jesus healed her with a drop of water. All I know is that your daughter was blind, but now she can see, perfectly I might add. I am a person who doesn't necessarily believe in miracles, but this, this has me questioning my beliefs. Could you please tell me the full story of how this happened?"

Mom explained to him in full detail what she brought, the anointing of my eyes with the Water from Lourdes and her prayer.

"Well, Mrs. Balestrini, your daughter was given that miracle. She was blind and now she can see. PERFECTLY!"

At that mom squealed with delight as she thanked God and Dr. McGraph for all he had done.

"Don't thank me, thank your God," and with that he said his goodbye. He turned to look at his colleague saying, "well I guess there is nothing else to be done, but to send Elaine home."

At the confirmation of my miracle Sister Martha, hurriedly, with an excited voice told all who would listen to her announcement, "Elaine can see, she has had a miracle."

The story of my miracle rapidly spread throughout my family relatives, and neighbors, along with the hospital, staff and patients alike. For some it was hard to believe, but for others like Vicky's mom Diane, the magnitude of the news brought her to her knees with a thankful heart.

Two days later after a 6 week stay, both doctors signed my discharge papers, and mom and dad came to pick me up to bring their full sighted daughter home, with a large reception of celebration waiting for us.

Hard to believe? Maybe for some I just have to look in the mirror at my disfigured pupil in my eye, (everyone calls it my cat eye because of its shape) to remind me of God's awesome power, mercy, grace, and unconditional love

My vision has served me well, I graduated high school, Nursing College, married, had five children, and became a Free Lance writer where I eventually became a Book Review Editor for a Catholic/Christian magazine along with writing this book. I received a gift of sight and I pray I have used it well, bringing Glory to our Lord, Jesus Christ, and honoring the Blessed Mother of Jesus through her gift of the little stream of water that turned into a river of healing and miracles.

To God Be The Glory

A celebration with friends after my miracle, along with my birthday party as I had missed it while in the hospital.

Hotel Dieu Hospital many of my nurses were nuns.

I remember my dad carrying me a few times, he smelled of cigarette smoke, which was somehow comforting to me.

My cousin Sandy who watched over me when I was a Flower girl & Sandy was a Bridesmaid. Not too long after my miracle.

Sandy

Lourdes France where our Blessed Mother appeared to a 14 year old pesant girl named Bernadette in the year 1848

Small bottle of Holy Water from Lourdes

Sandy and my mom some 30 years later. They loved each other so much, as did I.

Chapter Nine

Grandpa and the Madonna

The Virgin Mary had an important role in the lives of my family as we grew up. This next series of healings and miracles revolve around saying the Rosary as a family.

The rosary in its simplest terms is a tool used to aid prayer and meditation. The beads of a rosary count the prayers as they are recited out loud or in the mind. The importance of the Rosary is to reflect on the life of Jesus and His mother Mary who always points to her son Jesus. So, in short, we should always keep in mind the goal of The Rosary is, Jesus.

My family prayed the Rosary together every night during Lent, which is always forty days before Easter. It is a time set aside each year to remember the love of God and His gift to us through His son.

Jesus' death and resurrection defeated death, sin and satan, gifting us with Eternal Life.

I remember one specific Lent in 1961 when I was nine years old. My grandfather Luigi, although family and friends called him Louis, continued to grieve the death of his wife Anna, (Grandma) in 1956. She died in a horrific car accident, along with her sister-in-law. Although I was only four when Grandma Anna died, I will always remember the two coffins, side by side, and my dad picking me up to kiss Grandma's cheek to say goodbye. I remember trying to wriggle out of his arms crying, and my mom taking me from dad's arms telling him I was too young. This experience made me fearful of death and funerals; which reminds me of my three-year-old grandson Tanis.

When my mom died, on February 1st, 2005 she had an open casket at the Funeral Home. Before visiting hours, I walked into the large viewing, and reception room to find my beautiful daughter-in-law Sherri with her arm around Tanis who was looking into the casket. At first, I was upset at the thought this would affect him, but as I approached, I could hear Sherri explaining in a soft voice why Grandma Bea was so still. She was simply telling her three-year-old son in a way his little mind could understand.

I came up and knelt beside them saying to Tanis, "Grandma Bea looks like she's sleeping."

This was when I realized my grandson understood far more than I thought was possible, when he looked at me saying very seriously, "Grammy, Grandma Bea's not sleeping, she's dead!" and the word dead was emphasized as if he was telling me something I didn't know. I was shocked but very aware of the subdued laughter trying not to escape from the immediate family standing behind us. Now back to Lent.

After Grandma Anna's sudden death Grandpa went into a deep depression, no longer inspired by his wife to live a full life. Instead, Grandpa drowned his sorrows in wine, ignored his personal hygiene, stopped going to church, or having any other relationship with God.

Sadly, this was how I remembered my grandfather and the many arguments that came with his behavior from family members.

Grandpa was a brick layer by trade, and along with family and friends built his own house. I know he worked on the New York Central Railway but, I don't know if the two coincided with each other.

The house was a duplex, large and beautiful. When Grandpa could no longer care for the house, my dad and mom decided to move our family into the upper apartment of the duplex so dad could help.

I will always remember Grandpa during the spring and summer months, sitting under the big willow tree which seemed to mirror the weeping of his heart. There he sat day after day drinking the wine he made, while smoking his cigarette. During the winter I rarely saw him except for Christmas morning when he would hand us an envelope with five dollars in it which had been placed in the Christmas Tree.

My brother Rick would often sit at Grandpa's feet under that Willow tree talking to him about God.

It was during this time Grandpa was strongly urged to go to a church function, it was with great surprise that he decided to go.

Grandpa, fresh and clean walked into the church hall doors, and there he met a woman, also named Anna, and they enjoyed each other's company.

Grandpa began to go back to church with this beautiful woman, who did not resemble my grandmother in any way. They went on dates and after awhile Grandpa started calling her his girlfriend. She had a gentle loving way about her, a simple calming smile that accentuated her soft blushed high cheek bones, and Grandpa lit up when she would smile at him. I did not know this man anymore, he was a happy active man, I had only known a depressed, defeated man. This Anna was good for him, but when things became too serious Grandpa was harassed by certain family members to end the relationship. My parents were all for his happiness, but others felt he was trying to replace their mother, or did money play a part? As far as I know Grandpa was financially healthy, but by no means well off. I heard whispered conversations about it, and all too often yelling screamed up the stairway to our home above. Some family members tried to stop him from dating Anna. I didn't understand why this was happening. I remember hearing my dad tell my mom that those family members should leave him alone, as he was happy, and that was all that mattered. Knowing my dad, I am positive he tried as he was as boisterous as the rest of his siblings. I do not know if Grandpa ended the relationship or if Anna did. I tend to believe Anna could no longer cope with the drama and harassment, and of how my grandfather did not stand up to them. The fact remains the relationship ended, and Grandpa went back to his old ways, and the big Willow tree wept with him, and Rick took up his spot at Grandpa's feet again.

In 1961 our family did what we always did, we started saying the Rosary for the forty nights of Lent.

My brother Rick had won a waxed statue of the Blessed Virgin at school, one where you could put a small birthday candle in the back. Rick wanted all the lights to be turned off while we prayed so that the soft glow of the small candle would flicker in the darkness.

I remember thinking it would be too scary, but Rick insisted and that little candle stayed lit until the final prayer ended with an Amen. The candle went out leaving us in darkness, I didn't like that.

Rick was so happy, "Look, our Blessed Mother kept the candle burning until the final prayer."

"Rick, it's probably how long that candle takes to burn out."

"No mom, she waits for us to finish."

Rick was not talking about the wax statue being alive, but that the Blessed Virgin was present with us in Spirit, and that made me more anxious. Night after night as mom placed a new birthday candle at the back of the statue, it burned until Amen, and flickered out.

My dad was working afternoons and could only join us on his nights off.

We often prayed on our knees; at times we leaned on the backs of our kitchen chairs when our backs began to hurt.

One-night Rick announced he had invited Grandpa to come pray with us.

"Oh Rick," mom said, "I'm not sure he will be able to climb the stairs, let alone show up."

"He will come mom; we just have to wait for him."

"Rick, it's time to start and you know how long it takes, and you and your sisters have school in the morning."

"Mom, please, I know he will come."

So, we waited, and waited, then Rick jumped up and ran down the stairs to remind Grandpa we were waiting for him to join us, then ran back up to wait yet again.

It was with great shock to all of us except for Rick, when we heard Grandpa's footsteps on the stairs.

Grandpa came into the room, looked around to see an empty kitchen chair.

"Dad," mom told him, "Just sit on the chair, you don't have to kneel."

Grandpa just smiled at her and knelt behind the chair to pray, and the little candle flickered in the dark until we ended with the Amen, then the candle went out; and the lights were flipped on.

"Would you like something to drink Dad?" mom asked.

"No thank you Beatrice," he said in his broken, Italian language, and left the room to go back down to his place.

The next night we were all so happy when Grandpa showed up again, and on time.

Prayers were said, Amen, and the candle went out.

This time Grandpa didn't leave but stood to sit on the chair.

"Dad, would you like something to drink," mom asked.

"Do you have hot chocolate?" he asked.

Mom looked slightly surprised by his request, but quickly hid her expression, and said that she did.

When she handed Grandpa the hot chocolate in a light blue mug, he took a sip and began telling us what happened to him the night before.

"When I went to bed, as I lay there, the Madonna (FYI, not the singer, but the Mother of Jesus) came to me behind a veil. She no say nothing to me, I say nothing to her, we just nod, we know."

The Veiled Virgin is a Carrara marble statue carved in Rome by Italian sculptor Giovanni Strazza (1818–1875)

"Knew what Grandpa," I asked with goose bumps rising on my skin.

"Something that the Madonna (Blessed Virgin) and I know."

After Grandpa left Rick asked my mom, "do you think he really saw the Blessed Virgin?"

"I don't know Rick, he has stopped drinking alcohol, and the way he said it I tend to believe him."

Rick just nodded but my sister MaryAnn and I just looked spooked.

The next night Grandpa came back to pray, and as was the night before the candle went out at Amen.

Grandpa, asked for Hot Chocolate again, he seemed to enjoy the hot drink.

"The Madonna, she come again under a veil, I no speak to her, she no speak to me, but we know."

Now this was getting too spooky. I asked that the next time we prayed could we leave the lights on.

"No way Elaine," Rick said strongly. "The candle stays, the lights off. The Blessed Virgin is with us and she isn't scary, she loves us."

Mom told us to go to bed, but that whole night I wondered what Grandpa and the Virgin Mary knew. Was it all real?

The next night Grandpa came again, but this night was different, it didn't end with the Amen, instead as the candle flickered wildly Rick wanted to say a different prayer to end the Rosary.

"I have the prayer written in my notebook in my bedroom," and with that he jumped up.

"Rick, the candle is going out, we don't have time for you to find the prayer."

"Yes, we do mom, the Blessed Virgin will wait," and with that he left.

I asked mom if we could turn the lights on while we waited, as Rick was taking longer than expected, but she didn't answer. I think she was testing the longevity of the candle; or was it as Rick said?

When Rick returned, he knelt between my sister and I so we could read it too. The candle was flickering wildly, but Rick and mom stayed the course as we said the new prayer. I will always remember that prayer, called the Memorare, which took a little longer than the usual prayer.

In the middle of the prayer the candle went out, and MaryAnn and I asked, begged my mom to please, please turn on the lights.

"No mom, she will keep the candle going," Rick said, and with his words the candle came back to life. At Amen, the candle went out, and mom hurriedly turned the lights on. The Blessed Virgin did indeed keep the candle going, what other explanation was there. My nine-year-old mind wrestled between fear and curiosity.

I looked at Grandpa, he just smiled, and stood up to sit back in the chair. He didn't seem to be scared of how the candle responded each night.

"Hot Chocolate Dad?' mom asked him.

"Yes, please Beatrice," I loved to hear my grandpa say my mother's name, it was in Italian dialect, but soft like a whisper, and drawn out.

Rick asked as Grandpa sipped his warm drink.

"Grandpa, did the Madonna visit you again?"

Grandpa nodded yes, "she no speak to me, I no speak to her, but we know." I am sure we were all curious, and our thoughts wanted to scream; what do you know? But no one asked.

The next morning, Rick, MaryAnn and I were pulled out of school just before lunch time, and brought to a neighbor's house. Because Rick was old enough to understand the situation dad decided he could stay with him

It wasn't that long, but felt like an eternity when dad finally arrived to pick us up and bring us home.

We were told to sit down on the couch and dad told us that grandpa had died in his sleep.

"That's what Grandpa was telling us, he and the Madonna knew that she would soon bring him to her Son, and she did," mom explained with joyful excitement.

MaryAnn and I cried while trying to make sense of it, but how do you make sense of a miracle like this, a miracle shrouded in sadness, a miracle embraced by death.

God used Rick, a thirteen-year-old boy to bring Grandpa back to Him, and the Blessed Virgin was announcing his upcoming return home to Jesus.

Was it the Virgin Mary, Grandpa's Madonna that came to him that last night to bring him home?

There is no denying this miracle of God's love for my grandpa. He was lost but was found, and now lives in his new Home with his Savior, his Madonna, his beloved wife Anna, and other family members that were taken home before him.

I like to believe that Mother Mary came to bring grandpa Home to her son. It just makes sense, or otherwise why did she appear to him the last few nights of his life here on earth. Grandpa was escorted Home at the age of sixty-five, dying in a way we all hope to go; in his sleep.

We all received a most beautiful gift, for we knew where grandpa went when he died. Home!

"I no speak to her, she no speak to me, but we know."

To God Be The Glory

Chapter Ten
Unexpected Healing: And
Was That An Angel?

Sometimes miracles take on different forms, coming through a small child's prayer, or through no prayer at all. Sometimes a miracle comes in the form of a warning, or in the soft, gentle fragrance of God's tender love, anointing with Holy Oil or Water; or through heavenly hosts, and you may ask; was that an angel? Only God knows, but we do know that God often sent His angels to announce, warn, give comfort, protect, guard, and do what He asks of them, like our own personal Guardian Angels. Also God uses His people on earth to answer a prayer, not just adults, but often through children.

One day when my daughter Mary was three years old, she was playing with her brother Sean in our very simple play/family room.

That day I had a horrendous migraine and was laying on the couch in our front room. Mary came quietly to me and asked me if I was sick.

"I'm okay, sweetie, mommy's head just hurts inside."

Without hesitation she put her tiny hand on my forehead saying, "Jesus please heal mommy's pain in her head. Thank you, Jesus."

She left as quickly as she appeared, skipping away in that still awkward toddler way. As I watched her, I suddenly realized my headache was gone.

"Mary," I called to her. "Mommy's headache is gone."

"I know mommy, Jesus healed you," she answered confidently, while looking at me with an expression that seemed to question why I didn't know this. "Mommy, did you thank Him?" she asked.

"Yes, of course mommy will thank Him."

How old was she? Oh yes, three, just a toddler with childlike faith and tiny little transparent angel wings somehow tucked around her tiny body.

As she continued to skip away, I sat feeling stunned at the sudden answer to Mary's little but trusting prayer, and I sat there thanking and praising Jesus.

Another healing miracle came after my parents were in a car accident just before Christmas. Dad was driving and was at a stop light, he had the green light, but a car coming from the intersection ran the red light and slammed into their car, passenger side. Dad was not injured but mom was and in pain. Although mom flatly refused my dad told the police to please call an ambulance.

"Ma'am please stay in the car," the police officer said, "you could have a serious injury that needs to be checked at the hospital."

Mom knew he was right along with my dad but she refused to believe she was injured. "I'm fine," and proceeded to get out of the car, this movement caught her off guard as she cried out when a stabbing pain took her breath away.

The ambulance was called and to her dismay she was taken to emergency with sirens blaring. Once she was seen, with x-ray taken the doctor told mom and dad that she was fine except for the stabbing, throbbing inflamed soft tissue pain in her right side. It could have been much worse, and would take time to heal.

Day after day with Christmas being only three weeks away, mom's pain was making it impossible for her to get anything done. Mom usually made our two daughters Christmas dresses, but she worried that this would stop her from completing them. I told her not to worry about it.

"Mom, relax, the girls have clothes to wear, your worrying and being tense about what you can't do is only going to make your body tenser and painful."

I am so much like my mom, especially in preparation for holidays, and the many different celebrations a family of young children has. I was an undercover perfectionist, who was fooling myself. Everyone knew by my frantic actions and behavior; it was especially clear to all when my mother-in-law Edna would be staying at our house. If everything was perfect, we would have a good visit, when I was unable to keep everything the way she liked, well our visit would not go well, and this would put more pressure of my already burdened shoulders. When I look back, I wondered why I didn't heed my own advice.

A week after the accident Mom began to feel depressed and discouraged. She wasn't sleeping well, having a difficult time laying down and staying there as the pain interfered with her breathing. Actually, everything mom tried to do was met with searing, stabbing pain. One particular day when exhaustion overpowered her, she decided to try to take a nap. Of course, mom had been praying for a healing as we all were, but this day was different. Mom looked at the small painting she did of Jesus with angels hovering by his side. It was hanging on the wall just above her bedside table. She asked Jesus to bless her by allowing His angel to comfort her, and that is when she noticed the bottle of Holy water sitting on that table. Taking the bottle into her hands she asked the Lord to heal her as she opened the top of the bottle. It was difficult for her to do this small action of opening the bottle, but she did and put her finger over the opening, turned the bottle over to get a few drops on her finger, and then she slowly lifted her hand, and with her finger she made the sign of the cross on her forehead and side, asking the Lord to once again heal her. Immediately, and I mean immediately the pain left her body. She slowly and carefully bent her body, twisted her waist side to side; no pain! Mom ran downstairs calling out to my dad, "Joe, Joe, Jesus healed me, look," and she bent and twisted with youthful exuberance. Taking hold of my dad's hand she sat beside him, "Joe, I'm healed, I have no more pain," and they both thanked the Lord for this miraculous gift. Once they finished their thanksgiving prayer mom went to the phone to call me.

"Elaine, the Lord healed me," and she explained the simple action and prayer.

"What? Mom say that again, only slower this time."

"Elaine," she spoke slowly, and clearly, I'm healed, Jesus took all my pain away instantly."

"Mom, you know I believe you, but can you give me detailed information."

Mom did as I asked, with very slow and clear speech.

I began to laugh because now she spoke so slowly, she was difficult to follow.

"What's so funny Elaine?"

"You're talking so slowly now, almost in the speed of a turtle and it's hard to follow."

Mom laughed at my explanation and began to talk normally. When she finished, we both began to thank the good Lord for His merciful miracle of healing.

She told me later that when she looked at the painting she did of Jesus with the angels, she felt a nudge to anoint herself with the Holy Water. However, our healing miracle comes, always remember it is Jesus who is our divine healer.

To make this story more meaningful, as it says in;

Romans 8:28 (NIV Bible)

'And we know that all things work together for good to those who love God, to those who are called according to His purpose.'

This rang true, as an answer to another prayer came quickly after. Mom and Dad were not well off, if anything they just made it through each month by the skin of their teeth, so to speak. Because of the accident and it not being their fault, an insurance adjustor came to their home and offered them five hundred dollars in compensation for their pain, also paying for the repair of the car.

My parents were satisfied with this, they weren't the kind of people to take advantage, or milk the system for more money, they were happy to have this extra money for Christmas.

Mom repeated Romans 8:28 when telling me of the outcome. They of course spent some of that money on Christmas presents, which made them very happy, almost like the character Scrooge when he danced and laughed in his bedroom after his big transformation. Well, my parents were that happy when they could afford Christmas presents for the family along with helping other families have a more joyful Christmas.

It seems rather odd that a car accident would bring blessings, but it often comes that way. In desperation, at the right time God swoops in as the Hero, bringing Glory to His name. Did God cause the accident? No, that happened due to free will, and a person not paying attention running a red light.

But God did bring good out of it for their benefit. Praise God!

In another story good friends of ours from our prayer meeting had a miracle of warning and protection.

Sharon was traveling down a main street in our city with her daughter in the back seat. This street, is one of the main routes through our city of Windsor, Ontario, Canada. Actually, it has the largest international suspension bridge in the world. On average, more than ten thousand vehicles mainly truck, travel on the bridge everyday. It is one of North America's busiest international border crossings in terms of both traffic and trade volume.

Dave and I had just moved into a new house which faced this very busy road. I could see a stop light from my front room window, and decided to count how many eighteen wheelers went through this light in the supposedly sixty seconds it was green. I could hardly believe it, sixty-five trucks in sixty seconds seemed impossible, but it was true.

When the World Trade Center in New York was attacked on September 11/2001, commonly known as 911, by militant Islamic extremists, all borders were closed, the trucks were at a stand still, as was the world. In my city alone on the road my house faced traffic, mostly trucks, were backed up over twenty miles. Realizing the depth of the horror, knowing the trucks were not going to move for quite some time, our neighbourhood along with the Tim Horton's on our corner brought food and drinks to the drivers, often letting those who needed to use a washroom enter our homes and do their business.

Needless to say, the Ambassador Bridge, connecting my City of Windsor, Ontario with Detroit Michigan and Huron Church Road (which is the name of the road I am writing about), were important to trade, and very busy, but the terror that happened that day made us all realize the extent of that fact. We were just seeing the Canadian side, I heard the Detroit, Michigan side was blocked just as bad, or worse than we were.

One day, long before moving into our new house my friend Sharon was driving on Huron Church behind a long truck carrying large logs with a flag at the end of them. Sharon said that she stayed well behind the truck, while other drivers would weave in and out of the two-lane road, to pass it.

As Sharon was about to do the same thing, a car drove up beside her and a man rolling down the passenger window in his light blue Beetle Volkswagen waved for her to roll down her window.

"Do not pass that truck. Do not pass that truck," the driver yelled.

Sharon not seeing anything to be alarmed about wondered why he would say that; but something in Sharon's spirit spoke to her to heed his advice. This man stayed at the side of Sharon's car so she couldn't pass even if she wanted to.

Not one minute later the ties holding the logs securely gave way from the side. The side where Sharon would have been if she were passing that very large, long truck. Sharon, thankfully was still at a good distance behind the truck and was able to escape any contact with the falling logs.

Sharon and her daughter would have certainly been crushed under the impact, probably killed.

As traffic stopped, Sharon, trying to catch her breath at the thought of what could have happened if that man had not warned her, looked to her side to thank him. He wasn't there. He wasn't anywhere. How could that be? There were cars and trucks blocking her in, and this man could not have moved, yet he wasn't there. "Where did he go? How did he move his car through all the cars blocking him in?" Sharon said out loud.

Her daughter from the back seat excitedly proclaimed, "He was an Angel mom, God sent us an Angel to save us."

Out of the mouth of babes. What other explanation could there be? As people came out of their cars walking around, Sharon asked if some of them had seen the light blue Volkswagen Beetle car that had stayed beside her. Not one could recollect seeing that car, not even the couple driving behind him.

Sharon got back into her car, and looking at her daughter agreed with her, he had to have been an Angel, and they both said a prayer of thanksgiving to the Lord for His protection by sending an Angel to warn and save their lives.

I am reminded of another story my mother-in-law Edna told me. Now Edna was Dave's adoptive mother, and in my opinion, she was not what you would say a strong believer in the Lord, even though she was very active in her church and taught Sunday school when my husband was young. Whether her faith was strong at the time this miracle happened, the storm of losing her husband in his fifties of a heart attack destroyed what little faith she might have had.

She became a bitter woman who didn't go to church, and didn't want to hear any conversations about God. I must admit that when we had a children's devotional and a prayer every night, when Edna was

visiting, she was very respectful, she didn't say a prayer when it was her turn but we were thankful she respected our prayer time.

Our relationship was strained at best, but my husband and I held our tongues, and stayed true to our faith. We prayed for her always, but our faith became a divide that could never be mended. She was stubborn and turned her back on God, and family, unless you agreed with her. She tried to ruin happy healthy relationships, trying to pull my husband and I apart. In fact, she told me to my face that she wanted Dave to marry another young woman, not me. I was not the woman she planned for Dave to love and marry. I was overweight, Canadian Italian, and to her horror a Catholic.

"I show my love through my actions," Edna once said. The meaning was clear, she would never tell you she loved you, and stayed true to that fact. Throughout the forty-four years I was in her life, I had only heard her say it once, after a phone call with Dave and I. We always told her we loved her, but the day she said it back we were shocked. That was the one and only time. She did however show her love, in which I cannot deny by her actions, she made me and the whole family clothes, cooked and baked, but it was all conditional love. If she didn't like something we said she would retreat with a book into our front-room staying there for the rest of her visit. She always made my mother Beatrice feel very uncomfortable, that did not sit well with me, as my mom loved unconditionally. When I would try to defend my mother, mom would stop me. "Just love her Elaine."

Edna chose who she loved, and on her last visit to our home she told our five adult children, her only grandchildren in front of the whole family, that she only wanted our first two children as her grandchildren. The other three were not wanted, oh she didn't say that in those words, but her meaning was clear. That destroyed any relationship we had, as little as that was. She remained that way until her death at age ninety-two.

Dave's adoptive parents did much for him, they went on vacations, and gave him a good life materially. I didn't know John all that well before he died. He was a teaser, enjoying people's reactions to his very disturbing comments. When it came to our faith, he was cruel, and made fun of it at every chance he could.

Dave and I were maybe a little too excited in our new found faith in the Charismatic Movement, and to be fair someone should have locked us up for six months until we became subtler. But John went out of his way to ridicule, and demonize us in our walk with Jesus. One day when we went to their home to visit, he taught our very young son to say the Lord's name in vain, laughing as our son finally said it. John could be very nice at times, but most often we were the brunt of his mean-spirited jokes. It seems Jesus was the division that separated us. I silently prayed for a healing of our relationship when in their presence, but prayed openly when at home or at a meeting.

Jesus himself declared families would be separated because of Him, some would come to believe in Him and others would refuse. You can read about this in Matthew chapter 10, and Luke chapter 12. This was true in my life with Dave's family, and it brought me such deep sorrow.

I am a peace maker at heart and agonized over this undeniable acceptance of who I was and my faith. It was evident when I started dating Dave, and became much worse in our marriage.

I have to believe that God in His divine intervention gave John and Edna that last moment to come back to Him. John died of a massive heart attack at the age of fifty-nine, so young and his death grew anger and bitterness in Edna's heart.

Although Edna made our lives miserable, dreading every visit, I began to understand her, after asking the Holy Spirit to help me gain wisdom. I wanted so much to deeply feel the love I said I had for her.

Edna was brought up in a staunch British family, where everything had to be done perfectly. Her grandfather was an Orangeman in short, a member of a secret society organized in the north of Ireland in 1795 to defend the British sovereign and to support the Protestant faith. He must have rolled in his grave at his great, great, great grandson marrying a Catholic. Edna's father was a Soldier, and brought his family up in a non-nurturing strict way. Edna took on that persona. In my opinion she was unable, to love more than one person at a time, and she chose who she showed love to. Like my mother, Edna too grew up during the Great Depression, where at the tender age of fourteen found work caring for a family of five children. She had to care for the children, clean house, cook the meals and other duties. This family was well off, but treated her like a slave, paying her the least amount possible. It was a difficult time for everyone, but more so for a child of fourteen who should have been allowed to be a child. I gained more insight into what made Edna who she was. There was no excuse for her behavior, she had to own that, but her history helped me to gain insight in the why's of who she was. The saying 'before you judge a man, walk a mile in his shoes,' in effect, is a reminder to practice empathy. While long credited as a Native American aphorism, replacing the word shoes with moccasins, the saying came from a Mary T. Lathrap poem published in 1895. These are words to live by, and I tried, I honestly tried with Edna. When you have someone in your life like Edna don't stop showing your love, unless the relationship is so toxic there is a need to separate. Edna did that with us, she moved to England, Italy, and then settled in Toronto, Ontario, Canada four hours away from where we lived. We all tried so hard to continue to show love in the face of her insults, and tirades. When she visited, she ruled our home, making life unbearable at times. We did have some good memories, but not enough to ignore the bad, I had no regrets in how I responded to her, although I do regret that we didn't ignore her request to not be at her bedside when she was dying. So much needed to be said, but by then Edna had done so much damage that her request was respected. Sadly, we shed more tears when our dog died, than we did at the news of Edna's death. Edna had her good and loving moments and lived her words, "I show my love through my actions," meaning in making us clothes, cooking and baking, even helping to clean and do laundry. She was there throughout my first two pregnancies and births of Sean and Mary.

I don't want to demonize Edna, she had many good qualities, I just wish she could have loved us for who we were, and we her.

That said I will always remember this next story Edna told me while her husband was still alive. This happened when my husband Dave was young. He and his sister (two years older) sat in the back seat of the family car driving to a vacation destination when it happened. As John stopped at a stop sign, Edna saw a truck driving at an extreme speed heading right toward them. She yelled at her husband to get out of the way, but they had no time.to do so as the truck barreled down on them. They knew they were going to be hit. Edna told me she said a quick desperate prayer, "God save us."

"Elaine," Edna said, "I don't know how it happened, but all of a sudden, we found ourselves across the road in a small ditch, there was not a ding or any other signs we were hit, and especially not a scratch on us. Except for the skid marks from the truck, not ten feet away being the proof of a near accident.

The driver of the truck was as shocked as we were asking "how did we escape injury, or worse, death? How did I end up in the corn field? I don't know what to say about it, I drive this road all the time, I guess it would be considered a miracle of some sort. Maybe an Angel picked our cars up and placed yours in the small ditch and mine in the corn field on the other side of the road. The truck driver was also baffled, but she gave credit to God, and apologized repeatedly for her actions of possibly causing a devastating outcome. I remember her saying,

"We definitely had some angels watching over us," as she walked back to her truck."

Dave and I did consider it a miracle as there were no other explanations to be had. It was good to know that Edna thought it was possible at that time. I don't know what John thought; Edna didn't elaborate on his version of the story. However, Dave remembered it clearly.

This next story happened to me, a soothing miraculous happening with an Angel.

It was a time when I was distraught over my daughter Mary's rare heart condition, along with our finances in trying to pay the hospital bills with very little money.

I needed gas to get me to work, and I knew we had little to spend.

I was depressed, distraught and reaching for the hope and strength that only God could provide. I drove to a nearby gas station where Dave and I often went. I knew the owner, and men working there. Driving up to the pump, the attendant who pumped the gas signaled me to roll down my old tired car window. I only saw the gesture, not his face. My eyes were fixed on the twenty dollars in my hand, it was the last of our grocery money. I fought with my thoughts of splitting the money, ten dollars for gas, the other for needed groceries. "How much would you like me to put in your tank?"

Not recognizing his voice, I looked at the man to tell him, but lost my voice as my eyes were met with the kindest, bluest eyes I had ever seen. The kind of blue which to this day is hard to describe. As we looked at each other I seemed to breathe in a soft flowing warmth that weaved peacefully through my body. It was a cold Canadian winter day but all I could feel was a warmth deep in my body and spirit, pushing all negativity out and filling me with an all-consuming peace. What was happening? I had not seen this man before, but his smile shone like the sun. He had glowing white hair and beard, a beautiful white, everything about him took my breath away. What was happening?

"Mam," the man asked, "how much do you want me to put into your gas tank."

His voice was soft and gentle, and as he continued to smile, I answered saying twenty dollars while continuing to look into his eyes.

With that he left my sight to put the gas into the tank and cleaned my windows, front and back. I tried to come out of my white cloud of wonderment when he returned to collect the twenty dollars.

"Have a blessed day mam," he said and walked back into the gas station.

A car pulled up behind me and I had to move, or otherwise I would have sat there a little longer to collect my thoughts.

I drove about one mile and pulled over to the side of the road and fell into deep, cleansing tears. Healing tears.

My situation didn't change, my daughter was still extremely ill, our finances still lacking, but my spirit was light and hopeful.

Did I have an encounter with an Angel?

It hadn't occurred to me to look at my gas gage, but when I did twenty minutes later the gas tank read full. That twenty dollars I spent for gas filled my tank. That was impossible as my car was a gas guzzler, and twenty dollars filled it; twenty dollars usually gave me a half of tank, until my encounter with this possible Angel.

I didn't see that man again close up but, I did catch sight of him as I drove by the next day.

The next time I went to buy gas that man was not there. I asked the owner about him.

"Oh, Mrs. Vizard, he came by the day you are talking about, and asked if he could work for us. I don't know why I said yes as I didn't need anyone. But I said yes before I knew what I was saying. Funny thing, he only worked two days and when I went to pay him for those two days he had already left. I haven't seen him again," he answered scratching his head under his cap. As he left my car, I heard him mutter, "he sure was a nice guy."

My meeting with the Angelman, and after talking to the owner will forever live in my memory. That feeling will never leave me, a memory etched on my heart and in my spirit.

As time passed, I became positive that I had looked into the eyes of an Angel, and that God sent him to me when I needed a heavenly touch of strength and the peace that passes all understanding. God does act when we least expect it.

To God Be The Glory

Edna's story. Was it an Angelic
encounter? Did
God send an
Angel to protect them?
I believe so,
you can make your own decision.

My memory of what
the Angel at the
gas station looked like.
It was a deeply profound
experience that
made a huge difference in my life.

Was it a Angel that saved
their lives? Did God ordain
the miracle, holding them
safe?

Dave

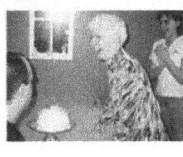

There were good times with John & Edna (not their
true names as they have passed) These photos show
there were good times with them.

Chapter Eleven
Heavenly Visit

Sometimes miracles come to us in dreams and if you have ever wondered if your dream was heaven sent; you just might be right.

My dad, Joseph Albert Balestrini died on Tuesday April 11th, 1995, at the age of seventy-eight. He died the way many of us hope to die, laughing and suddenly. Although dying in my sleep is my preferred way to go, waking up in the embrace of pure light, love, and with Jesus. It is a good way to go, but hard on family members.

Dad died at Easter time and his funeral was delayed due to it being

Holy week, which consist of...

Palm Sunday (Palm Sunday commemorates Jesus' entrance into Jerusalem. As he rode into the city on a donkey, his followers spread palm branches at his feet and called him "Hosanna" meaning Saviour. Palm branches were considered symbols of victory and triumph at the time.)

Holy Monday to Wednesday, (Jesus continues His teachings, and Judas plans his betrayal of Jesus)

Holy Thursday (The Last supper celebrated during Passover, where Jesus washes the feet of His disciples, giving them His last instructions. Judas leaves to betray Jesus receiving money for his betrayal by the Leaders of the Church who were afraid of Jesus, wanting to get rid of him.)

Good Friday (Good Friday, although a horrible day is called good because it led to the Resurrection of Jesus and His victory over sin and death, and to the celebration of Easter)

Holy Saturday (is the last day of Lent, and the last phase of Jesus' messianic mission, during which he is said to open heaven's gates for the just who had gone before him)

Easter Day (Easter is celebrated by Christians as a joyous holiday representing the fulfillment of the prophecies of the Old Testament and the revelation of God's saving plan for all mankind through His son Jesus. It is a celebration of new life in Christ, a completely new relationship with God the Father, and Jesus' defeat of death and the hope of Salvation)

Back to my dad's funeral, which took almost a week due to Holy week. When the Funeral Home could hold his three days of visitations (per my mother's choice) it was Easter weekend. It was an exhausting week, not only grieving for my dad, but waiting to have closure, and worrying about the stress on my mom who just lost her husband of forty-eight years. I put my grief on hold to care for my mom and sister. It was a week of frustration, anger for some in the family as they tried to cope with dad's death. Sadly, it was made much worse for my immediate family as my husband's adoptive mother, Edna was over for the two weeks of Easter. She always made life more difficult. I had hoped she wouldn't come as I knew our stress would be magnified, and it was. I felt fragile, like a frayed rope on the verge of ripping apart, yet letting go would be disastrous, for me, for my family. Everyone looked to me for decisions, although my mom had the final say she seemed to make the decisions just to get them over with. Funerals were expensive then and now. Mom opted for cremation.

Dad died in a Nursing Home, one block away from where I lived. I was very stubborn in my choice of where he would be cared for, I needed him to be near me so I could monitor his care. We were blessed that the Nursing Home, I wanted him to be in had a semi private room/bed.) I knew the good Nursing Homes, and the ones that were not so good. In dad's nursing home I knew many of the health care workers and knew he would get excellent care. Most nurses know the secret of making sure your loved one receives good care; I hope this tidbit of information helps you. Visit your loved one daily at different times. If you have other family members take turns visiting, having two of you visit daily is optimal, this way the staff never knows what time you are coming, keeping them on their toes. This is not as important if you know the staff or have been referred by a good friend; still, keep the nursing home staff on their toes.

As a Charge Nurse working in Nursing Homes, I was very active in his care, monitoring his medications. I did his wash, visited him almost daily as did our older children, but mom lived thirty minutes away, which was hard on her, plus she didn't drive. My sister MaryAnn lived with my parents and often brought mom to visit dad, other family members did likewise. Dad improved as time went on, but I was still very much aware that he was not himself. He was a great Euchre player, making a point on a ten and nine. Now however as I watched him play with other residents, I noticed he wasn't as sharp, making many mistakes, but he loved the game, and it made him happy.

My dad's laughter was something I will never forget, it was exuberant, boisterous at times, it was an immediate genuine laugh; sometimes forced when the joke wasn't all that funny.

Once he began laughing it was contagious, and embarrassing as in the incident of his being an usher in church.

I was around ten years of age, and dad and his good friend Harold were both ushers. As they walked up the main isle in the church my dad passed gas, rather loudly. The more he laughed the more he tooted, then Harold began laughing and he too tooted.

Mom, my sister and I were walking behind them, but as this musical journey continued to grow louder with each deep laugh, we quickly found a pew to escape into. By this time the whole congregation joined in the laughter, and the church was filled with this musical overture of epic proportions when other members of the congregation joined in. I don't know what everyone had eaten the night before, but it sure made a grand entrance, and my dad started it. My mom kept trying to shush his bodily function by saying, "For gosh sakes Joe get a hold of yourself," waving her hands in the air, which only made it more comical, with more laughter. At that moment as I tried to hide my face, I remember wondering how much gas could one person hold.

Our Priest came out eventually to try to calm his congregation, butt (pun intended) it was obvious to see he was struggling to quiet his own laughter. Eventually everyone calmed down as dad and Harold escaped through the side door. It took a while to calm the laughter, but I can safely say Mass was late the day, and if anyone looked sideways to find someone smiling, giggles could be heard. It was a delicate balance of calmness which could be disrupted at any time, and it was. The older women in the congregation were disgusted by this unholy performance, but their husbands, despite their being shushed by their wives, held their smiles all through mass. Needless to say Mass was certainly not its usual solemn, holy celebration, and although my family was embarrassed, we could not deny the entertainment dad and Harold had presented. Thinking about it now I am sure Jesus was laughing with the congregation.

Death seems to usher in, if you are blessed, an avalanche of good memories, and although there are bad ones too, the good seems to outweigh the not so good.

Memories invaded my thoughts that Saturday night before the final day of visitation. Although I had a difficult time falling asleep, when I did it was deep, until something woke me. I became aware of someone softly touching my cheek as if to wake me. I then became aware of the stillness, I no longer heard the clock ticking, or any house noise that is usually heard. With the quiet came a sense of peace, and love that washed over me. The only sound I heard was the soft voice of my dad, warning me yet comforting me at the same time.

"Elaine, something is going to happen but don't be afraid everything is going to be fine."

Normally, anyone would be alarmed at this, but I continued to breathe in that peaceful, loving presence until I began to once again hear the ticking of the clock, and the creaking of the air vents as the furnace brought warmth to every room.

Why was I not sitting up, fearful of what was going to happen? Why wasn't I alarmed at the voice of my dad who was dead? There was no explanation I could give to explain my feelings, only that of the undeniable peace that embraced me as I was lulled back to sleep. This in itself was a miracle, as I was not a sound sleeper, and what happened would have kept me up jumping out of bed worrying and wondering why.

About thirty minutes later, my daughter Mary woke me up in extreme distress. Mary was born with a very rare heart condition, so rare she was one of five in the world with this congenital heart defect. But at the time of diagnosis the other four had died, leaving her to be the lone recipient of this unwanted diagnosis. The doctors couldn't give us a written paragraph at what to expect, and Mary made medical history with each passing new health problem.

Her full story will be told in another book in which I am writing titled 'A Fragrance So Rare.'

At age fifteen Mary had received an experimental surgery in Toronto, Ontario, Canada, and with it came many warnings of possible problems.

That night after taking heavy antibiotics for strep throat Mary went into distress and rushed to my bedside.

"Mom, Mom, something is wrong, I need help, the pain in my chest is bad."

Being Mary's mom and a nurse, I jumped out of bed and followed her to the bathroom so I could assess the problem. Mary was vomiting what looked like coffee grounds, and dark red blood. I yelled for my husband to call an ambulance. Being the amazing, observant nurse I was, I failed to ask Mary if she had been drinking anything. "Yes, grape juice." Although, the grape juice became the reason for believing Mary was vomiting blood, the warnings we were told after Mary's experimental heart surgery in which the surgeon used Gortex to repair the absent left side of her pericardium. "If Mary develops any infection, the infection could go right to her heart, and possibly kill her."

That was foremost on my mind. We lived in the county, thirty minutes from the nearest hospital. Often in an emergency I would rush Mary to the hospital in our car, as an ambulance usually took anywhere from ten to fifteen minutes or longer to get to us; but that night I wasn't taking any chances.

Surprisingly, the ambulance arrived within five minutes, just giving us time to get dressed. Mary was examined, put on a stretcher, loaded into the ambulance leaving our driveway with lights flashing and siren blaring. Was it my imagination, or were the paramedics nervous? One knew of Mary's history, the other was relatively new in his job, but whether new or experienced her condition could be overwhelming.

As the ambulance roared quickly down the streets, Dave and I followed in our car, very aware if we tried to keep up with it, we could be the next ones in an ambulance.

Mary was a frequent patient at the hospital, known to many in the emergency department, and pediatric ward. Although Mary was now nineteen and more stable in her health, the doctors and nurses were still very aware of the fragility of her heart and lungs.

Before leaving our driveway, the paramedic who was staying at Mary's side contacted the emergency unit to let them know who they were bringing in. At Mary's name the emergency unit rapidly prepared for her arrival. Her Cardiologist Dr. Pete, was called in, and the unit was set up for any equipment that might be needed.

As Dave and I rushed to the hospital the thought crossed my mind that Mary could die. Would God take my daughter and dad in the same week? At that thought I was too raw to keep my composure, I cried, was short of breath and my heart was probably racing faster than the ambulance. Dave too was fighting his emotions, he had to keep it together in order to drive, so we both practiced deep breathing to calm our bodies which helped us enough to be able to talk.

I tried to calmly tell Dave about the visit from my dad, not completely understanding the complex simplicity of it all.

"Why was my dad allowed to come to me to warn me and tell me everything was going to be fine?" This was so hard for me to grasp, to believe, let alone others believing it. Since my being enticed innocently into the occult, I questioned everything, worried over whether it was God, an angel, or the devil?

"Was my dad's voice his? Was it an angel with his voice, or worse the devil tricking me?" I asked Dave.

Dave knowing what I went through in my early teens with the occult, understood my worry. Dave was always logical and prayerful before answering: he knew me, he knew the same, magnificent God I did, and how honesty was a value we held on to strongly. We were/are a couple rooted in integrity.

"Elaine, you know I believe what you're saying, and we have to be careful in what we don't understand. We know that if it's from God it will happen. We can't hold God in a box or our understanding of Him. Does he let someone we love speak to us after death? Is it a ghost, a demon, an angel, or your dad? We don't know for sure. But remember the overwhelming peace and love you felt? I want to believe that was God, and He allowed your dad to come to you to warn and comfort

you; let's hold on to that. Mary's going to be fine." God has always blessed my husband with the insight needed at the right time.

When we arrived at the emergency department, I forced myself to stay in the car until it stopped. We were met by a nurse as we entered through the revolving door, telling us that Mary was being seen by Dr. Pete and undergoing tests.

"I know this is difficult, but Mary is receiving the best of care as you know. Could you please come and sit and sign the necessary documents for Mary to be seen?"

Mary being nineteen could sign the papers, but as her parents we gave the clerk what she needed, and Mary if needed could sign the papers later.

As the minutes dragged on, and on, and our restless, worried pacing continued, we finally saw Dr. Pete coming toward us, we became like statues bracing for what he might say. He was smiling, "Dave," I whispered, "he's smiling!"

"He shook our hands saying, Mr. and Mrs. Vizard it has been a while since we last met; Mary's fine." My dad's words echoed in my spirit. At hearing the doctor say Mary was fine, Dr. Pete's smile widened as we exhaled.

"Please sit so we can talk."

Thankfully the emergency waiting room was almost empty, which was a miracle in itself.

"Mary has had a reaction to the antibiotic she is taking causing her chest pains, shortness of breath, nausea and vomiting, along with confusion."

With that information I interrupted him by blurting out, "Oh, that's why she was talking about flying saucers and aliens coming to get her."

Dr. Pete laughed, "Aliens and flying saucers? You will need to remind her of that. So, as I was saying, Mary is fine, her tests came back as normal as Mary's heart can be. There are no indications that the infection has attacked her heart. The coffee grounds and blood that you saw were actually the grape juice she was drinking just before this happened. She told me about your dad's passing, I am so sorry for your loss. I gave Mary a new antibiotic prescription: she will need to rest for a few days, but she is talking about going to the funeral home this afternoon. I advised her against going, but I will leave that with you knowing Mary can be very determined. Also have a blessed Easter!"

Oh, I forgot it was Easter and was apologetic for taking him away from his family.

"No need to apologize, it's still quite early, I have plenty of time to celebrate it with my family."

Dave asked him, "was this your weekend off?"

Dr. Pete just smiled, touching Dave's shoulder, "anything for Mary," and left.

As we went to our car with Mary I thought, Best Easter Ever. Thank you, God, thank you for allowing my dad to comfort me.

Mary was fine! My heart sang at the realization of this miracle gift God had given us. Eventually when my mom was able to let it sink in our story comforted her in her grief.

When a loved one dies, we are separated from them for the rest of our lives. I know many will find these stories of dreams God has given me unbelievable, and I am the first one to pray about them.

When I told my cousin Irene what happened, she took my hand saying with her beautiful smile and soft voice, "Elaine, I believe that with all my heart, I feel that God allows our loved ones to visit us, usually in our dreams, but this time it was a true God sent message he allowed you to receive."

Irene was always a strong Christian and I always respected and cherished her loving thoughts and advice. I agreed with her one hundred percent, and this next story took my breath away.

Often when I had a dream of significant meaning it was always in my past home, but this time the dream took place in the new home I presently lived in.

In my dream I heard the front door bell ring, when I opened the door there stood my dad, looking more handsome, and youthful, yet still the same age at the time of his death.

"Dad? What are you doing here? You're dead!" I asked rather breathlessly. I looked around him hoping to see my mother but she wasn't with him.

"I came to visit you, Elaine. I look like this for your benefit," he answered walking in the opened door.

He walked up the stairs, looked around and said how beautiful our home was. He looked at the soft multi floral couch and sat. I sat in my chair next to him.

I asked him what heaven was like, but he just smiled.

"It must be heavenly, right?" again he just smiled.

"I have something for you," he said, and a yellow rose appeared in his hand.

It was the most perfect long stem yellow rose I had ever seen, delicate and strong.

As dad handed it to me, he said he grew it himself in my mother's rose garden. My mother had died about three years before this dream. Mom loved roses, it was her most favourite flower of all, especially red roses.

I was overjoyed, "mom has a rose garden?"

"Yes," dad answered," and it's heavenly," he winked handing me a long stem red rose that suddenly appeared in his hand.

The thing that surprised me was the absence of thorns on them. Dad must have known my thoughts for in the next second he said, "No thorns in Heaven Elaine. No thorns."

I ran my fingers up and down the stems to feel that truth. Dad smiled, saying "Mom told me to make sure that you know how much she loves you. We both do."

I started to cry, and my dad stood and held his hand out to me. "Let's dance."

I always loved dancing with my dad, sometimes when we were in the kitchen while mom made her delicious spaghetti sauce, or as some would say: gravy. Mom simmered her sauce for twenty-four hours, (something I still do); and dad would grab my hand and dance with me while he sang an old familiar Italian song.

I took my dad's hand and suddenly a song started playing as my dad twirled me around my front room. I wasn't familiar with the song but I remembered a verse,

"If I could get another chance
Another walk, another dance with him
I'd play a song that would never ever end
How I'd love, love, love to dance with my father
again."

My dream ended slowly while still dancing with my dad. I laid in bed embracing the peace and love that came with it. My heart was filled with warmth, and I just wanted to lay in bed all day to bathe myself in God's grace in allowing me to have this, (words escape me on how to describe the dream,) beautiful doesn't describe the heavenly realm that enveloped me.

When I finally decided to enter the reality of life, I eventually went to my computer to google the song's verse.

🎵 "If I could get another chance
Another walk, another dance with him
I'd play a song that would never ever end
How I'd love, love, love to dance with my father again." 🎵

What I found blew me away, not literally, metaphorically, and I

researched it until I was sure it was the right song.

The song was titled, Dance with My Father, sung by Luther Vandross and written by him and Richard Marx. It was released in 2003 but I had never heard it. I wasn't one to listen to the radio, I had my favorite artists and genres but R&B wasn't a genre I listened to.

Had I heard it before, and that's why it was in my dream? I was positive I hadn't, and when google led me to a YouTube video of Luther Vandross singing it, I wept, that was the exact song that swirled and flowed like a soft ribbon in the air throughout the dance. The song came from nowhere yet everywhere as Dad and I danced.

One night as I watched the news the death of Luther Vandross was announced. Usually, I wouldn't give it a second thought except to pray for the family of the deceased. This however meant something to me, God had chosen this song for me to dance with my dad in my dream.

I often wanted to contact Mr. Vandross' mother to tell her how her son's song brought me such great joy, and how God used it in the context of the song's meaning. I didn't contact any family member of his for the simple reason of not knowing who to contact.

So, what was the miracle? The healing?

Well, when my mom died I for some reason didn't want her to visit me in my dreams. I had had some horrible dreams before her death, yet nothing to do with her, they were satanic dreams. Now I know my mother would never scare me, but I did ask her after her death not to visit me, and she didn't, and to this day I am saddened that I asked God not to allow it. It wasn't until I asked God to allow dreams of her to come, but it took some time to happen. I have had two dreams of her and each one more beautiful than the last.

God allowed, I believe, for dad to visit me in this way so I would know of mom's heavenly rose garden and her joy at giving me a red rose. How amazing is that, through this dream I knew my parents were together planting a garden of God's love, in my life.

All roses symbolize God's love at work in the world. The yellow rose in the spiritual world symbolizes wisdom and joy. The red rose symbolizes passion and sacrifice.

I prayed on what the yellow and red rose meant. Finding the spiritual meaning of both meant so much to me. After mom had died, I lost all interest in the book and although written, not published, I had put it on the shelf letting it collect dust, until now.

With the meaning of the roses becoming clear I realized it would take wisdom and joy in the amount of work it would take to revise the book, along with passion and sacrifice.

I went through many stages in trying to get the stories out, a blog, YouTube videos, but everything seemed pointless; until God reminded me, that He had told mom and I to write the book, and publish it throughout the world. That was a daunting project. So, I have now come back to the book doing exactly what God asked of us, His will be done. It took a most precious dream, a song, and a gift of the yellow and red rose to turn me around.

To God Be The Glory

Chapter Twelve
Jesus and Mae

Some miracles come to us as teaching moments, in disguise of not being miracles at all; but when eventually you look at it you realize how painful the learning process was, and the miraculous impact it made on your life.

First, the greatest miracle God gives to us is through His son Jesus. What the name of Jesus means; and how His sacrifice paid the price.

All too often we forget that fact, forget the miracle that is Jesus Christ our Lord and Savior.

Jesus made it possible for us to have a close relationship with God our Father, by taking on our sins. What does that mean? Well, God is Holy, and we need to remember that sin is unholy. Sin is a wall we build up between God and ourselves. Jesus takes down that wall when we accept Him as our personal Savior and all that comes with accepting Him into our lives.

The world today minimizes sin as a simple mistake, or just plain human behavior; but to our Holy God sin is sin and we have to learn to recognize it. In the Catholic faith there are two kinds of sin, Venial and Mortal, Venial being the not so bad sin, and Mortal being the worst. However, this is not biblical, and in my own belief God is so Holy sin is plainly sin, all are abhorrent to God, He is the judge of our mortal souls. If you feel something you are doing is wrong, well God must feel that same way, and that is sin. The Ten Commandments are a good guide as to what is wrong and what is right. This is where Jesus comes in, God our Father in order to have a relationship with Him gave His son Jesus as the ultimate sacrifice so we could have that close relationship with God the Father.

In the New Testament of the Bible it says in **John 3:*16-17***

"For God so loved the world that He gave His one and only Son, that everyone who believes in Him shall not perish but have eternal life. 17 For God did not send His Son into the world to condemn the world, but to save the world through Him...."

Jesus' death gave us forgiveness of our sins when we humble ask Him to, He knows our hearts. Jesus also gave us eternal life. How can that be? In my belief it means when we die Jesus brings us new life. We don't just simply die, we live.

Death is a miracle, not a punishment. It is God welcoming us home, in heaven, in paradise. It is said we should imagine what heaven is like, and multiply it more times than you can count.

My daughter Mary isn't afraid to die. Why? Because she had a glimpse of heaven when one day, she saw an Angel who touched her head. With that came the glorious insight of Heaven's delight. She knows heaven is real, but most of us have to go on faith, and faith grows in the presence of He who created us

I know Christianity is difficult to understand, but in reality, it is the simplest gift of love that God could give us, so profound that people will die rather than denounce their relationship in Christ.

Too many people put their own spin on Christianity, and too many wars have been started in the name of religion. Ireland is an example of what personal belief in Jesus meant. How long did terrorism kill Protestants and Catholics alike, all in the name of Jesus. We are better than you, God is more on our side than yours. This is just a very simplified explanation, but it boils down to who feels they are defending the true faith, whose faith is better and, more Jesus inspired than theirs. There are other reasons this war between the different religions exists, but what many forget is that we all worship the same Jesus, and if we follow in His footsteps, peace does not surrender to war.

The same could be said of people believing white people are better than people of color. A horrible belief going back ages, centuries, where people forget that Jesus came from the middle east and was himself most likely a person of color. Deception and falsehood passed on down from one generation to another cause's hatred and belief that one's color is supreme. This is still shown in the world today, and I often wonder why this world has not learned the valuable reality of being equal.

Enough of that, as it is an ongoing continuing saga of destruction and hatred. We are all God's children, but it seems evil in the hearts of people cause more damage than those who peacefully fight against the injustice, hoping for change, praying for change, dying for change.

An example of this was shown to me through a good friend of mine named Mae. She was brought up in South

Carolina, in a family riddled with alcoholic violence and belief in their superiority as a white person.

She was horribly abused by her dad, and it was a miracle of God's love through His son Jesus that changed her life.

I first met Mae at a Catholic Retreat in our church hall.

I had watched her throughout the weekend; she was brash, loud, and opinionated. When she was speaking to a person, she would invade their personal space. She was not a person I could or would relate to, nor want to be friends with. I had people in my life like Mae, and I was not about to add another one into my life, it was exhausting.

On the last day of the retreat, I felt a tap on my shoulder, and when I turned around there was Mae with a big smile on her face.

"Hey," she said in her deep southern drawl. "Ahh been watching y'all weekend an I reckon wees gonna be good friends." My attempt to write in southern drawl is I'm sure lacking, the words aren't spelling mistakes, just my attempt in writing southern drawl, which is slow and drawn out.

After she introduced herself, I thought, no way, no possible way, I don't need a complicated friendship with a woman I don't like. Jesus calls us to love, but like is a different emotion, different expression, a different way of feeling. You can love the person Jesus calls us to love, but you don't have to like them. So, this next question often is asked, "if you don't like a person, how do you respect them?" Well, and please remember I am not a professional, but in my way of thinking respect means that you can accept somebody for who they are, even when they're different from you or you don't agree with them. You can respect someone's position, like a politician, a boss, people of authority, but you don't have to like them.

Getting back to Mae, I just smiled back not knowing what to say, not realizing my judgement of her would become clear in the next day, and how the realization of judgement was so very wrong. My thoughts were quickly interrupted by our parish Priest telling my husband and I that there was an emergency at home concerning my mom, and we needed to get there immediately.

Mom was taking care of our four children so we could attend the weekend retreat. Our retreat was during the day, but mom slept at our house so we could be sure to make the morning sessions.

After our Priest told us Dave and I ran toward our car, we couldn't get out of the hall fast enough, leaving without saying goodbye to anyone.

We made it home before the ambulance arrived. I noticed my dad was struggling to compose his fear in front of his grandchildren, and at seeing my mom I rushed to her side, she was pale, and breathless. I took her pulse and felt she was in Atrial Fibrillation. I said this to the paramedics when they arrived and they quickly assessed her, one applied the sticky electrodes to her chest to attach the wires to the heart monitor, while the other gave her oxygen through the mask placed on her nose and mouth.

Dad and I followed the ambulance both in our separate cars, and sat in the waiting room while we waited for someone to come and talk to us. My dad was never one to sit still, especially where the health of his wife and family were concerned. He paced, and paced, and paced; it made me wonder what he was like in the waiting room while my mother labored and gave birth. I had no doubts that he was smoking back then, but cigarettes were no longer allowed in the hospital, he would have to go outside to do that; he wasn't about to leave to smoke, so he paced, and paced and paced.

I truly felt my mom was in Atrial Fibrillation, (A-Fib for short.) It can be a very serious rapid arrhythmia (irregular heartbeat) causing the heart to quiver, often causing blood clots, strokes and other cardiac problems if not treated. Oddly enough it is somewhat common, and most often can be controlled with the proper medication and or treatment.

Mom had been going through a difficult time with her Thyroid which is a butterfly shaped gland in the front of your neck that produces

hormones that help control many functions within your body such as the heart.

When the medical staff settled mom's heart and she was admitted for observation, dad and I were now able to visit her in room #402. The first thing I did was to hug her, telling her repeatedly how much I loved her, I then scolded her gently for not telling us how she was feeling.

"Mom, you are more important to me, church retreats come and go. I only have one mom, and taking care of four children while your heart was beating crazy was just plain ridiculous, serious not to mention dangerous."

"I know Elaine, it was important to me that you and Dave attend this retreat. I know I wasn't being wise, but God took care of me."

I could not argue that, but wasn't that putting God to the test? I bent down to give mom another hug, thanking her for her sacrifice in caring for our children.

"But please mom don't do that again, how could I live with myself if something serious happened to you."

I left mom resting comfortably in her hospital bed, with her heartbeat returning to normal after receiving medication. Dad remained at her side.

The next day was like most others, caring for the children, making meals, cleaning, the usual day to day life. I had called the hospital throughout the night and morning checking on mom's condition, knowing she was in stable condition I still jumped when our phone rang. I picked it up, no cell phones back then, just a landline with a long and winding cord attached to the receiver, a trap that often wrapped me in its fish net like grip. More than once I struggled to keep the cord from winding around me as I tried to keep my youngest children away from it. What is it with children? They are playing nicely in a different room, but once they hear the phone ringing, they are all over you, seeking your undivided attention, knowing you were going to be tied up for a few minutes in more ways than one? Struggling with the cord and keeping the kids in check, (how is that not considered exercise?) I finally answered the caller, "Hello," and then I heard it, that slow southern drawl.

"Ahh Elaine, ahhs just calling to see how your mamma is? Ahh been praying for her, you, 'n,' all of em. I assumed she meant the whole family.

I smiled at the new but familiar accent, "Hi Mae, my mom is still in the hospital but doing well." I explained to her what happened.

"Bless your momma's heart, if y'all need something just give me a holler," and without warning to get pen and paper, she gave me her phone number.

Mae, despite my judgmental thoughts in which I asked forgiveness for, to God not Mae, as it would have hurt her feelings to know that, she eventually became a good friend of mine. I was reminded what I had always known that the heart of the person is more important, not the way they present themselves that matters.

Mae and I often went to the same Church and Mass on Sunday mornings and eventually she started attending the same Prayer Meetings in our church hall on Wednesday evenings. We grew closer as time went on, although it was quite difficult for me not to say anything about her profanity. She swore a great deal, or as she would say, cussing. I didn't mind her saying shit, as I have been guilty of that myself. In fact, it was my first baby Sean then eighteen months old who brought attention to me swear words. I was eight months pregnant for Mary and was having a difficult time trying to put his clothes on with all his constant turning and wiggling on the changing table.

I sighed heavily and just looked at Sean who then said, quite accurately, "oh shit, you little bugger." I tried to hide my amusement but I then became very aware from that moment of the language I used.

Mae used the F… word often, along with other unacceptable words in my opinion. I didn't correct her, that was not my place to do so; yet! What was more disturbing to me was her use of the Lord's name in vain. In the Bible James brings attention to this in,

James 3:10; "From the same mouth come blessing and cursing. My brothers these things ought not to be so."

Another word Mae used that made my spirit cringe was nigger. I know she was brought up that way, and thought nothing of it, but for me, and I hope most people, it was just wrong. I was hoping our priest would have said something to her but maybe she didn't talk like that in front of him. I know when we were at church events Mae's language was very respectful, but in a comfortable environment Mae let her true self hang loose.

Mae was new in her walk with the Lord, so I waited for our friendship to grow a little more before I brought them to her attention.

First came using the name of Jesus in vain. When I brought it to her attention very carefully, I might add, she was shocked.

"I don't do that Elaine, I don't," she stated rather forcefully.

I didn't disagree with her, I just left it for her to think on it and pray as she said she would.

The day after I told Mae she called me; "I am sorry Elaine, I do use His name in vain, but y'all know I wasn't knowing I was doing it, not until you said something."

"I know you didn't use His name in vain intentionally Mae, and so does He."

After I had brought it to her attention, she became more aware and eventually His name was only used with deep love, respect, and worship.

As for the, (I hate saying this word), nigger, she actually didn't think there was anything wrong with it.

"Down south we say it all the time."

"Mae, then is Jesus a nigger, is He a kike?" seeming confused by my question, I continued.

"Nigger is an insulting slur hurled at people with black, or dark skin. It demeans the very fabric of who they are. kike is another insulting demeaning word against Jewish people. chink the same against Asian people, wop against Italians. All are disrespectful and so many more causing great harm in this world. Have you ever thought that Jesus could have dark skin? I believe he did as Israel is part of the Middle East. The point I am trying to make Mae is that even though you were brought up using the word nigger you are insulting the very people God created. No one deserves to be disrespected, or demeaned regardless of who they are, where they were born, the color of their skin, their religious background, physical differences, even mental illness. We all need to be aware of harmful, hateful words, because those words can turn to action through violence, and destruction."

Mae sat quietly for a few minutes, "I have never thought about it that way Elaine, it is just the way it is, has always been where I come from., but I will honestly try to be aware to what I am saying. How did y'all become so smart?" she asked.

"Not smart Mae, I was brought up differently, and I have always been aware of respecting all people. I sometimes have a hard time with those who are hateful causing harm and violence. I just remember I am not their judge; God is. Also, we are always taught to be careful of those who could harm us or others. There is good and bad alike in our world, but we can pray for everyone."

Mae grew in her walk with the Lord, and the more she learned, the more her words mattered.

I consider this a miracle of transformation. Mae told me from the time she was a little girl she wanted to learn about God, she said she wanted to be a Catholic. Her parents however refused to allow her to go to a Catholic church with her friend's family; she was told she was a Baptist. She didn't know what that was at the time because her family didn't go to church. She laughs at the memory, "I just remember thinking, "what the hell is a Baptist?"

Mae chose to formally accept the Catholic faith, this was her path, and she lived it to the full with her Canadian born family.

Mae became one of my dearest, closest friends through the years. Through her once hard exterior, she grew from what I can only describe as a caterpillar into the most beautiful butterfly. She had a tender heart and cared for people in their homes. She was a hard worker, even though her chemo and radiation treatments for breast cancer, she never missed a day of work. Mae was able to ring the bell at the end of her chemo and radiation treatments marking the day she was cancer free.

One evening Mae came to my house with her husband Wes. She was very upset and grabbed my hand leading me to my bedroom, I turned to look at our husbands, but she just waved her hand saying they would be fine.

Shutting my bedroom door, she quickly sat on my bed, I remained standing still not understanding what was happening.

"Well, aren't ya gonna sit down too. You'll need to sit Elaine, I think I did something very bad."

"Were you at a party?" I asked as she was dressed for one.

"Yeah, but not the kind of party I should have been to. Well it was a good party that turned out to be not a good one."

Sitting beside her on my bed she grabbed my hand tightly as if I could rescue her from drowning. "Okay Mae, slow down, I'm not understanding what you're trying to tell me,"

I eased her grasp on my hand, "Oh sorry Elaine," but her eyes held the same fear she displayed in her hand.

"What is wrong Mae?"

When she finally calmed and was able to speak more clearly and slowly she said, "I did something very bad, and ya'll have to help me."

"My sister had a Thanksgiving get together, in Detroit, and the whole family came. While we sat eating dessert her next door neighbor popped in. I knew who she was and what she did, but I guess I was weak."

"What does, or did she do to make you this upset?"

"She was, is a fortune teller, tarot cards, palm reading, ya know all the occult stuff you warned me of. But I needed to know what my son's future was, I needed to know if he was going to be successful and happy."

She looked at me with the wildest and fearful look.

"And…" I asked

"Well I let her, no I invited her to do her hocus pocus so I would know my son was going to be okay?

I sighed heavily, "Mae, why? Was trusting God not enough? Is your faith so lacking that you had to get answers from the occult? If you knew it was wrong why on God's green earth did you not call me before relenting to this temptation?"

"I just wanted to know Elaine, I just wanted to know. Ya'll can understand right?"

"No Mae, I can't understand it in any way or form, but then again, I know how slithering, and conniving satan is. I guess you were weak and easily lured into his web.

Mae, I warned you before about the occult, didn't any of my horrific experiences with it sway you."

"No, I just wanted to know," and Mae sobbed the tears of regret.

When she finally calmed, she asked if God would punish her.

"I can't answer that Mae, but remember God sees the heart, the part that we cannot, we have a loving God, a God who forgives, so let's pray."

We joined hands and Mae sobbed her wrongdoing asking for

forgiveness?"

After we talked for a little while longer Wes knocked on the door saying they had to get home, reminding her he had to get up early the next day for work.

After they left Dave asked me a hundred questions, but Mae had asked me to not tell anyone, not even Dave. Poor Dave, he went to bed with so many thoughts and questions running through his mind. Whenever I ask someone to keep it quiet, I never ask them to keep it from their partner, unless it is so private it would embarrass the person.

I don't remember how long after her brief experience with the occult, but I believe it wasn't that long when her cancer returned. We were devastated, and Mae believed it was because of her involvement with the occult, how brief it was, it doesn't take satan long to sneak into that sliver of a door opening to raise hell on one's life. I couldn't tell Mae one way or the other when she asked me whether it was her action that caused the devil to do it. I only knew through my experiences that it didn't take much for satan to slither in.

The fact remained Mae was now diagnosed with fourth stage bone cancer. She fought hard, and the day I quit a job that had tested my endurance as a nurse, causing very high blood pressure, my doctor stated very seriously "you need to quit your job, or have a stroke, and you know what a stroke can do. You will always need money Elaine, but death should not be an option to consider."

Dave and I had discussed it, and we decided my health was more important, so I quit that abusive, job as head of the nursing department. I often found that the stress didn't come from the work itself, but from the many levels of management. But I had to remember that they too had to answer to their higher ups, and I don't mean

God, although it would do us all good to remember that He was the ultimate 'Boss.'

When I was working, I always carried in my pocket a hard acrylic reminder that a friend gave me. It was a cross embedded into the middle of the round clear acrylic form. It was smooth, and comforting to touch and hold, a lovely reminder to myself that I worked for God. Some days when my job was beyond coping with, that little round reminder got me through the toughest of days. God was always with me.

The day I told Mae, she exploded into song, praising God, and thanking Him for answering her prayer.

I was still very raw emotionally, but Mae's words took me by surprise.

"God answered what prayer Mae?"

"I asked Him to set you free from that job so I could have you as I fight this damn cancer."

Mae knew the job was taking a toll on my health, and she thought I would be better off helping her. She was right, and with receiving sick benefits that would last a year I was able to be with her through her fight, and still not drown in debt.

I took her to her chemo treatments, and on the way home we always had to make a stop at the nearest Burger King so she could have two regular hamburgers, which she ate with gusto, somewhat like cookie monster from Sesame Street would inhale his cookie. After that she would fall asleep for the thirty-minute ride to her house.

After many chemo treatments it became clear not just to the doctors, but to Mae and all who loved her, that the chemo was not destroying the cancer cells, but physically killing her, cancer was winning. She decided to make a pact with me, "Elaine, keep me fighting until I tell you to stop." WHY? Why would she ask me such a thing? She was my friend; how could I tell her to stop and die.

I visited Mae often, I even started recording her life's story and was appalled when she laughed at the memories, often in my opinion tears should be flowing as she recounted her abusive past.

She laughed remembering her alcoholic dad driving her home from the grocery store. He wondered where she got the money to pay for all the food, but she wouldn't tell him that she knew when he was paid and took most of the money in his wallet before he had the chance to spend it all on alcohol at his daily "watering hole."

Mae said, "he never remembered how much money he had, so I made sure my family had food to eat and clothes to wear."

The day her dad drove her home from the grocery store he was "drunker than a stinky skunk, that man's elevator doesn't go all the way to the top, if you know what I mean." Sadly, I did understand.

Mae continued, "I knew I should have called a cab but dad saw me and I loaded the large amount of food in the car and he told me to get in. As he drove, he almost hit other cars, people and trees. I had enough and told him to stop because I wanted to get out and walk. He didn't stop but when he slowed down I jumped out. He was madder than an old wet hen on a dry day, and came after me with the car, fixing to run me over. That man just isn't right in the head."

"Did he catch you? I asked.

"Nah, by the time he got home he forgot what he was trying to do and went to bed. That gave me time to put the groceries away so he wouldn't ask about the money on seeing them in grocery bags."

That story was bad enough but then she started on another story that had me in tears. "My dad was a mean ole drunk, and one day I was twirling around in the main room and accidently knocked over his bottle of beer. He stood up so fast, took off his belt and grabbed me by the arm. He started whipping me hard, and I kept running in a circle, he kept telling me to stop but the whipping was so bad I couldn't and peed my pants, then he whipped me harder and longer. Once he took all his anger out on me, I stood there crying with him looking down at me. "Why did you whip me so hard daddy?"

"Because you ruined my beer, then peed your pants,"

Mae laughed at the horror on my face, "It's okay Elaine, that was

normal in my family."

"Mae, that's not normal, that's abuse, horrible abuse. Did you ever confront him about this as an adult?"

"Yeh, with my husband, but daddy wouldn't listen to me, said he was a good dad. He didn't say he was sorry or nothing like that, and I really wanted him to say he was sorry for the way he treated us kids, treated me. I tried so hard to get him to understand, and I left him with not so much as a kind word. Did I ever tell you how I got my name?

She didn't wait for me to answer, "the way my momma tells it her and daddy went for a walk and her water broke. She said it was the first time he wasn't drunk, so he took momma to the hospital and wouldn't leave her side, they didn't do things that way back then, but daddy refused to leave the labor and delivery room. Momma said her nurse was cute but clumsy, she wore glasses, and her one shoelace was always untied. I guess daddy made fun about her. Anyway when I was born daddy said out loud, "not another damn girl." So daddy cursed me when other dads would have been happy I was a girl, and blessed me, kinda what I think your daddy probably did. Momma asked what they should name me, daddy looked at the nurse and asked what her name was, she replied, "my name is Mae," "aright then that's her name, Mae," daddy said, then left to celebrate at his watering hole. My poor momma."

Either Mae had a way of coping with her life with humor, and laughter, or laughing when she spoke about it was a way to stop any tears from flowing. Every time she spoke about the abuse there was a sadness behind her smile, because her smile never reached her eyes.

Although I didn't want to agree with Mae's pact, I did just that, even when she was diagnosed as terminal, and all treatment stopped as the cancer had spread throughout her body. We didn't give up hope, we stood on the word of God, we prayed together all the time. But one day, when it seemed cancer had won, and she was so weak and sick she pulled the plug asking me to help her die. No, not yet God, please, please heal her.

Her words broke my heart, we knew a physical healing was not in God's plan, but could we give in? Give up?

One day when Mae was telling more of her story she would stop and look out her front room window. I hated that window because it faced the Funeral Home across the street.

"Someone's having a big ole funeral."

"It's not a funeral Mae, it's a visitation."

"Do you know the person that died Elaine?"

I didn't want to say yes; I didn't want to tell her that I would be in that very long lineup to pay my respects to the family later in the day.

"Who's the person Elaine?" couldn't she just leave it alone.

"It's the sister of a friend I worked with Mae."

"Looks like a big turnout. Is it a large family?

I wanted to scream, "STOP" but I knew Mae would not until her questions were answered. She was a stubborn woman.

"Yes, it is a very large family, I believe twelve brothers and sisters, along with many relatives and friends."

"How old was she?"

"Not quite sure but I think in her forties."

I knew what was coming, I knew she would ask that final question, that question that would bring our world, our day to a complete stop.

"How did she die?" and there it was, the question I had hoped I wouldn't need to answer. But there it was, and Mae kept staring at me begging for an answer. Did she want me to say car accident? Hit her head falling in the tub? I could lie to save us both grief but lying wasn't an option. Damn cancer!

I looked Mae in the eyes with tears fighting to be released; why is life so cruel?

I wanted to whisper the answer, hoping by whispering it wouldn't make it true.

"Breast cancer, she died of breast cancer," I said loudly, and there it was, the words that stopped our world.

My lips quivered, life was so unfair, so unkind, and even though Mae wasn't afraid to die, so she said, she didn't want to leave her family, she didn't want to die, and neither did the woman lying in the coffin across the street.

On my way home I listened to Christian music on the radio. I needed something to distract my thoughts from the inevitable, in reality I shouldn't have been driving as my thoughts kept straying toward death. I had to get home to change to go back to the Funeral line up to pay my respects, I just hoped Mae wouldn't see me.

When I returned home, I parked on the street, the song I was listening to help me in its grasp, hopeful yet giving in to God's plan. As I sat there listening to it I began to cry, no, sob, pounding my fists on the steering wheel like I had so many times with my daughter's illness, sinking in to the unfairness of all that was happening.

Mae had asked me to come sit with her during the funeral of her daughter-in-law's father, who was diagnosed with cancer around the same time she was.

Death clung in the air like a dense fog, one that would not clear, one that held our thoughts as hostage, it took us awhile before we started talking.

Whether we wanted to or not, it was clear to see her now cancer ridden body, the weakness in her movements. Mae was so sick with diarrhea; I had helped her to the bathroom and went into the next room while she took care of her bodily functions. "Elaine," her voice called out to me just slightly higher than a whisper. "Elaine, this is it, I was told what to look for at the end, the color of my bowel movements are what the nurses at the cancer clinic told me about."

Mae was very strong willed, she had to be growing up as she did, she wanted to know every stage, every symptom, every change in her body, what to look for when the end was near.

I helped her get back into bed but as she sat she secreted a small amount of diarrhea. She looked up at me saying she was sorry over and over again, it wasn't something that was foreign to me, as a nurse I was very familiar with bodily functions.

"C'mon Mae, you don't need to apologize, let's just get you cleaned up, I washed her, put a clean nightgown on her and sat her in a chair as I stripped her bed to put clean sheets on it. She looked at the sketch photo I had brought her sitting on the dresser. This in itself was a miracle, I had gone shopping with my mother at a Christian bookstore and a picture caught my eye. It was a sketch of Jesus bending down to pick up a little girl, and I felt the strong nudge of the Holy Spirit to buy it, frame it and bring it to Mae. When I gave it to her the next day she cried saying the little girl looked just like her, hair, clothes and all. It gave her great comfort, and as she looked at it again, she asked if I would hang it on the wall so she could see it when lying in bed.

Still seated on the chair I heard her whispered, shaky voice say, "It's time Elaine."

I looked over at her from the opposite side of the bed as I tucked in the sheet.

"Time for what?"

"Time to stop fighting and help me die."

"The pact? You want me to help you die instead of praying for your healing?"

"Yah." As she sat there, she seemed to question her decision and then said, "well, maybe not." I smiled and said, "why don't we leave that up to God but still pray."

Mae nodded and I went to her and helped put her back into bed making sure she could easily see the picture on the wall.

After I helped Mae get back into bed I quickly cleaned up and put her sheets in the washing machine, then went to sit down and watch the television that Mae had asked me to keep on. She loved western shows, Bonanza, Wagon Train, Rawhide, The Rifleman to name a few. I wasn't a fan of The Rifleman but sat watching it while Mae slept. It was a long day and as I sat waiting for a family member to get home Mae called out to me, "Elaine, go home, I will be fine, someone should be here soon."

I refused to leave but we both knew I had an appointment with

Unemployment to keep my benefit money coming in, and not going meant I would lose it, which I was willing to chance, but Mae being the stubborn, strong-willed woman she was would not let me. She repeatedly told me to go until I gave in and, put the phone in Mae's reach, kissed her, told her I loved her and left feeling painfully guilty for abandoning her. I called her after my meeting and her son answered telling me he arrived soon after I left. Thank you Jesus!

The next day, I received a phone call from her daughter-in-law, they were in emergency as Mae's breathing was compromised. Her last words to me before they admitted her flowed breathlessly from the background, "Elaine, keep praying." I told her daughter-in-law to tell her I was and will, and my connection to her had ended on Good Friday, Easter weekend.

Mae had always stated that Easter would be the best time for God to take her home. The next day, Holy Saturday, I received another phone call, this time from Mae's husband, "Elaine, they are saying that Mae had a massive stroke, and could die today, can you come."

As it was still morning, I jumped out of bed dressed, ran out the door to jump in the car with Dave in the driver's seat. "Elaine, I am driving you, you need to get there safely." Dave was right, and all the way to the hospital I prayed, and prayed, and prayed. What I was praying for was simply for Him to take her quickly.

During that time in 2003 the whole country was fighting SARS, a Severe Acute Respiratory Syndrome, a coronavirus, but not as deadly as the pandemic in 2020-21-22-23 called Covid-19 which kept mutating.

During SARS only one person was allowed to be with their family member, but as Mae was dying, I was allowed to be with her and the many family members who had gathered at her death bed.

As we all sat in silence, I was comforted that the CD titled The Gaither's Homecoming I had given to Mae was softly playing in the background. Mae loved that CD, and the comfort came from knowing Mae was going Home bathed in Heavenly songs. Although the songs were beautiful their music could not soften the sound of Mae's death rattle, a sound I had often heard as a nurse.

Mae's husband broke the silence, "Elaine, how long do you think it will be before she goes home to the Lord."

I know hearing that sound coming from Mae was upsetting for me, ever more so for her family. "I don't know Wes, it could be today, it could be tomorrow, there is just no way to tell, except for it being soon."

Wes nodded and I excused myself and left the room, almost running to the elevator to get to the chapel. There I took the pencil and pad laying on a table with a box to put it in. I wrote, 'please God, take Mae home today, actually Lord I ask in your name to take her in the next hour. Thank you, Jesus.'

I rushed back to Mae's room, and once again sat beside Wes. A nurse appeared stating the Chaplin was in the building asking if we thought Mae would want to receive the Sacrament of the Sick, (last rites) an anointing with holy oil to simply ask God to give His grace at the time of illness or death.

Everyone's heads turned toward me with Wes asking, "What do you think Elaine?"

Mae had received the sacrament many times over the course of her illness. She had told me how much she loved receiving this sacrament, it often strengthened her, giving her comfort. "Wes, Mae would love it."

That said the Chaplin was called to the room, and anointed Mae as he began the prayers. It was at the end of the hour of my prayer request, and I was beginning to think it wouldn't be answered, but as God often does, for whatever reason, He answers the prayer at the last possible minute as He did with Mae. As the Chaplin said Amen Mae took her last breath and was carried like that small child in the photo, in the arms of Jesus to her eternal home.

Mae was always so animated at times, I could almost see her spirit taking a bow, saying 'ta da,' as her death coincided with the final word Amen. Now that was dramatic to say the least; but that was Mae, this was the day she was transformed into her new life, and I know without a doubt I will see her again.

I have witnessed transformation in many lives, living and in dying. Some who had given up on life, some with addictions. The miracle of watching those who have found Jesus turning their lives completely around, giving up the drugs, alcohol, and whatever else held them bondage, is nothing less than miraculous. Although my story isn't steeped in tragic history, and I don't pretend to know the depths of pain the spider web traps of personal battles many people live with, I do know that I am flawed, a sinner, and although I live each day to do good, I still fall short of the person God created me to be. That said, He loves me just as I am, and I am bathed in His mercy, grace and forgiveness living each day in the

presence of a miracle worker, Jesus!

To God Be The Glory

The picture Mae loved which I hung on the wall for her to see clearly.

Mae, my beautiful friend!

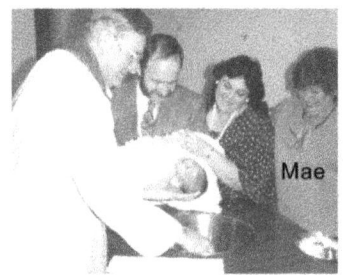

Mae

Mae was Godmother for our youngest son Adam

I can only imagine the look on her face when she met Jesus face to face.

Chapter Thirteen
Aunt Gert

Some healings and miracles come to us through what are known as healing ministries. A result of people who God has chosen to work through with the power of the Holy Spirit.

One such miracle happened to my Aunt Gert at a Kathryn Kuhlman service. Kathryn traveled extensively around the United States and in many other countries holding healing crusades between the years in the 1940's-70's.

Always remember it isn't the person who heals, it is Jesus, and all glory is His.

Aunt Gert, developed Rheumatoid Arthritis, if I remember correctly in her late forties, early fifties, and I believe it wasn't long after she had a heart attack.

Rheumatoid arthritis is an autoimmune disorder, occurring when your immune system mistakenly attacks your own body's tissues. It causes painful swelling that eventually can result in bone erosion and joint deformity.

Today the medical field knows much more about this disorder. New medications are more helpful than when Aunt Gert suffered with it, and she truly suffered.

My aunt never complained although she did not hide it from my mother. Mom knew her suffering. Needless to say, we her family helped her as much as we could. The only enjoyment she had in life was that of her daughter, grandsons, and extended family. Everything caused her horrific pain; just the simple fact of sitting, laying in her bed, taking a shower, getting dressed were all contributors to her excruciating pain.

Aunt Gert was able to attend my wedding due to an injected treatment called a gold shot, which wasn't a pain reliever but lessened the inflammation in the joints resulting in less swelling and pain. A series of these helped her move around easier. Gold shots are no longer readily available due to their toxicity and in some cases, dangerous outcome.

I am not sure how many shots Aunt Gert received, but in her words, they helped her. She looked so beautiful at my wedding, and I was so thankful she could attend.

I had what was called a honeymoon baby, although I lost the baby through miscarriage. My doctor was very sympathetic and told me I could, if Dave and I wanted to become pregnant again with no waiting period. We didn't know it back then but Dave and I were a fertile couple, my mom often said that all Dave had to do was hang his hat and I became pregnant. We all know that hanging a hat doesn't cause a pregnancy, it takes a little more than that, but needless to say, we were fertile.

The next month I did get pregnant, and due to a freak accident, I was confined to my bed for a little over five months, this story will be told in the next chapter.

During that time my mom kept me updated about Aunt Gert's condition, and how her suffering continued.

The day Dave and I brought our baby home my mom was taking my aunt to a Kathryn Kuhlman service in Detroit Michigan USA; just across the bridge from my city Windsor Ontario, Canada. A group from our church were attending the service, and they hired a bus to bring them to the arena, with hopes God would move in miraculous ways.

That day Aunt Gert's body had doubled in size, her knees were beyond recognition, her every step excruciating but she was determined to go and go she did. She had long prayed, hoping for a miracle along with many others on the bus who also longed to be healed.

Mom told me later that my aunt said, "even if I'm not healed, I pray God gives me the strength to endure and accept this pain." In her suffering Aunt Gert offered it up in prayer for others who were suffering in the world.

At the healing service thousands of people were praying for the release of illnesses, strokes, cancer, being paralyzed and so much more. My cousin and his wife who had been diagnosed with a debilitating disease as a young adult also attended but not with the same group.

I have often wonder how God chooses who will be healed and who won't. Is someone more worthy? Does He love that person more? I came to the realization that, no, He doesn't, we are all His children, and His plans are not ours. We can't understand the mind and heart of God, after all He is God, and we are human. We are called to trust in whatever He chooses to do. One of my good friend's boyfriend, later her husband, was angry with God, because He didn't answer his youthful teen prayer to heal his cousin of Muscular Dystrophy. This man wasn't a believer in God, let alone Jesus, but he thought he would take a chance in asking for this healing. Only God knows our hearts, the true measure of our prayers, and the reason why this prayer was unanswered. The fact remains that this man harboured an undeniable hatred toward God, even before he said that prayer. I often wondered why my friend married him when they were so incompatible. They both had their issues, but they were a true example of two different people, who did and didn't believe, causing much friction and damage in their marriage and children. I didn't realize their issues with mental illness were deeply rooted in their lives, and they struggled with it, but his bitterness and anger with God grew as my friend tried to get him to believe. You can't make an unbeliever believe, that is their choice, not yours, mine or even God's. In fact, God can put situations in one's life but because He gave all people the gift of free will it is up to that person to choose Him as their Saviour. Sadly, his heart remained hardened against God, although he is still living I am not aware of any change in his choice.

Eventually their marriage disintegrated, and their children's sense of security had long been lost with the existence of spousal and child abuse. Dave and I tried so much to help them, but not all can be saved physically, emotionally and spiritually. I pray for the whole family by name daily, hoping that somehow the presence of God reaches into their lives healing them from the pain they have all long endured. My heart aches for them.

Getting back to Aunt Gert's story, mom recounted what it was like in the arena as they waited for Ms. Kuhlman to appear on stage.

Mom stated, "Whenever I have gone to a conference the noise within the facility was often loud, until it began. Excited voices would fill the air, until the conference was officially started. This however was an arena, holding more people than I could count. I am sure the arena was filled with thousands of people, and although there was a choir with live music, there was a calm almost silent atmosphere within the noise, a whisper that seemed to whisper, 'you are sitting on holy ground.' The only voices I heard were of whispered prayers, and the hushed anticipation of hope that surrounded me. As the choir sang songs that many of us were familiar with, we joined in.

When Kathryn appeared on stage the Holy Spirit became a tangible electrifying presence that flowed throughout the crowd."

Mom said Ms. Kuhlman was very dramatic and flamboyant, which bothered some people who had seen her television shows, but most accepted her for who she was, a vessel guided by the Holy Spirit in which Jesus was the author of her gifts. As some people felt they were healed they were brought up on stage to confirm their miracle. Wheelchairs sat empty as those who could not walk for different reasons were healed. There were many different miracles, healings but not everyone who experienced a healing made it to the stage.

Aunt Gert was one such person. She said she felt a gentle breeze flow through her and around her, and then watched as her swollen body returned to her normal pre rheumatoid arthritis shape. Her crippled hands, and fingers were straightened, her knees now normal in size, her pain vanished, gone in an instant. Aunt Gert received her miracle, and as mom stood stunned witnessing the miracle as it happened, she said it reminded her of the godmother in the animated movie Cinderella when she was transformed for the ball. Like a twirling magical wand that wrapped its miraculous ribbon, from toes to head, and so it was with Aunt Gert. After the shock of what had happened mom grabbed her sister, gently at first, but Aunt Gert no longer in pain, with physical disabilities no longer a factor, grabbed mom in a strong hold, jumping and laughing with her in youthful excitement.

On their return home the bus was filled with glorious praise and joy, as others announced their healings. As the sisters stepped off the bus, they saw my dad and ran to him to once again laugh and jump. Dad didn't join in with the physical activity, but his laughter met theirs in joyful celebration.

Dad didn't bring Aunt Gert home as she and mom wanted to share the good news with me, and to hold our newborn baby Sean who we had just brought home that day.

I will always remember their faces as they walked in the door. Aunt Gert lifted her arms to show her hands, lifted her knees to show their freeing movements; "I received a miracle Elaine, I am healed." I stood there crying, thanking Jesus, and as my aunt held out her arms, I placed my newborn son into her arms. My aunt was made whole, her miracle a reality of God's divine and glorious grace. Everything was right with the world. Thank you, Jesus!

As for my cousin's wife, I was told she had asked for a fifty-year remission of her disease, but it would take time to know the outcome.

God's grace didn't just heal bodies but renewed souls, and Kathryn Kuhlman didn't heal Aunt Gert, Jesus did, and just a note on ending this chapter, some evangelists are true to God, and some aren't. Be very careful who you follow, who you give money to for their ministry. Research them carefully, and if the Holy Spirit lives within your spirit, let Him guide you. I was unsure of Kathryn Kuhlman, and I think the way she presented herself, almost like an actress on stage, caused me to be doubtful, but after Aunt Gert's miracle I became less suspicious of her motives. God uses who He chooses to touch peoples' lives. All healing and miracles come from Jesus, when my eyesight was healed it was through the water of Lourdes, connected to Jesus' mom, but Jesus is always the healer. Sometimes people are healed alone at home in prayer, but each healing, each miracle is God's doing through His son Jesus and the power of the Holy Spirit.

Kathryn Kuhlman was an earthen vessel, a jar of clay for God to use for His purpose, in her case, a healing ministry.

2 Corinthians 4:7

⁷But we have this treasure in jars of clay, to show that the surpassing power belongs to God and not to us.

To God Be The Glory

Aunt Gert was Maid of Honour at Mom and Dad's Wedding

Enjoying a Pic-Nic with Aung Gert

Aunt Gert on my Wedding Day

Chapter Fourteen
Wedding, Sex and Pregnancy

Some miracles come to us in small bundles as did this next miracle. The last story where I spoke about my Aunt Gert touched on this precious, miraculous gift from God. But first a little history of a very personal nature.

I always had from the time I can remember very painful and heavy periods, (menstruation.) As I didn't want to have my cycle during my wedding week and honeymoon my family physician, Dr. Smeetin suggested I go on a low dose birth control pill which he felt would resolve this issue, and it did. We had a beautiful wedding day, in fact I had long been praying for a day of no rain, with flowers blooming, you know the whole Disney movie dream. In the grand scheme of things, it wasn't that important, but it was my dream and prayer. As I still lived with my parents, I was in my bedroom about to get ready when I heard the doorbell ring. The next thing I knew mom was knocking on my door,

"Elaine, it's mom can I come in."

"Of course, mom, what's up?"

"Mr. Chambers from down the street told me something very interesting," she said as she sat down on my bed, looking up at my wedding dress hanging high from the ceiling.

"I can't wait to see this on you," her thoughts went elsewhere for a few seconds, "Oh, Mr. Chambers told me he had been praying for your wedding day, and that you are not to worry, the day will be completely rain free warm and blooming."

"That is interesting mom, since I am the only one who knows I have been praying for the perfect wedding day. Dave and I went to the park just yesterday morning to see if the flowers and trees were blooming for our pictures, but all we saw were buds."

"Mr. Chambers was positive that this was going to be the day you prayed and hoped for."

"From his mouth to God's ears mom;" at that moment my cousin Sandy arrived to help my sister Mary Ann (Maid of Honour) and I with our makeup and hair. The house became wedding central as my bridesmaids and flower girl along with the bouquets all arrived at the same time. It was an exciting time, and when the photographer arrived it was a blur of activity, especially with my Uncle Ted filming us at the same time. Although the film had no sound it was a very precious gift to give us, although he recorded it on a Super 8 film, my husband surprised me on our forty-fifth wedding anniversary when he had it changed over to a CD. I had wanted this for many years, but it was too expensive, until it wasn't and as Mae would have said, "God bless his heart."

My dress was made by the woman I baby sat for, her wedding gift to me. It was a simple empire waist with the most beautiful lace accenting its flowing beauty. I felt so guilty as every time I went for a fitting, I had lost weight due to working double shifts and working out at the gym I went to. The biggest problem was the pearl buttons at the back of the dress, she had to continually adjust them after each visit until she gave me fair warning to stop losing weight. My veil was long, made of the same flowing material as on the dress, it was so long my dad accidentally stepped on it as he tried to step over it after giving me away. No damage was done, except I might have had a slight case of whiplash.

My cousin Patti said my wedding was like a fairy tale, and it truly was, with a very celebratory reception of two hundred and fifty guests. What was more important was the fact we all came to a decision on who would take responsibility to pay for the wedding. With my parents and Dave's, we all came to a compromise, Dave and I wanted to pay for our wedding, but our parents were very much against it. I knew this would put more pressure financially on my parents as Dave's parents were more financially set, not wealthy but comfortable.

Dave's dad was a caterer, so he catered the meal with his very reliable staff, making it relaxing for him, the day of, but not the days leading to the wedding. They also paid for the reception venue as being a caterer he had many contacts offering discounts.

Dave's mom and sister made all the bridesmaids and flower girl's dresses. My dad and mom paid for the live band and liquor, leaving Dave and I to pay for the rest, which wasn't very much. We were truly blessed as most couples pay for their own weddings.

Our wedding day was just like I had hoped and prayed for, just like Mr. Chambers told mom. The day was warmed by a gentle breeze, and the park where our photos were taken, was now in full bloom which highlighted my bouquet of pink roses, and white baby's breath. The birds happily chirped while gliding in the stunning blue sky as white fluffy clouds floated above making the day picture perfect. Truly my cousin was right about a Fairy Tale Wedding, the whole day was like a Disney movie, dreams did come true, but more importantly prayers were answered.

Because I hadn't worked for a full year at the hospital, I was only able to take six days off for my honeymoon. We decided to stay in Canada and go to Niagara Falls finding it the perfect place meeting many other newlyweds from all over the world.

The day of our wedding Dave decided to hide our car, a blue Ford Pinto, in the hotel open garage where we were staying for a night before we left for our honeymoon, which we thought was a brilliant idea.

On our wedding night we didn't consummate (sexual intercourse) that night, we were just too exhausted and decided to wait until we arrived at our honeymoon destination. That night we fell asleep in each others' arms, only to be woken at four thirty in the morning when the complimentary champagne bottle's cork popped making a very large noise. As we were just falling back to sleep someone knocked on our hotel room door, for the second time that night, but no one was there.

"I think someone is trying to warn us," Dave said.

"Warn us about what?"

"That possibly someone is decorating our car."

Our two best friends were pranksters, and they often spoke about decorating our car, after the wedding. Although we thought our car was safely out of their reach, we realized our brilliant idea was not so brilliant after all. This couple was committed to pranking us, and they succeeded.

Walking to our car after checking out of the hotel we found our car was covered in small blue sticky notes. When I say covered, I mean every inch, every space on the car was painted with the sticky notes which overlapped each other. People walked by commenting, and laughing at our predicament, but no one, I mean not one person offered to help remove them. Dave and I began laughing, although our laughter and good humour diminished after two hours of removing them. We were relieved to find that the car had not suffered any damage, and we vowed to do the same to our friends when their wedding came, three months later.

Taking the birth control pill worked but had its' side affects, especially making me very nauseated. I thought about stopping them so I would feel good for the wedding but then I was wearing white, and if my period started, I knew I would be worried about an accident, so I stayed on them. The side effects didn't last too long, saving me from the needless worry of what to do.

In Niagara Falls we were escorted to the bridal suite, but I almost changed my mind when the attendant mentioned how lucky we were.

"Tiny Tim and his bride stayed in this very room on their honeymoon."

Tiny Tim was an eccentric ukulele playing singer made famous by his song, 'Tip Toe Through The Tulips.' He was married to his first wife who he called Miss. Vicki on the Tonight Show hosted by Johnny Carson. It is said forty million people were watching the show, but I wasn't one of them. He just wasn't my cup of tea, so to speak.

"That's interesting," Dave said blandly to the attendant's excited announcement.

For me, it was just too much information and I wanted to tip toe right out of that room.

It took me a little time to adjust to Tiny Tim having stayed in the same room, but I was comforted knowing they were there four years before us. I don't know why I felt that way, I just didn't like that man's eccentric behaviour.

Dave was very patient as I am sure he was biting at the bit to make love, and the full extent of what that term meant. I was nervous, and although Dave and I were intimate in the last year before we were married, we did not have intercourse.

The first night in our honeymoon suite as we tenderly showed our physical love for each other, I screamed out in pain as he tried to penetrate me.

I was devastated. What was wrong with me? Each time we tried my body betrayed me, to the point I dreaded trying again. Dave and I were so innocent, the blind leading the blind comes to mind, but we kept trying. One night the hotel was filled with kids on a school trip running through the halls, and when once again my body betrayed me and I yelled out in pain, Dave put a pillow on my face to scream in to as he finished penetrating me, that was something we had talked about, and did.

The wedding was perfect, the honeymoon not so much. I felt as if I was a failure, a disappointment to Dave. I just wanted to go home to familiar surroundings.

It took awhile before I was comfortable in our love making. I thought something was physically wrong with me. Yes, I was a nurse; no, my mother didn't prepare me for the physical part of consummating our wedding vows. I had no knowledge that sexual intercourse could be so painful at the beginning, but it was, and it put a shadow over our honeymoon. Dave was very patient, but I was distraught, and felt this may never happen for us. It wasn't until my cousin Janie's wedding when I spoke to my other cousin, Sandy.

We were born on the same date, July 31st thirteen years apart. Sandy and I were extremely close especially when I was a teenager, I often babysat her two children at the time. She was an amazing woman, so much like my mom in her beliefs and faith. She always seemed to be aware of when something was bothering me.

"Elaine, let's take a walk outside, I need some fresh air."

Outside we walked breathing in the cool refreshing soothing air.

"What's wrong Elaine?"

"What do you mean Sandy?"

She stopped walking and looked into my face, "I know when something is bothering you, so what is it?

"It's embarrassingly personal Sandy," I whispered as tears welled in my eyes.

"Embarrassing? Personal? not between us Elaine. If you let me know maybe I can help you, or at least try."

I then held her hand as she reached out for mine and told her.

"Oh Elaine, didn't Aunt Bea tell you it could hurt?"

"No Sandy, she didn't say anything. When it comes to sex mom is somewhat lacking in information. She must have thought I already knew; I am a nurse for goodness' sake."

Sandy just laughed, "I don't think your nursing education covered painful sexual intercourse, but I am surprised Aunt Bea didn't tell you. Elaine, it is perfectly normal for many women," and she continued to give me all the information, and relief I needed.

I laughed when she stopped talking, "geesh Sandy, who knew sex could be this complicated."

"It's different for everyone, but you and Dave will find your way, and as time goes by it will continue to become much more pleasurable."

"You know Sandy, I am thankful Dave and I didn't have intercourse before our wedding, I might have changed my mind on going through with it," I joked.

We both laughed as we walked back to the reception hall.

There are always people giving out wrong information on sex, like you can't get pregnant if the man withdraws before ejaculation. I knew that was wrong, and even if I had a doubt my getting pregnant on my honeymoon proved that fact. Those little sperms are activated on the very thought of sex. The fact that I was on the pill should have stopped my becoming pregnant, but one night in Niagara Falls I forgot to take one pill. One pill? Honestly? That along with not having had the complete sexual experience made it difficult to understand.

Dave and I discussed having children early, as Dave's dad had a bad heart, and he wanted his dad to hold a grandchild. Dave didn't think his dad would live much longer as he was having angina attacks every day. At that time heart bypass surgery was just coming into its own, but Jack was not a candidate for it. His condition was far too progressive, a ticking time bomb, however his nitroglycerine pills helped his symptoms. He was a very hardworking man, stubborn too as he would not let his heart condition hold him back.

When we told our families I was pregnant, they were all excited, but I began to have problems with cramping and bleeding and lost our baby three months into the pregnancy.

Much happened in those three months, but to go into detail is another story you will read later.

After our baby died, in August of 1973 we were told our loss was due to my being on the pill when becoming pregnant. Our baby was deformed and would have never lived. We were heartbroken but life continued, and my doctor told me I could get pregnant right away again if we wanted.

After speaking with the doctor Dave and I decided to follow his advice, to try other means of birth control. The next month, September 1973, I became pregnant again, and this time we were not surprised. We were happy and worried about losing this baby, as were our families.

During the first trimester everything was going well except for the horrendous nausea I experienced. At that time, we lived in an apartment which was for adults only. Dave and I decided to buy a house and found a cute little one with two bedrooms, one bathroom, and a breakfast nook off the kitchen; I fell in love with that little nook. I could picture Dave and I with our baby sitting, laughing, talking and eating. Our parents checked the house before we bought it, and everyone fell in love with it. When we received the good news that the house was ours, we decided to go out and celebrate at a very nice restaurant. Not the little diner we often went to, this was fine dining.

This restaurant had a very large heavy wooden door with no glass to see if anyone was leaving or entering the restaurant. As I went to grab the large pull door handle, a man came rushing out swinging the door wide hitting me in the lower abdomen, taking my breath away.

Standing there trying to breathe the man apologized but didn't wait to see how I was.

When in the restaurant Dave went right to the manager to tell him what had happened, "…you need to replace that door with a safer one, my wife could have been seriously hurt."

The manager apologized and said he would see to it, but that door remained there for many more years.

I told Dave I was fine, and we continued on with our romantic celebration. The food was great, we ordered appetizers, then talked and waited for our main course. I love steak, and ordered that medium rare, a baked potato and salad. In a fine dining restaurant in my opinion the salad always looks like the food, food would eat, not a typical salad of iceberg and romaine lettuce, tomatoes, cucumbers, celery, shaved carrots, cheese, with added croutons. I am not a fan of leafy coloured lettuce, the kind that rabbits chew on.

I did however enjoy the fine dining salad while waiting for the entrée to be served. When it came the aroma made my stomach gurgle in joyful anticipation. Dave loved sea food, so he had lobster, and enjoyed all the side dishes that came with it, especially the butter he dipped the lobster meat into. Halfway through our meal I felt a strange sensation, as if I had peed my pants.

"Are you okay?" Dave asked looking at the expression on my face.

"I think so, I just need to go to the bathroom, it feels like I peed myself, maybe the door hit my bladder."

I wondered, worried that I may be bleeding, thankfully I wasn't and went back to finish my meal. I reassured Dave I was fine; I just wished my heart would believe in the words I was speaking

The rest of the evening went well, until in the middle of the night I ran to the bathroom when I felt another gush. After checking the spot on my nightgown, and yes smelling it, I knew the gush did not come from my bladder. Fearing the worst, I thought of the amniotic fluid that surrounded our unborn baby.

The next day found us at our family doctor's office being examined, what really unnerved us was when Dr. Smeetin called an obstetrician to check me.

He confirmed it wasn't urine, and that in fact I was losing amniotic fluid. If I had been further along in my pregnancy I would have been sent to the hospital, instead I was sent home on complete bed rest. No getting up for anything, except for bathroom privileges for bowel movements, urinating would have to happen in a bed pan. No shower, only bed baths, and since I was at the end of my first trimester it would be a wait and see.

Agonizing as it was, fear was my daily companion. Every cramp, every symptom brought me to tears. I leaned on my faith, trying to trust in God's plan for us, but all too often my fears overcame that trust.

The day we moved into our new home in February of 1974 the first item to be put in our new home was our bed. I laid on the sofa in the apartment until Dave came to get me putting me in a wheelchair to go to our new home.

I had to climb five stairs to the front door which entered immediately into our front room, our bedroom was right off the front room, on the left. My mom had the bed made waiting to tuck me in, and she did. I was on the verge of tears but fought hard to hold them in as I didn't want to upset anyone.

Dave and I decided to hire a moving company, which was much easier on all the family. Our moms Beatrice and Edna, along with my sister MaryAnn were at the house to help put things away. It was difficult to direct them in where to put things, although the house was small, they had to keep coming into the bedroom to ask where I wanted specific items to go. I found this so frustrating, longing to be up and organizing my new home. Don't get me wrong, I greatly appreciated everyone's help, but self pity and disappointment crept in. I was helpless, feeling exasperated as some decisions were made without my input.

My mom noticed the tears I was struggling to hold back and suggested they put a chair in the middle of the kitchen, that way I would have more control.

I think the reality of my confinement was sinking in that day, I felt useless, vulnerable as my independence was taken away from me.

I understood that being on bed rest would save my baby, but that wasn't written in stone, so every day was much like the other, my mom, sister and mother-in-law Edna took turns to help care for our home and me. Feelings of guilt often overpowered me knowing both moms had their own homes to care for. Edna always reminded me of the Donna Reed television show, which aired from 1958-1966, the perfect wife and mother, where nothing was out of place. I had much time to watch repeats of older television shows; and Edna fit right in to the 1950's expectations of a wife and mother. She did not mesh well with my mom who was less demanding, more relaxed in her house keeping, something Edna pointed out every time it was her turn to help. My sister was even more relaxed, she lived with my parents and housework was not something she readily did, and Edna complained a great deal about it. Growing up MaryAnn would rather give me the money she made babysitting rather than clean. I had no problems taking her money in doing her chores.

Our house wasn't always in need of cleaning, as Dave did it on the weekends.

Every day my heart would skip a beat when I heard Dave's footsteps on the stairs coming home from work. My spirit soared, wishing I could jump out of bed to meet him at the door, instead I sang 'my husband is home' in my mind and heart.

Eventually Edna became the primary care giver as my mom took sick with pneumonia and pleurisy, and MaryAnn started to work full time.

I spent almost six months in bed, and as time went on with my baby bump growing, I was able to have complete bathroom privileges, able to take a shower, however short but very welcomed.

Something that didn't sit right with me was the fact that I still had to go to my doctor's appointments. It just didn't make sense that one day out of the month regardless of the weather, I had to shower, dress and go to my doctor's office, which wasn't far from where I lived, but still a risk.

The winter months were dreary and long, especially living in my part of the country. Canada is larger than the United States in land mass, and is separated by thirteen very large provinces. I live in Ontario, my city being the most southern part in all of Canada. I often call it our version of Florida especially as the weather has changed though the years.

February turned into March, which ushered in an ice storm while Dave and I slept, taking Dave by surprise as he fell down the icy front stairs going to work. I heard his painful yell and ran to the door, opened it and saw him lying on the ground.

"Dave, are you okay?" I cried.

"Yes," Dave whispered trying to catch his breath. "You need to go back to bed."

"No, I need to know you're okay."

Dave slowly crawled back up the stairs, the ice made it difficult for him to grasp a stair to pull himself up. With each stair accomplished the ice grabbed him bringing him back down, but he was determined and finally made it.

Entering the door which opened immediately into our front room he laid on his back panting like a dog.

With Dave on the floor, I checked him for any broken bones or wounds.

"Did you hit your head?" I asked.

"No," his voice became louder, "Elaine, go to bed."

I did no such thing until I knew he was up walking around with no serious injuries.

My husband is stubborn, a man of integrity, and strength. I had hoped he would stay home after that horrible fall, but no, he made sure I was tucked back into be and then left for work using our back door to get to the car. When I heard the door shut, I got out of bed and from our bedroom window watched him carefully walking on the ice until he entered the car and drove safely out of sight. I found it hard to get back into bed, as I needed to walk off the adrenaline that built up from the stress of his fall. I knew I had to get back into bed for the sake of our baby, but I lay fully awake for a very long time before my emotions calmed. His fall made me very anxious as later that day I had a doctor's appointment. I called Edna telling her not to come as I was going to cancel the appointment, "you will do no such thing," she firmly stated, "it's warming up and the ice is melting." I coward under her demanding voice, showered, dressed and walked on the ice from our back door. Edna said nothing as the ice still very much frozen threatened my ability to walk safely without falling. I wondered why her pride came before the safety of her grandchild. When we reached the doctor's office my doctor's nurse was shocked, "what on earth are you doing here?" Exactly! Scolded by her and my doctor for taking such a risk I wanted so much to pull Edna in front of me to take the scolding. It wasn't Edna's way to apologise let alone take the blame for making me go to the appointment. I was a wimp when it came to her, it was easier to follow her directions instead of dealing with her wrath, but one day, one year that would all change.

On April 3rd a severe spring storm brought with it a tornado. Dave and I were playing a card game on our bed when we heard the thunder roll. I was so happy as I loved thunderstorms, if they weren't violent. This one was everything and more. Suddenly we heard the wind howling and went to the window to see our huge trees bending to touch their roots, but thankfully stayed strong.

Anxious and feeling uneasy I asked Dave if he thought this was a tornado. Something was making the hairs on my skin stand up, my body seemed to vibrate with an eerie sense of doom.

"I don't know," Dave answered, "But we probably should go to the basement, but don't rush Elaine, you still need to be very careful."

Don't rush? If this was a tornado taking our time was not an option. As we started to walk toward the basement stairs, we became aware that the wind had calmed, but that electric atmosphere continued to hover, as we stayed upstairs.

"That was weird," I said, and that's when we heard and saw them, sirens, police cars, firetrucks, ambulances, all rushing to a unknown destination. Dave and I immediately held hands and prayed, knowing it must have been a tornado.

We eventually learned the statistics of that day. It was listed as the sixth deadliest tornado in Canadian history.

That tornado was one of one-hundred and forty-eight that ripped across North America that day, most in the United States, all from the same storm system.

We also learned that the tornado had jumped over our house damaging part of the factory that sat just a block away from us. It hit many buildings, our large shopping mall, but the worst was when it ripped the roof off the Windsor Curling Club building, collapsing one of the tall, heavy brick walls killing eight people. Dave's parents belonged to this club but thank God they were not playing that evening, but many of their team mates and friends were, and eight died under the very heavy collapsed wall.

Nine people died that dark, stormy night, and dozens more injured. Rescue workers worked throughout the night and days that followed. It truly was a most horrible time for our city, but like most cities the community rallied around the families of the dead and injured. In our darkest moments a light often shines brightest in the hearts of many.

After that night, with every approaching storm Dave and I made sure our television or radio was always on to notify us of any danger. Back then notifications of possible tornados were not as quick as today, so most times we sought shelter just in case.

April turned into May, and as our family celebrated our wedding anniversary on the fifth, we were entertained by the newest member of our family, our puppy Buttons.

Much to our parents' dismay Dave had gone to the animal shelter and brought home a playmate to entertain me while I continued my bed rest orders. Buttons was immediately embraced by us, but not so much by Edna who was now coming over every day to help. When I look back, I realize how unfair it was to her, not only did she clean our house, make our meals, but now she had a hyper puppy to care for.

During lunch when Button's slept in the big box beside my bed, Edna would bring me a cup of tea and a sandwich. She would often sit in the rocking chair stuffed on the other side of the bed, knitting a Christening shawl for her first grandchild due toward the end of June. We would often laugh as I placed the teacup and saucer on my now large belly bump and watch the baby move it up and down and sideways. Edna would often lay her hand on my tummy to feel the baby's kicks and movements. It was a sweet time of bonding for both of us, although she always had to be in control, and was very opinionated. Edna grew more calm in our relationship toward the end of my pregnancy, accepting each other for who we were, or so I thought.

In early May, the first thing Edna would do when she arrived was to open the windows. I loved the aroma of the fresh late spring air, while watching the fluffy white curtains dance as the gentle breeze nudged them into a calming action. Edna would then tend to Buttons and make us tea, which she insisted was good for me. I always drank it even though I disliked the taste, she seemed to find pleasure in drinking it. She would sit in the rocking chair, sipping her tea while we both enjoyed the sweet songs of nature charming us. Those were the mornings I wanted to sing the song from the movie Oklahoma, "oh what a beautiful morning…"

Dave and I always made time for worshipping God and doing a Bible study. I missed my prayer meeting, although many members would come to visit, praying with me for a healthy baby. I didn't have the experiences most pregnant women I knew had. I didn't have a baby shower; I wasn't spoiled by little precious gifts. My sister MaryAnn however made sure she celebrated her niece or nephew who would be coming into the world every time she could. She always made my heart smile.

By the middle of May, I was given permission to get out of bed and walk around the house. Although I still oozed amniotic fluid, it was not a large amount, and didn't seem to be harming the baby's growth. I was eventually given permission to go outside into our backyard and sit in the comfy padded lawn chair, enjoying the sun on my face with Dave sitting beside me. It was there where I met some of our neighbours especially the elderly British couple next door. I so loved their accents. Helen and Alfred had an interesting history. They met in their late teens, but Helen's parents were strict and said she was too young. Alfred was entering the army and with the added pressure from her parents, the young couple separated. Helen said she was 'gutted,' (extremely disappointed and unhappy.)

She moved to Canada, fell in love, married and had a baby. She had a happy life but was marred by the death of her husband in his early sixties.

Unknown to her Alfred also moved to Canada with his wife who also died in her sixties, they did not have children.

They both told us that they thought of each other every day, after all they were each other's first loves.

One day in her late seventies as she took the bus to go shopping, a familiar face, "a face I would know anywhere," came on to the bus, and she gasped. Alfred looked in her direction and was met with a familiar and "beautiful," smile.

He walked to her side, and with romance in the air, sat in the empty seat beside her. "We talked for hours," Helen said laughing; "we didn't get off the bus, we just rode the same route all day long. The bus driver was kind and allowed us to remain seated for as long as we wanted to."

It wasn't long until this young at heart couple rekindled their once flaming relationship and although Helen's son did not approve the couple now in their eighties, married.

"It took us a long time," Alfred said, "but I was finally united with my first love."

They bought the house next to us six years before we bought ours. When we met them, they had been married six blissful years. Alfred became ill soon after we took possession of our home and was diagnosed with cancer; Helen never left his side. After Alfred died, we tried to help her as much as possible, but her son decided she should enter a care facility, where she died soon after being placed there, but like Helen said, "I had a lovely life," and I know her eternal life takes lovely to a new level.

Dave and I prayed over our baby bump every night; I knew it was a boy as God had whispered it into my soul.

"You will have a healthy son," and although I felt sure of this small still voice, I always sought biblical confirmation, and even with that I needed to wait and see. The day God told me we were going to have a son, I told Dave; he just nodded, "if it was from God, it will be."

Our baby was due June eighteenth, on my mom's birthday, however early morning on May twenty-first I started feeling some cramping. They weren't painful just uncomfortable. Mom had slowly recovered from her pneumonia and pleurisy and took her place once again in helping me. It was my mom's day to be with me, but I called her earlier than usual, she came right away, and we timed the contractions together; fifteen minutes apart, but regular. I got up to go to the bathroom, and while on the toilet my water ruptured. I found out later there are two sacs of amniotic fluid that are held together cushioning the baby in the uterus. The amniotic fluid that slowly oozed out of my body all these months was from the first sac, and with this large gush there was no denying the sacs had ruptured; five weeks before our baby was due.

As I sat in the bathroom Edna arrived, to this day I don't know why she came, as it wasn't her day to be with me. Edna was angry that I called my mom and not her first. I explained that I wasn't sure I was in labour and was just about to call her now that my water had ruptured. It seemed to calm her; I wanted to ask her why she had come over but thought better of it. As my water was still leaking, I stayed on the toilet and asked Edna to call Dave's work to let him know, she was happy to oblige.

Dave rushed home as fast as he could, and Edna made him sit down as he was very pale, and we all worried that he might pass out.

I kept saying, "It's too early, the baby isn't due for another five weeks."

My mom Beatrice just tried to encourage me in God's love knowing He had a perfect plan. When I went to get dressed to make the short drive to the hospital mom came with me. She wanted to remind me just what the Lord had told me out of Edna's hearing range. "…a healthy baby Elaine, remember that" kissing me on the cheek.

I was nervous, almost frantic, as I hadn't packed a suitcase for the hospital, and trembled as I tried to do so. Dave now fully present helped me while Edna hovered over us, telling us not to worry about it, that she would do that while I was in the hospital. This just added to my already frayed emotions, I wanted to cry, but Dave took control and told his mom that we wanted to do that, "Elaine knows what she needs and wants for her and the baby in the hospital." Edna understood, I think, and left us to join my mom waiting in the front room. My mom had her faults, but she always held back knowing Dave and I were quite capable in living our lives.

It is a different scenario when you have children in committed relationships. When your child is grown and independently single, they may want to still be dependant on your helping them. When your child is in a strong relationship, and in my case married, parents should step back, and that can be hard to do. You might feel you are being replaced but need to remember your child now has a partner to stand with, building a life together. The last thing a couple needs is to have interfering parents overstepping boundaries. My mom knew how to step back unless called for, Edna, not so much, she was a take control person, and did so at every opportunity.

Being five weeks early I knew the many complications that could happen for our baby, and it was all I could think about on the short drive to the hospital. Dave held my hand, and on parking turned to look at me, "I know you're scared, I am too, but we need to trust God in this. Do you want to pray before we go in?"

"Yes, please," and we did, praying that God would embrace us with his merciful peace, and our families too. We asked Him to take control of the situation, holding our baby safely in His care, giving the nurses, doctors and all medical staff His wisdom; Dave always the gentleman stepped out of the car and came to my side, took hold of my hand, kissed the top of it as he helped me out, we then walked toward our tomorrow.

I was admitted quickly, my pregnancy history was already given by Dr. Smeetin by phone, and then of course by me.

At the time, 1974, there were no monitors to observe the baby's tolerance of the contractions, stethoscopes were the only method to hear the heartbeat. No ultrasound to see the baby's position, or anything else, just the experienced hands of the staff to determine that.

As I lay in the uncomfortable bed in the labour room, the bed where the sheets would not stay tucked in when in a sitting position. Back then I was unable to get up and walk, the movement of walking can help ease the intensity, progress and position of the baby in hopes of a shorter, easier labour and delivery.

Labour was made worse by the routine practices where shaving the perineum for hygiene reasons, and any woman who has been shaved knows the agony of itching as it grows back, worse if you have stitches. Then there was the 3H enema, high, hot and heavy, it caused painful cramping adding to the already labour pain. The enema usually backfired on the doctor as the baby traveled down the birth canal, and on bearing and pushing the baby out. Let's just say pooping is a natural happening in delivery, often collected in a pail positioned just right; but an enema made the natural a noisy explosive happening, usually spraying on the doctor. Although the doctors wore protective gear, it couldn't have been a good experience for them or anyone. Most of these practices have been discontinued and no one is more thankful than the mom to be.

Another routine practice was to have an intravenous, for hydrating the body, or for possible injections of medications. A needle was used to enter a vein usually placed in the top of your hand or arm, where the fluid could be efficiently ministered.

I have always had deep veins and many a nurse or lab technician have had difficulty finding a good vein in my arm, or hand. I was so happy when the nurse found one right away, and that Dave was not present when she put it in. Dave, however, was the first one to notice the needle in my hand went interstitial, simply meaning it came out of the vein, causing the fluid to leak and my hand to swell, with blood backing up into the intravenous tube.

Dave has an aversion to needles but for some reason he decided to stay in the room saying he would just look away, when the nurse replaced it. While the nurse removed the offending needle and slapped my hand to make another vein more visible to put a new one in, Dave collapsed to the floor, he forgot to look away.

As Dave lay on the floor two nurses quickly went to his side to assess him. They told me he was fine, just fainted as many new dads have done. They helped Dave back on his feet and brought him to the waiting room where he could relax and get something to eat.

I remember thinking after I knew Dave was fine, that the wrong person fainted, it should have been me. I must have said it out loud as the nurse at my side responded, "Oh honey, you're in too much pain to faint, it is always the dads," we both laughed but secretly I was praying to faint, anything to relieve my pain. Someone once told me that labour was like your menstrual pain. NO! it wasn't labour far exceeded my horrible menstrual cramps.

Carol Burnett a comedian once said on her television show that labour was like taking your top lip and forcing it over your head. Because I was in bed for most of my pregnancy, I was removed from most labour and delivery horror stories, unless seen on a television show.

Dave returned after a short break to recover from his fainting spell, and tried to soothe me in between contractions by reminding me of the nursery our baby would soon be sleeping in.

Our nursery was not my doing, Dave and my in-laws did everything. Edna gave me the choice of wallpapers, all in the Winnie-the Poor design. I chose one and she ran with it. I must admit Edna and Jack (my in-laws) were very generous, buying all the necessities our baby would need. They bought the crib, in white, Winnie the pooh bumper pads, and sheets, a Winnie the Pooh changing table; it was a Winnie the Pooh explosion in a tiny room, and I was so thankful for all they did and gave. This was their first grandchild, and I knew this baby would lack nothing as far as they were concerned.

Dave and I chose the name Corey, but Edna and Dave's sister were completely against that name and wore me down until I agreed to call a boy, Sean. That was okay as I did like the name. If it was a girl, I wanted to name her Mary, in which again was a battle with Edna, but I stood my ground, this I could not be deterred from. I continued to believe I was having a son, but I couldn't tell them that. I told my parents, but Dave's parents would have argued and ridiculed us at the very thought that God would tell me our baby's gender. We only told those who we knew would understand, and wait with us for the confirmation at our baby's birth.

My parents were not well off and could not monetarily contribute to the baby's nursery, not that they were asked. Still mom was very talented as a painter and in sewing, creating many beautiful and treasured gifts.

As I laboured the waiting room was filled with our family members waiting for the blessed event to arrive.

I went to the hospital around eight in the morning, and at five in the afternoon everything went wrong, so wrong.

Dr. Fry the Obstetrician was called in for an emergency consult, I tried to breathe normally while he examined me inside and out.

I was not told why everyone was so concerned even though I begged for someone to tell me something.

"What's wrong?" I asked Dave.

"I'll be back Elaine; the doctors want to speak with me."

"No Dave, they can talk to both of us. I need to know."

Dave just slipped out of the room to meet with the doctors, I just cried and gave into the heavy waves of pain and fear that threatened to drown me.

When Dave returned, he took my hand and told me what was happening.

"Elaine, the nurses and the doctors have said our baby is breech, coming bum first," he hesitated for a few seconds to catch his breath and fight the tears that struggled to be released, "they also can't find the baby's heartbeat, and think a C-Section would be the safest way to deliver the baby."

"Are they saying our baby is dead?" I asked in full blown panic, searching his face for any signs of hope.

"Yes, they believe Sean might be dead."

I couldn't breathe, the pain of labour sought to consume me, but the pain of having a stillborn was more painful than any physical pain I was feeling. I needed to see my mother, I needed her encouragement, to hold me tightly in God's promises. Could my faith cope if God's promise was only my desire? Did He tell me I was having a healthy son? Or was it all a beautiful lie? A deception born in the longing of my heart. At that moment all hope dwindled. I wanted to be able to say with strength, 'the Lord giveth, and the Lord taketh away, Praise be the name of the Lord.' Could I? Would I turn my back on God? At that moment I had no answers, the haze of insurmountable pain, doom and death covered my mind in hopelessness. I didn't think of Dave and on what he was feeling, but I know he was feeling the darkness also surround him, like a stormy cloud threatening to release its destruction. I sobbed in Dave's arms while his tears fell on my trembling head. I am sure the doctor's waited for our tears of disbelief to fade to enter my room.

Dr Fry entered with a grim look on his face. I am sure he has faced this many times in the years he cared for women and their unborn babies.

Dr. Smeetin was extremely sad, almost to the point of crying. He took my hand, "Elaine, Dr. Fry and I feel it is wise to bring you to the operating room, but Dr. Fry is going to try to deliver the baby naturally, but if there are any complications, he will do a C-Section. We have ordered an epidural, because there is a slight chance that because the baby is breech, we are unable to hear the heartbeat. We were not going to allow Dave to come into the operating room, but he was very strong in telling us that we could not keep him away from you, so we have agreed to let him be at your side."

All I could hear was the words of a slight chance our baby could be alive. I kept repeating the words 'slight chance' repeatedly in my thoughts.

Everything went so quickly after the doctors left, I had heard about epidurals but they were not readily used or available. It just happened the anesthesiologist on site was experienced in this relatively new pain-relieving anesthesia.

I had to lay very still, at this point Dave left the room, first to tell the family the news, second so he wouldn't have a repeat of fainting when seeing the needle.

I learned later after Dave told the family, they decided to turn the baby's nursery into a sitting room. Mom and MaryAnn went to the pay phones in desperate need that prayers be said for me and the baby. The first-person mom called was her aunt, aunt Nellie, then our prayer community families and friends. They all went into action calling others to pray.

"Pray for a miracle," Mom and MaryAnn said with every phone call.

When Dave returned my body was quiet, no longer quivering uncontrollably in pain, feeling no physical pain at all, just numbness from the waist down. I wasn't in the right frame of mind to enjoy the results of the epidural, no pain. I clung to the wonderful miracle of 'slight chance,' but my mind, heart, and spirit were as numb as my body.

As we waited to be called to the operating room, Dave held my hand tightly trying to keep my focus on a positive outcome.

"Dave," I cried, "I guess I didn't hear God's voice telling me we were going to have a healthy son."

Dave spoke with an authority he later said he didn't think he had at that time.

"Elaine, we need to trust God and His word to you. We are going to have a healthy baby boy, don't give up, trust and believe. We need to trust God through this, because He is faithful and will see us through the good or the bad."

Seconds after Dave finished talking the nurses came to bring me to the operating room, while another nurse helped Dave get into the protective gown, mask, hat and foot cover.

Dave and the doctors seemed to arrive at the same time. Dave was told to stand just in back of my head, my feet were already propped up in stirrups and the doctors began their work.

The operating room was quiet except for the doctors talking between each other. As Dr. Fry picked up an instrument I have seen before as a nurse, the cold steel tool called forceps which looked like oversized salad tongs, I prepared myself for the ultimate invasion into my body. It was a good thing I was numb from my waist down and couldn't feel the solid intrusion.

I was not told what was happening, but as a nurse I had witnessed the birth of babies and knew the instruments used.

My body was numb as numb as my thoughts, I prepared myself for what could be the inevitable, but Dave's encouraging words continued to whisper in my ears and spirit.

With the forceps invasion I suddenly felt and heard my pelvis crunching, I thought it was the baby's head being crushed. But if I had remembered that baby's bones were soft, I would have realized it was my bones being crunched. With the disturbing noise I thought, 'well if my baby isn't dead, he is now.'

I couldn't feel pain but I could feel the pressure as they turned our baby's body around so that his head was in the birth canal, not his bum.

As they pulled him out at 1951 (7:51 pm) that evening, he gave a slight cry.

Dave hugged my head, "he's alive, he's alive."

Dr. Fry said aloud, "he's a keeper."

I didn't know what that meant, but later found out that as a fisherman (angler) the term meant 'a fish you don't throw back, you keep it.'

Although our son, yes, our son, gave the small cry at the beginning, he stopped breathing, and the worry of losing him again became another reality.

It felt like hours, actually seconds, as they fought to get the baby breathing. It wasn't until Dr. Fry picked him up from his feet and slapped his tiny little bum twice when our son's indignant cries filled the room.

Dave and I laughed and cried with relief, thanking God aloud for this miracle. Everyone in the operating room laughed and cried at Sean's breathing on his own. We were in a glorious heaven filled musical of joy as our celebration bounced off the walls. Our son is alive!

We constantly thanked God, and the doctors for bringing our son into the world. God and doctors are not in competition with each other, in fact doctors are the instrument that God blesses us with to help us.

Dr. Smeetin looked at Dave, "I think it's time for you to announce your little miracle to the family."

Dave left for a few minutes to give them the good news and returned.

I was on the operating table for a long time while the doctors stitched my body together.

Sean, our son, thank you God, was brought to the nursery to be checked by a pediatrician. Except for the many bruises he sustained during the very difficult birth, he was healthy. Being five weeks early and having all the markings of a preemie, Sean weighed 6 pounds 10 ounces and was nineteen and a quarter inch long.

I was anxious to get out of the extremely cold operating room. I finally asked Dr. Fry, "how many stitches are you putting in?"

Dr. Fry broke out in a song I was familiar with from the musical the Music Man; "seventy-six trombones led the big parade."

I gasped, "really Dr. Fry, seventy-six stitches?" I asked.

Dr. Fry and Dr. Smeetin just nodded yes.

"A small price to pay for a healthy baby boy, although you will need some time to heal. Remember Elaine you have been on bed rest for months and will need to return to normal activities of daily living slowly. By the looks of all who are in the waiting room, you will have a lot of help doing this," he smiled.

Eight hours later I was brought to the maternity floor on a stretcher. I came to appreciate that ride with my other four children. Looking up and seeing the lights on the ceiling as we passed gave me comfort that all was well with the baby, and me, it somehow soothed my mind and body.

Although in a great deal of pain from the stitches, every-time Sean was brought to me, every four hours back then, I would just hold him amazed at this precious, beautiful gift from God.

Sean looked like a little Italian boxer at birth, my dad's description, but he grew into a chubby, perfect baby. The only mark that he continues to have, maybe still does, not sure, I guess I should ask him, if the discoloured blue permanent bruise is still on his coccyx. It was a continued reminder of his struggle in the birthing process, a continued confirmation and miracle that was placed in our arms.

To God Be The Glory

Our Wedding Day, it was definitely a most

At our friend's wedding, the next day I was in the Hospital where I eventually lost our first baby.

 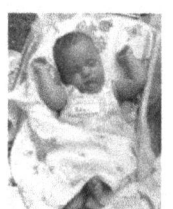

First day home with Sean and Aunt Gert's Miracle Healing.

At our Prayer Meeting's and Sean's first picnic. Praise the Lord!

Sean's first Christmas, a very happy baby!

Dave with our son Sean. at a men's Promise Keepers Convention. Although Sean described himself as a athiest, he honoured his dad by going to this very Christian convention.

Chapter Fifteen
A Common Miracle?

I once heard someone describe pregnancy and birth as a common miracle. I do agree with that, however for those who desire to become pregnant, and are unable, common might not be the way to describe it; my heart goes out to them. On the opposite side of being infertile, we were blessed with fertility. In fact, we had four children aged five and younger, a baby born beginning with Sean in 1974, then 1975-1977-1979, the fifth came six years later in 1985.

It was a different time back then, there were those who either made fun of my pregnancies, such as when I was carrying my third baby, "what are you, a bloody rabbit." This did hurt my feelings, but most people were kind and happy for us, not so much my mother-in-law Edna, who almost caused me to have a miscarriage. It isn't my intention to demonize my Mother-in-law, in spite of all she said and did I loved her, but the facts remain she was a very difficult woman to have a relationship with. I was not without fault, but I tried to like her, and I'm sure she felt my struggling with that emotion.

Edna felt I was putting too much pressure on her son, "he can't cope with this much responsibility." Granted Dave and I were young at age twenty-five on having our third child, but we had dated for three and a half years discussing everything, especially when we became engaged. Dave and I wanted children; Dave wanted six, but we settled on five. The fifth being a different kind of miracle.

As for Edna our relationship became more strained since the day of Dave's sister Ann's bridal shower. I was sitting at a table with my mom when Edna decided to join us in conversation. From the moment she sat down it was easy to see she was intoxicated, as she slurred her words, or at this point I would call it venom. Her conversation was somewhat nice at first, but soon turned into a verbal attack toward me.

"Elaine, Ann feels you are robbing her of having a baby."

I just sat there waiting for the next verbal onslaught, I was sure she was going to continue; and she did.

My mom asked her why my having children would stop Ann from having a baby.

"Ann," Edna continued, "feels the world's population is growing much faster than should, and with each baby born it puts more added pressure on the world's economy, plus other things," as she said this last sentence her spit hit me in the face.

"Do you feel the same, Edna?" my mom asked.

"Yes," Edna's voice grew louder. "Elaine has no right bringing another baby into this world, plus she is not being fair to my son."

I, not wanting my mother to be verbally attacked by this intoxicated woman quickly entered the conversation.

"Dave and I are very happy with our choices, having children is what we both want."

Edna exploded, yelling, "you're Catholic and decide alone how many children you have. You are a heavy woman, and what happens if something happens to you? We will be the one's supporting your choices."

I could feel my blood pressure rising, as the other guests turned to look at us. Were they taking her side? They didn't know me and were siblings and relatives to Edna. I felt the tears of shame fighting to escape, but I was not going to give Edna the satisfaction of shedding them. As she continued her verbal assault, not one person in the room tried to stop her drunken tirade against me. What made matters worse was the smile on Ann's face, approving of what her mother was doing.

I felt betrayed, and horribly sick at the thought that she was denying her grandchild growing inside of me. When Edna's attack was taken off me, she decided to attack my mother. I can't remember what she said because I suddenly felt a gush rushing out of my vagina. I took mom's hand and told Edna we were leaving. She continued to demean us, yelling at us as we left, her words were like burning knives piercing my heart and spirit. I didn't give her the satisfaction of looking back, I just held my mom's hand and rushed to my car.

By the time we settled into our seats I was trembling so much I had a hard time putting the key into the ignition. My car was parked far from the house which was a blessing as mom suggested we sit and try to calm down.

"I think I'm bleeding mom," I told her as my hand reached to feel the liquid in between my legs. I was afraid it might be amniotic fluid, but blood would also be as devastating, removing my hand it was confirmed, blood.

Mom said we should go to the hospital, but I just wanted to go home. "Mom I'm in my first trimester, if this is going to be a miscarriage then that is what it will be."

As I let my tears flow mom took my hand and prayed asking God to take control of the situation, she then took my keys and drove us to my house.

Back then there were no cell phones, and I didn't want to call Dave from the wedding shower, he did however meet us at the door.

"What's wrong?" he asked looking at my mom and me.

"I have to go to the bathroom, come with me please?" I asked Dave.

Mom took care of her two grandchildren while we went to the bathroom.

I was bleeding heavily, with formed clots. Dave quickly called Dr. Smeetin who was on call that weekend. He told Dave what I already knew, "go to bed, and if the bleeding gets worse, go to emergency."

Once dad came to pick up mom and had left, we fed our two babies, bathed them and tucked them into bed, Dave doing most of the work. When Dave tucked me into bed he took hold of my hand, and with both of our free hands placed on my abdomen, Dave began to pray. He asked God to save our baby if it was His will, to give me peace and to touch his mother's heart.

Edna was a controlling, opinionated woman and expected Dave to follow her choices. If Dave tried to choose otherwise, she would quickly put a stop to it, so Dave continued to accept his mother's intrusion other than strive to be his own voice.

At first, I was upset that Dave didn't stand up to his mother about her behaviour, but like him I too coward under her dominating personality. It was easier that way, if you were kind and let her rule the roost, she was happy, even if the roost was not hers. Eventually, years later when Dave stated it took a long time to "grow some balls," where his mother was concerned, he finally did, we both did. That broke the frayed thread that connected us to her, by then we had, had enough, and our children were now all adults and could make choices where Edna was concerned.

I didn't want Edna to help us, to even know I was put on bed rest so Dave took a one-week vacation so I could stay off my feet as much as possible. During that time all bleeding had stopped and with the confirmation of not having lost our baby, I was out of bed living in the day-to-day duties of my life, choosing to trust God, that doesn't mean I didn't have times of worry, but I decided to praise God through those moments of doubt.

Was this a miracle? Very much so, and in my opinion, not a common miracle.

Edna never apologized; she just entered our world again as if nothing had happened. I chose to forgive her every time she stabbed me in the heart, and with prayer and forgiveness I asked the Lord to help me feel what my mind was saying as forgiveness didn't come easy in the face of Edna.

Our baby grew as the month's passed causing my hips to come out of their sockets as my body tried to adjust to the spreading girth. Maybe that's somewhat overdramatic, but the pain was so severe I felt it was a real probability.

Dave often worked midnights, and once Sean and Mary were tucked in bed for the night, I would sit in my overstuffed recliner that Dave bought to help ease my pain and rest with my feet up. I would stay in that recliner hugging my body until I felt restless and needed to change my position, then I would go to bed.

I always waited until Dave left for work, this was our time to talk and enjoy each other without interference from our toddlers as we took time for our nightly Bible study.

I used to dread being alone when Dave worked the midnight shift, and although I still felt uneasy, with time I became more relaxed enjoying my quiet time praying and watching television.

It was one of those quiet times when the phone rang soon after Dave's car drove away from our house, I wasn't startled as usually it was my mom or sister checking to see how I was.

"Hello," I cheerfully answered, expecting a loving hi back. There was no reply, so I repeated my hello and was met with a heavy disturbing almost angry breathing.

I hung up quickly, those kind of phone calls were common back then to most households, and I didn't become worried until I realized that same phone call repeated each night when Dave left for work. Someone must be watching the house, knowing when Dave left for work; it felt like an Alfred Hitchcock movie reaching out to grab me in its psychological horror thriller. Thrilled I was not!

What really upset me was the fact that it never happened when Dave was home on the weekends.

Dave became alarmed when I begged him to stay home, "take a week off for your vacation, anything, just don't leave me alone with the kids."

That was not something Dave could easily do, as I wasn't working and we needed Dave's pay to meet all our monthly bills.

My sister MaryAnn stayed a few nights, and on those nights, no calls, I began to think my family thought I was imagining the phone calls, as the only proof was in the phone calls themselves, and they never came unless I was alone. This person knew when I was alone, and I was positive this person was watching our house. We had called the police, but until something happened, they were limited at what they could do unless this man decided to escalate his behaviour by something other than just calling.

I tried not to answer the phone, but the ringing would continue until worried that it would wake my children I would answer.

Finally, I gave up and began to pray about what to do. Why didn't I do that first? I always went to God first, and

Dave and I had prayed about it, and for the person, but I hadn't prayed on what to do.

A thought popped into my head, instead of this heavy breathing intruder wasting my time to fuel my fear, I would do something and not waste his. So, I got my Bible, opened it to the New Testament to;

John 3:16-21,

[16]"For God so loved the world that He gave His only Son, so that everyone who believes in him may not perish but may attain eternal life.[17]"For God did not send his Son into the world to condemn the world but in order that the world might be saved through him.[18]Whoever believes in him is not condemned, but whoever does not believe in him already stands condemned, because he has not believed in the name of the only-begotten Son of God.[19]"And the judgment is this: the light has come into the world, but people preferred darkness to light because their deeds were evil.[20]Everyone who does evil hates the light and avoids coming near the light so that his misdeeds may not be exposed. [2] However, whoever lives by the truth comes to the light so that it may be clearly seen that his deeds have been done in God."

I then waited in my comfy chair with my Bible close by, I couldn't keep the Bible resting on my lap as my unborn baby had taken that place. Even though I knew the phone would ring I jumped when it did, as did my baby. I prayed and with a shaking hand, answered it. I was not disappointed when the heavy breathing began seeming more sinister this time, or was that my imagination, whether it was or not, it was go time for me.

"I don't know who you are, but I am sure you live in this neighbourhood." Was it my imagination, or did he stop breathing at my statement. That was the only brief response and, there it was again, the heavy breathing continued.

"Since you have decided to try to scare me and waste my time, I have decided to not waste yours." Not waiting to listen if the heavy breathing had stopped, I began to pray for him, then I read John 3:16-21. I was surprised that he had waited to the very end of my one-sided conversation. After I had finished only silence came from the other end. Was he rendered speechless? Not quite, it must have taken him a few seconds to gather his thoughts, and then, **"Lady, you're crazier than I am,"** and he hung up never to call again. My response was to Praise God out loud and to continue praying for that man, I didn't know him but God did, whether he was mentally ill or just a mean, disturbed person I had to believe God would answer my prayer in helping this man become all that God had planned for him to be.

As time grew closer to my due date so did my girth. I found it hard to crawl out of bed when Sean and Mary would begin their morning routine of baby talk and laughter. They often threw their stuffed animals at each other. Sean was now almost three, and Mary eighteen months. I decided to wait a little while before I clawed my way out of bed. They sounded so happy and knowing they were safe I didn't budge.

As I listened to them, I finally heard tiny footsteps, running somewhere, and then I would hear the squeal of laughter with the word, "wee," coming from Mary's joyful response.

What were they doing? Listening closely, I heard the tiny footsteps, and then heard the tap in the bathroom sink running. I flew out of bed worrying that our little culprit Sean was turning on the hot water. We had a little plastic cup on the side of the sink for their much needed, cry outs for water. As I reached their bedroom I found the empty cup in Sean's hand, and the content all over Mary with her sleeper and diaper drenched practically falling off her body. The water also waterlogged the crib, wall, etc., Thank God it was cold water. I stood there looking at the work they made for me to clean, it was only water but my body was not in the best of shape to bend down to wipe it up. After that morning Dave and I decided to do more baby proofing, especially of the taps.

The day before I went into labour, I was so depressed, so tired, so exhausted from the pain in my hips. I didn't want to make anything to eat. MaryAnn was staying with me and took over the care of Sean and Mary. At breakfast I took out a Sarah Lee frozen chocolate cake from the fridge freezer, I didn't care I cut a piece frozen and ate it for my breakfast.

MaryAnn looked at me as if I had lost my mind, "are you going to eat that for your breakfast?" she asked me.

"Yes I am, and for lunch, snack and supper. Don't judge me it's my choice," and I did just what I said. That whole day I ate only that chocolate cake. It was a selfish indulgence, not sharing it with anyone, an attempt to soothe my inner beast at not having had the baby.

It wasn't long after eating the cake that I began to show signs of labour. I waited until I knew for sure and woke Dave up. He was on midnights and was sleeping so I quietly walked into our bedroom to wake him.

"For real Elaine, are you positive this time?"

I felt insulted at his comment, but to be honest this was my third time announcing I was in labour.

"Yes Dave, I am sure. My contractions are four minutes apart and I am bleeding." With that news Dave was up and getting dressed. "We have to get the kids to your mom's."

"Already done, MaryAnn slept over and brought the kids to moms. She asked me if I was sure this time, just like you."

Dave laughed, "well you can't blame us, you have had false labour twice, hopefully the third time is the charm."

Our baby was due on our wedding anniversary in May, but to my pleasure he decided to come early, not too early, just nine days early.

It was a difficult labour, and a very busy night in the labour and delivery unit. I remember Dave flicking my ear every time I held my breath, it came to the point I threatened to throw him out the window if, "you do it once more," I said between clenched teeth.

Once again, throughout my pregnancy I heard the small still voice telling me I was going to have a son. We would name him Joseph Dennison after both grandfathers.

As I laboured intensely my roommate who came after me seemed quite happy and tolerating her pain extremely well. I thought this labour and delivery would go fast like Mary's, four hours from beginning to end; but no that wasn't to be for my third.

There were nine women in labour that night on April 26th,1977 and although fully dilated my water had not yet broken. I remember begging the nurse to break my water and call my doctor "… and the baby will come. I know my body, just break my water membranes."

The nurse didn't answer and walked out of the room only to be met by my dad, Joseph. Now my dad was a good man, and loving dad, but could make things happen when they needed to be. He was upset over my suffering lasting so long.

I understood the unit was busy that night, but my delivery was delayed for four hours and I was very worried how it could affect the baby.

As the nurse left my room she was met by my dad. He told her, "I have a dime, either you call the doctor or I will," she called my doctor.

As I suffered in that bed, another nurse came to check my roommate and was told she was ready to deliver. I quickly looked at my husband who continued to flick my ear in spite of my threats, "that's not fair, we were here first," I told Dave.

"Sorry buttons," a name he called me because in his thoughts, I was as cute as a button, "it doesn't go that way, it isn't a first come first serve, plus she had an epidural, that's why she's so comfortable."

That upset me, why wasn't I given one? I found out my doctor had not ordered it because of Mary's birth when the epidural didn't take. Honestly, he couldn't have allowed me to at least try it?

That was enough, I told Dave to grab the hook looking like a crochet needle hanging in its protective sterile package by the door. "Dave, go get it and give it to me I'm a nurse, I will break my own water."

This was no laughing matter, but Dave thought it was until I gave him the look. Most husbands know the look, but Dave wasn't going to follow my directions, and my look was not a threat to him. About another half hour of deep-rooted excruciating pain, I was checked again by the nurse who broke that stubborn amniotic membrane. She checked me again, I don't know why, I had been at ten centimeters for the last four hours, and there wasn't an eleven centimeter that I knew of, the Cervix only stretched so far.

Finally, it was my turn and I was taken to the delivery room when I was given permission to begin pushing. I had been told not to push for the four hours I was fully dilated. If you have experienced going through the delivery process, then you know that telling a woman fully dilated not to push was like telling a river to stop flowing.

Finally, after I was prepared and Dave was situated to safely watch his third child's birth, I was ready to deliver. My doctor handed me a mask, I thought it was for pain relief, and was trying to eat the air flowing into my nose and mouth.

"Elaine," he laughed, "that isn't pain medication, it's oxygen." It's funny now but at that time I was deeply disappointed and told him so.

I was then asked if I would allow a small group of nursing students to enter the room and watch the birth of our baby. Having been in that situation myself I quickly said yes in between pushes.

Our baby had large shoulders, and the doctor announced the baby had shoulder dystocia, which is a birth injury that happens when one or both of a baby's shoulders get stuck inside the mother's pelvis during labor. In most cases, babies are born safely which was in our son's case. It was good for the nursing students to witness how our doctor gently guided our baby out of this serious position.

Joesph Dennison Vizard was born at 7:30 a.m. at 8 pounds 11ounces healthy and crying loudly. Those cries are the most wonderful sounds a mother can hear. It was a very difficult birth, but we were all healthy, Praise God!

The next day my doctor came to examine me, but my curtains were pulled around the bed as I was having a heat light treatment on my stitches. I guess he felt I should have privacy and spoke to me from outside the curtains.

"Elaine, all your blood tests came back fine, except for your blood sugar, which has always been normal. When you were labouring at home did you eat anything that could contribute to this?"

I was so thankful I was behind the curtains as my smile would have given my secret away, that I had eaten a whole Sarah Lee chocolate cake, and nothing else that day.

"No," I lied," I don't know why my blood sugar is high."

"I am ordering another blood test to monitor the increased level."

The next day when Dr. Smeetin returned he told me my blood sugars were back in the normal ranges.

"Could labour have caused that?" I asked sheepishly.

"Possibly, but I will make a note of checking it for awhile. Still, it is baffling," he muttered as he left.

I understood I should have told him about the cake, but it was a secret only God, sorry God, my sister and I knew, and I made her promise to take it to her grave. Years later she was released from that vow of secrecy. I needed to make amends from this lie, but could not locate my doctor as he had retired, I did ask my sister who was a reluctant contributor to my lie. I did ask forgiveness of it with a humble heart, and it has not been a secret for many years. My weight has always been an issue, and I have told many lies through the years. I had to remind myself when asked about my weight not to lie, lying was not so much the problem as was my pride, although lying is lying however I tried to hide the reason to make it seem less of a sin.

How could I confess my sin to my doctor as I was in a ward, four beds with four moms who could hear my every word, so I remained silent and let mystery take the blame.

All four of us bonded in between the times our babies were brought to us for feedings, which was every four hours, night and day. Back then the mom's and babies were separated, the babies were in the nursery and only brought to the moms at feeding time We also stayed in the hospital for five days back then to recover.

On my fifth day instead of the nurse bringing Joey for his last feeding before being discharged, the doctor came.

He looked concerned, so concerned in fact that I asked him what was wrong.

As he looked at the baby clothes, I had laid out to bring Joey home in, he then looked into my eyes.

"Elaine, we need to talk about Joey's blue spells."

At first, I tried to concentrate on what he was saying, "what blue spells?" I asked breathless with my heart racing.

"You haven't noticed Joey having blue spells?"

"No, his complexion has been pink and healthy looking every time I have had him."

Dr. Smeetin took in a deep slow breath, "the nurses have observed Joey having blue spells. We can't send him home until we know the cause for these spells. Joey is going through some tests right now and I have called in Dr. Gatts, a pediatrician. You should call Dave and have him come sit with you." I nodded with tears flowing freely, and he touched my shoulder as he left.

I immediately called Dave, my parents and sister were at the house to care for Sean and Mary so Dave could pick us up.

"Dave," I cried, "something is wrong with Joey, and they won't discharge him until they know how serious it is."

As we didn't live far from the hospital Dave was at my side in minutes.

The other moms in the room had a difficult time looking at me, but each one came to give me encouragement. As the nurses brought their babies, they all tried to hide their healthy bundles, but I asked them to "please act normally, don't hide your beautiful babies."

Dave and I sat holding each others hand, praying, waiting, praying, waiting, praying, waiting for the doctor to return, to hopefully give us good news.

Two hours later both doctors came to talk to us with the pediatrician taking the lead.

"Mr. and Mrs. Vizard, I have examined your son and the tests he has had. I'm confident the blue spells are caused by Joey's heart. We think Joey can go home with you, but we have set up an appointment with a pediatric cardiologist at the Children's Hospital of Michigan. It is about a half hour drive from their side of the tunnel. The hospital will be contacting you as to directions, and time of the appointment. If for any reason you believe Joey is in distress please bring him here to emergency, they will contact me right away. I am sorry to give you this news, and I wouldn't discharge Joey if I thought he would get into an emergency situation. Try, I know it isn't easy but, try to relax," and with that he gave us his card with his personal phone number and left. Dr. Smeetin gave us each a hug, "you know where and how to reach me, call me any time," and he too left. I watched him leave in my hazy filled mind, a slow-motion haze of what seemed like smoke surrounding him. Was this a response to the amount of blood I had lost.

About twenty minutes later the nurse brought Joey, and as it was customary at that time, she dressed him. Another nurse brought a wheelchair for me to sit in, Joey was placed in my arms, and we were taken to the entrance ramp where Dave was parked. The nurse took Joey from my arms holding him until Dave had me settled in the car. Joey was placed back into my arms, car seats were not mandatory at that time, and with being officially discharged, we brought our son home.

Arriving home my mom and dad met us at the car. Mom tried to hold her tears back as I walked up to her placing her newest grandchild into her arms. My dad pulled me into his waiting arms where I finally let my tears fall, then with his arms around Dave and I we walked toward the house with mom and Joey following. I had to gain control of my emotions and waited a few minutes at the bottom of the stairs, then walked up the steps to the front door. I entered first and was met by Sean and Mary who were excited to see me. I couldn't pick them up as I was unable to lift above ten pounds due to a hemorrhage, I had experienced two days after giving birth. As I sat on the couch Sean and Mary had all my attention, hugs, kisses and more hugs and kisses.

Mom had placed Joey in Dave's arms who then joined us on the couch. The squeals of delight lifted our hearts and spirits when Sean and Mary met their baby brother. Like a birthday celebration mom had made a meal for us to come home to, with cake and gifts for Sean and Mary so they could celebrate the arrival of their new baby brother. Although the day was marred with Joey's health issues, we were all able to enjoy the celebration of family love.

When MaryAnn, Mom and Dad left I was beyond worried, I was almost panicky at being alone with Joey. Actually, not alone, Dave was with me and tucked the kids into bed while I fed Joey. Instead of breast feeding I had decided to bottle feed Joey due to his health, not knowing if he would need heart surgery. I was so thankful that the hospital had sent a care package, including formula along with information as to which drug stores were open all through the night.

That first night was met with much anxiety, worry being our constant companion. I called MaryAnn to see if she could spend the night, she was always a source of strength and support, but she had to work. I paced the floor with my infant son in my arms eventually stopping to look at the dark sky. That was how I felt, dark without any light to encourage me. Dave and I prayed over Joey and then placed him in his bassinette beside our bed, in hopes we could all sleep. I was a mess as sleep eluded me. Every move or noise Joey made had me sitting up watching him, but Dave made an executive decision he got out of bed and to my shock lifted the bassinette and placed it just outside our bedroom door.

"What the hell are you doing Dave? Joey needs to be by my side so I can watch him."

"You need to get some rest Elaine; we will hear him if he needs us."

"Really Dave, really! This doesn't make sense; we have always had our newborns at the side of our bed."

When Dave returned to bed, he brought me close, "this is different, you need your sleep and being up all night and day will not solve anything. We need to trust God in His care for Joey and all of us." I was too weak, too exhausted to argue so I let him pull me closer, and I cuddled into my husband's side and allowed the even rising and falling of his chest to lull me into a sleep I was determined not to do, but did.

As the sun shone on our bed Dave and I woke up to the yellow light of dawn at the same time. Facing each other. Dave asked, "how was Joey's night feeding?"

It was a sickening realization that Joey had not woken up for a feeding. I looked at the clock, it was six-thirty and not even our other children were awake. Joey had slept for just over seven hours. How could that be?

"Dave, Joey didn't wake up for his night feeding."

At my words Dave jumped out of bed, and I just sat back against the headboard hugging my knees crying calling out to Dave, "is Joey dead."

My mind could not grasp the horror of such a thought. What was God's plan in all of this? Before I could think another horrible thought, Dave was at my side, "Elaine, I think our son is hungry," while he placed him in my outstretched arms.

It was at that moment I realized my bleeding had not woken me up either. It's a good thing Dave doesn't faint at the sight of blood, because he had much to look at. I quickly gave Joey back to Dave, grabbed the bottom sheet which was already ruined, and ran with it between my legs to the bathroom. Sitting on the toilet, then taking a very quick shower I thought of the protective mattress cover on our bed, well at least that saved the mattress.

By the time I exited the bathroom Joey was in full blown feed me mode. His crying woke the other kids up, and a new day began. Joey continued to scare and spoil us by sleeping through his night feedings. Dave had taken two weeks off as vacation time, to help care for the kids and me. Did we settle into a routine? No! Everything wasn't normal, nor would it ever be.

The next day after our scare with Joey, Children's Hospital contacted us asking if we could be there the next day. I immediately said yes, and they gave me the directions on how to get there.

I am not great with directions, but I was great at reading maps. Maps although useful were frustrating when needing to get them folded back into their original shape. Things are so much easier than they were forty-four years ago, back then there were no monitors to tell you if your baby stopped breathing, no GPS in your cars to help you get to where you are going, although at times a GPS can be misleading.

My sister MaryAnn babysat, while Dave and I made our journey to the hospital, Joey was just eight days old.

The drive from our Canadian city to the far side of Detroit, Michigan was approximately one hour, depending on how quickly we were able to get through customs, the tunnel, and on how smoothly the traffic was on the highway. We would make this trip so often that we often joked the car should be able to drive itself.

Using the map and the directions the receptionist had given me we found our way to the hospital easily. I was surprised that it was situated in a rough neighbourhood, but then I was always nervous going to Detroit. I'd rather be in my own country, where murders were not a daily happening. As we entered the parking garage, I was surprised that security was present at the entrance but not so much in the parking garage itself. I'm not sure what I expected, but the garage smelled of urine, and the elevators were dirty. I held Joey close and covered his tiny body from head to toe so he wouldn't breathe in the stench air.

The elevator was slow but brought us right to the Cardiac floor, and arrows led us to admitting, a slow process due to the many parents lined up to register. The longer we waited for our turn the more fearful and anxious I became. Who was this doctor? Would we have faith in him? Would we like him? Questions, questions, questions circled through my thoughts, along with prayers.

After registering we were told to follow the yellow arrows, I felt like Dorothy on the yellow brick road, it was never ending. Finally, we entered the very busy waiting room where we could sit down. The chairs were hard, and increased the pain of my perineum and its stitches, which were already throbbing from the car ride and time walking.

After what felt like hours our names were called and we were ushered into a room to wait for the doctor. I was so relieved that I had packed the bottled formula hot, as Joey now restless and making it clearly known, he was hungry. The formula was at just the right temperature, and Joey latched on to the nipple and began satisfying his hunger.

As Joey ate there was a knock on the door and a doctor came in, well actually it was a resident who gathered all the information from before I became pregnant to the present. He checked Joey, interrupting feeding time with Joey complaining to this intrusion. I found it exhausting as one resident after the other entered asking the same questions, over and over again. Finally, the Cardiologist, or so we thought, came in the door, but no, it was his Fellow. A Fellow is an accredited physician who has decided to get more training in a specialty area, like pediatric cardiology. It was exhausting telling our story, Joey's story repeatedly. We felt as if the main cardiologist we were there to see was a coveted prize in which we had to earn. In fact, the purpose of seeing so many residents, and Fellows was for their training. Getting the why's, the who's, the what's was important for each to obtain and decipher to figure out the code as to what tests would be needed to help in the diagnosis.

Then came the tests, multiple tests, but the x-ray was the most difficult to watch as they stuffed Joey's little eight-pound body like a sausage into a tube-like infant holder. Today it is called a Pigg-O-Stat. In this tube his tiny body was held tightly with his arms raised above his head, with no possibility of movement from him. That was the beginning of Joey's screams and cries whenever entering a doctor's office, or hospital, which was often. This one test made my whole-body shake, I knew he wasn't hurt, newborns cry, but this, this was disturbing and all I wanted to do was run and take him out of that pediatric torture chamber and hold him in my soft, warm arms.

The other tests were blood tests, another test that alarmed me as his cries pierced my inner being. Then came the ultrasound, but we were able to keep Joey quiet by giving him his bottle of formula. After that came the electrocardiogram, (ECG or EKG) by then Joey's energy to fight was spent, sucking on a soother Joey fell asleep thus protecting the electrodes being placed on his chest.

After that came the very crowded waiting room, again. By this time my nether region was screaming for relief. As I switched sitting from one butt cheek to the next, to standing to sitting again, Dave went into my purse and held out the Tylenol and Advil I kept for pain relief. Dave went to the water cooler that was tucked into a corner and brought me a small paper cup. I gladly took the pills hoping they would help, but this pain was not easily comforted, I had to get off of my feet, my whole body was screaming but laying down was not an option so I tried to concentrate on talking to other parents sharing our different and mutual stories. One of the mothers said she noticed I was uncomfortable, I reassured her I was fine until Dave told her the story of my pain.

"Oh, you poor thing, you should still be at home healing, but our babies are more important than our pain, aren't they?"

"Very much so, I wouldn't be anywhere else other than here in hopes of my baby getting the help he needs."

Her child was now three years old, but she remembered that pain vividly. Before we were able to further discuss our children's health issues our names were called. As I stood to leave, she called out, "ask them to give you a cushion to sit on."

We were ushered into a medium size room, with two more of those hard chairs I had come to dread.

Once again, another Resident asked for the history, I wanted to scream, but held it in even though my stomach was churning with a painful anxiety. Finally, the main event, the doctor in charge, Dr. Green walked into the room with the Fellow we had seen before and shook our hands. As the Fellow shook our hands, she asked us to call her Julie, we did but added doctor to her name. By this time Dr. Green had been given all the information, but of course he wanted to hear the story from us. Dr. Green was most comforting, his voice was calm and pleasant wrapped in a southern drawl. I immediately liked him. He was the same height as Dave, five feet eleven inches, with greying hair, and deep blue eyes. His smile put you at ease, this man was very personable and loving, a Pediatric Cardiologist, one of the best, he was at the top of his field.

"So, this is Joey," Dr. Green said, "He is beautiful, look at those dimples, just like his mama's, he will be fighting those young ladies off when he is of age," he laughed.

"Dr. Gatts and I golf together, and he called me about this little guy asking if I would see him. Of course, I wanted to check this little boo out." Dr. Green called all his patients his 'little boo,' but made it seem like he was saying it for the first time, which warmed my heart

Dr. Green stood up, held out his hands asking if he could hold Joey and then placed him softly on the examining table. He then began removing the warm blanket and sleepers from Joey's tiny body. I readied myself for his immediate reaction as he was taken out of the soft warmth to the cool hard table which briefly became his new environment. We were all surprised when Joey didn't squirm and wake up.

"He must be too tired from the day's activities," the Fellow Dr. Julie stated smiling.

"His mama and daddy must feel exhausted too," Dr. Green added, "I know this is a very long day, but a necessary one for us to get the full picture of what led to Joey's condition."

As Dr. Green examined Joey, he spoke aloud to his Fellow informing her of what he was doing and hearing.

I understood most of what he was saying, but waited until he was finished and able to tell us of the results of the tests and his examination.

After he redressed Joey, who continued to sleep, he placed him back into my arms and then both doctors sat to tell us all their findings. But before they began talking Doctor Julie informed me that one of the mothers in the waiting room had stopped her telling her that the mother of the eight-day old baby that just went into the examining room, needed a soft cushion to sit on.

"Mrs. Vizard, is that you? You do look uncomfortable, and if you need something softer to sit on, I asked one of the nurses to find one just in case," and at her words came a knock on the door and a thick, soft cushion appeared. I must have turned all shades of red at the sensation of heat oozing from every pore of my body.

Doctor Julie asked me to stand up, and in doing so she placed the cushion on the chair saying, "Dr. Green she just gave birth and if I'm right, sitting isn't a position that is very comfortable at this time."

Dr. Green immediately apologized, "I am sorry Mrs. Vizard, I should have asked sooner, my wife would be scolding me right now for not being so observant to your pain. Please don't feel embarrassed, I can't feel your pain, but I am the father of four, three of them girls; I am fully aware of the pain associated with birthing, and on how long it takes to heal after a difficult birth."

As I was still standing, he asked me to sit down unless I wished to remain standing, I decided to sit and felt some relief, with thankful thoughts to the waiting room mother, the nurse and both doctors.

"Well then let's get this first appointment over so you can be back on your way home. It has been a long day for both of you," he said looking at Dave and I.

"I have checked Joey's test results, and I am positive Joey has an ASD, which is a congenital atrial septal defect."

"An atrial septal defect is a birth defect of the heart in which there is a hole in the wall (the septum) that divides the upper chambers (atria) of the heart. A hole can vary in size and may close on its own or may require surgery. Joey's is quite large and usually this size will not close on its own, but the surgery to repair it is often done when they reach age four unless there is more danger of leaving it then the surgery would be done much sooner. In Joey's case I feel confident we can wait. We will be checking him every three months at first then every six months as he grows. Until then Dr. Gatts will keep a close watch on him, and I will see this little boo every three to six months. Don't be too alarmed when his skin colour turns blue, when that happens slap his bare feet, undress him just get him uncomfortable enough to make him cry; that will keep his blood flowing enough to make his colour pink again." Dr. Julie then told us of what signs to look for if Joey's condition was to deteriorate. She then gave us pamphlets to read.

"Dr. Green," I asked, "How could this have happened? There were many births that night and I was fully dilated for four hours, and as my water didn't rupture, they felt I was okay to wait."

"The delay could have contributed to the chamber not closing, or it could have happened as the heart formed within the womb, or genetics could have played a part. Often there is no cause found, it just happens. Whatever the reason Mrs. Vizard, the hole can be closed."

Dr. Green and Dr. Julie said their goodbyes and with that we were checked out with another appointment made for three months. As we walked the long yellow brick road to the elevators Dave and I felt a sense of relief in knowing that Joey would be closely monitored, but still very aware that his condition could change for the worse at any time, which left us feeling like we were walking through a thick fog with no hope of it lifting

As we drove back home Dave and I sat in silence as Joey slept, each of us trying to digest our baby's condition. Okay I know I was a nurse, but I don't think any training can prepare you when it happens to your child.

I broke the silence, "How can Dr. Green tell us not to be alarmed when Joey turns blue?"

Dave thought about it for a minute, "Well, I think he knows most parents will be alarmed, we just can't panic. One thing we need to make sure of is that we know infant CPR, and everyone who will care for Joey if we go out."

Go out? I felt very uncomfortable at putting that kind of responsibility on my sister or mom, in the case something horrible happened.

Every time Joey turned blue, which was often, we did exactly what Dr. Green told us to do, we made him cry. At first it was alarming, but we soon became pros at coping with Joey's blue spells.

When Joey was three weeks old Dave and I drove my parents to the airport. We had given my dad a retirement party, and everyone contributed to his gift, a trip to Vancouver, British Columbia, Canada. While we waited for them to board the plane a woman came running up to me frantic and breathless saying, "your baby is blue, your baby is blue."

I looked at her and calmly said, "I know."

As Dave and I went to a bench to lay Joey down and get him crying the woman followed closely. I told this woman about Joey's condition, and what we had to do when he turned blue.

"Oh, my goodness, I don't think I could cope with that."

"I am sorry you were so frightened and worried but thank you for your concern and bringing it to my attention. Sadly, and I mean this with all sincerity, we don't have a choice when it comes to coping, we need to take each situation and do our best to keep our son healthy." It was then I heard sighs of relief from the crowd that had gathered around us.

My parents didn't want to leave, but we assured them their grandson would be fine, and to enjoy themselves, and they did, but called us each day to make sure.

During the time my parents were gone Joey had a new symptom, one so terrifying it took my breath away, along with his.

I just happened to check on him as he quietly slept. So quiet, almost deadly, and that is when I noticed; Joey had stopped breathing. Thank God my sister MaryAnn was with me that day visiting and helping with the children.

I grabbed Joey, rushed to the small kitchen table calling for MaryAnn, to help me. I unwrapped him stripped him naked, and began slapping his feet, putting the knuckle of my finger into his sternum to cause him pain, and after what felt like hours, yet only seconds he started breathing again. MaryAnn was still on the phone with 911, but I told her Joey was breathing and instead I would call our doctor.to see him.

Everything went so quickly, and yet so slowly; our doctor told us to get to his office. I called Dave at work, and he arrived within ten minutes, and we rushed to the doctor's office.

I couldn't tell you the time, I only know it was sometime in late morning. When we rushed into the doctor's crowded waiting room, his nurse was already waiting for us with an opened door to the examining rooms. She took Joey, disrobed him and went to tell Dr. Smeetin we were there but he entered the room with Dr. Gatts, the pediatrician. It was a great comfort knowing Dr. Smeetin called Dr. Gatts right after I talked to him, and that Dr. Gatts left his busy office with a crowded waiting room to check Joey.

"What happened Elaine?" Dr. Smeetin asked while Dr. Gatts was examining Joey.

"Joey was in his bassinette sleeping, but when I looked at him, he seemed abnormally still, and that's when

I noticed he had stopped breathing. I grabbed him, stripped him naked, slapped his feet, and put my knuckle into his sternum to cause him pain, and that's when he started breathing again."

"Was he cyanotic? Dr. Gatts asked as he turned to look into my tear-stained face.

"Dr. Gatts, Joey is always blue, and to be very honest, I am ashamed to say I didn't look at his colour, I was just trying to get him to breathe."

"Frank," Dr. Gatts asked Dr. Smeetin," could you examine Joey also."

As we waited for Dr. Smeetin to finish, I looked at Dave who was trying to stay calm, but the movement of his shaky hands told me otherwise.

Dr. Smeetin asked me to dress Joey, and both doctor's left the room to discuss what to do next.

On their return they informed us that they contacted Dr. Green at children's hospital.

"We can't find a change in Joey's condition," Dr. Smeetin said, "however we both feel that Joey should go back to see Dr. Green, who said he could see Joey tomorrow at noon. Will you be able to get there?" he asked.

Dave quickly answered, "Yes, we will be there."

Dave took the day off and the next for the appointment. MaryAnn stayed overnight to support us and care for Sean and Mary. Once again, we found ourselves driving to Sick Kids, smelling the same smells and walking the yellow brick road, (arrows) as we had nicknamed them.

I did not call my parents as I didn't want them to worry and fly home, I wanted so much for them, to enjoy their time in Vancouver. What good would it do to worry them when we ourselves didn't have answers. Better to wait until they came home.

Dr. Green and Dr. Julie saw us after Joey had another ultra sound.

"Did you miss your lunch," I asked.

Julie answered, "don't worry about us Mrs. Vizard, tell us what has been happening."

I told them what had happened, and they then turned to examine Joey.

"Mr. and Mrs. Vizard, this can and does happen, and short of putting Joey in the hospital connecting him to machines to monitor his breathing, we believe this would not be beneficial at this time. Joey's condition remains the same, and we hope he just had an episode that he would have pulled himself out of."

This made no sense to me, how could he possibly pull himself out of not breathing?

"I don't understand Dr. Green, Joey stopped breathing, I know he stopped breathing. Don't you have a monitor which we could use at home to alert us if he stops breathing?"

"Unfortunately," Dr. Green said with sadness in his voice, "technology has not gotten to the point where these machines are portable. I'm sorry but let's try to stay positive and believe this was a one time happening. You will need to watch him and check on him more often."

More often than I already have been doing. How is that possible? I was already in a state of sleep deprivation, not because Joey woke for night feedings, but for my own peace of mind in watching him and knowing he was okay.

We had no choice but to follow Dr. Green's advice and took our infant son home. What was wrong with technology? Why were they not further advanced in making portable monitors?

I often woke up through the night to check Joey before he stopped breathing, but now; now we needed to monitor him ourselves every minute of every day. How do you live like that? How other then having family members take turns watching him, how do we do this.

We decided to buy a small crib that fit in our small bedroom, and placed it close to my side of the bed where I could sleep, well not sleep with my hand under Joey's chest.

As time marched on Joey's breathing improved, although his heart defect showed no improvement and he continued to turn blue. Dave and I prayed over him nightly, joining the many that held him and us in their prayers. I eventually came to terms with God and placed Joey in His tender care, desperately trying to trust Him, no matter what.

The next heartache came on August 2nd when Joey had just reached three months old.

My mother-in-law Edna called me. Her voice was shaky, and I could tell she had been crying.

"Elaine, I don't want you to get upset, but I am calling from the hospital, Jack (Dave's dad) had a massive heart attack and has died. I am going home could you call Dave at work and let him know." Jack was only fifty-nine. I can't say it wasn't expected but I thought it would have happened much later in his life.

My breath caught in my throat, I could hardly speak, but I did manage to tell Edna I was sorry and that I would get Dave immediately.

Dave worked for the city as a Garbage collector, he had been at this job for six months with better pay and benefits.

I called the number I had used a few times for Joey's health and told Dave's boss about the sudden death of his dad.

"He needs to be home as fast as possible."

Dave's boss called his truck in, and when Dave arrived there was a police car waiting to escort him home. Dave was not told that his dad had died, his boss just stated, "you are needed at home."

The police asked Dave if he wanted a ride, Dave thinking it was about Joey told the police he could drive home and did.

When he arrived, I was there to meet him, "Where's Joey? I have the car running, are we taking him to the doctor's or to the hospital?"

"Dave," I spoke softly, "it isn't Joey, its your dad. Go turn off the car and come back in a sit down."

He hesitated as if trying to make sense out of my words but turned to go back to the car and turn it off.

When Dave returned, I met him with a cup of tea. All the children were napping, with Joey at my side.

"What's going on Elaine? What's wrong with my dad?"

He sat and I told him as softly as I could, however there is no soft or easy way to tell someone of a sudden death, especially when it is your own spouse. I had experience as a nurse, but having to tell my husband was heart wrenching.

I was surprised at his calmness, and quiet acceptance of this news. It would take Dave a few years before he would grieve his dad's loss.

"I called my mom and sister; they will be coming soon to pick the kids up and take them to their house. They will take care of them for as long as needed. I have all their clothes, toys, and Joey's bottles ready."

"Elaine, can they take care of Joey? What if he stops breathing?"

"Dave, Joey will be fine, you always remind me to put him in God's hands, now I'm telling you to do the same. Your mom is probably at home now and needs you," and he went to shower and change. Mom and MaryAnn came quickly to take the kids, Joey just being three months old was hard to let go as with him came many ifs. Was it the right thing to do giving them the responsibility of caring for Joey? Should I stay home to care for him and our other children, with MaryAnn helping me? I was torn between supporting my husband, going with him, or staying home and caring for our children? I was playing the game tug of war in my mind, and either way there were no winners. However, mom soothed my turmoil by saying they would all be fine, "God is with us, and you and Dave. You need to be with your husband Elaine, and don't worry, your sister has cared for them often, and Joey is in good hands, we will be watching him closely." I tried to say it might be too much to cope with, three babies aged three, and under, along with Joey's health. I knew MaryAnn could cope but my parents just entered their sixties, it just seemed more then they could cope with. As I hugged my mom she whispered in my ear, "it isn't too much, we are not alone." Then they hugged Dave warmly and left.

 I ran to take a shower and joined Dave as we drove to his mothers to support her. When we got there, her apartment was already filled with other family members to help support her, Dave's sister Anne who lived four hours away had left her home to be with her mom.

It was a long four days of grief, mourning and exhaustion. Dave was strong, and his mom Edna said something I would never hear again, she asked God to help her, get through this.

After the funeral normal life resumed, (if anything can be called normal after a tragedy such as that), but everyone continued to walk on.

Jack had died at the breakfast table, collapsing onto the floor, Edna called 911 and began CPR to no avail. Dr. Smeetin comforted her by telling her that Jack had died before he hit the floor.

A few months before Jack died my Aunt Gert, a second mother to me died, at the age of fifty-eight. Two deaths of two loved family members were difficult to cope with, but life has a habit of going forward for the living, and we must bravely walk on.

I remember thinking about the old saying that bad news, usually comes in threes. Was Joey next?

There was not a third and thank God Joey grew into a beautiful, dimpled, curly head, red tipped nose active boy of three.

As he grew, he continued to turn blue, but after six months he had no further episodes of apnea lasting more than ten seconds. We had continued to take him for his check ups but there were no changes, no evidence of deterioration or improvement, it stayed the same.

During those three years our daughter Mary, eighteen months older than Joey became ill and, was found to also have a heart defect at age four and a half. Her condition was rare, one of five in the world and much more complicated. I will be continuing to write a book about her story, after this one is published.

Mary needed heart surgery and as life would have it so did Joey. At times it was too much to cope with having two children with heart defects, but with surgery looming over both coping was not a question, it was expected.

Mary's surgery was booked in the summer of 1981. Dr. Green was also her cardiologist. As Joey was due for his pre surgery examination for some reason Dr. Green along with the surgeon decided they would perform surgery of both, just two days apart. Did they think we were super humans? How on God's green earth did this make sense. Although both extremely necessary, caring for two children after heart surgeries felt almost incomprehensible.

Joey was familiar with the tests, but had white coat syndrome, which usually describes people whose blood pressure increases around doctors or nurses. Joey's white coat syndrome became the simple fact of screaming, crying when near any medical facility or staff.

At age four he was better at not panicking but we constantly stayed alert at the possibility that it would come to life at any given time.

We brought Joey for his last x-rays and ultrasound before surgery. As Joey rested comfortably on the ultrasound table, Dave and I looked at each other praying, hoping Joey would remain calm, and to our great surprise, he did.

The ultrasound technician did her thing, talking to Joey the whole time. She took longer then usual, and we began to worry. She looked up saying she needed Dr. Green to check something out and would one of us stay at Joey's side. Dave jumped up to go to Joey, both of us now more worried than the minute before.

The wait was about ten minutes but felt like ten hours before she returned with Dr. Green.

"Hey boo," he said smiling at our son giving him a little tickle on his tummy. "Hey Dave and Elaine, are you holding up?" he smiled. By that time, we were on a first name basis, although with respect for his position we called him Dr. Al. not just Al.

"We're good Dr. Al, how about you?

"Good but busy as usual."

He then took the ultrasound probe putting it to our son's chest, carefully examining every inch of our son's heart.

"Do you see it Dr. Green?" the technician asked.

"Not yet, so let's take another look, "and they did just that, taking much longer than usual.

Dr. Green finally looked up with a confused expression on his face.

"If you don't mind, I need to leave the room for a few minutes so I can compare this ultrasound to the one we did three months ago. I know this is worrying you, but I need to be sure before I give you the results."

The technician left with him, and Dave and I beyond worried, prayed for peace and for God to help us in whatever news we were going to receive. What could be worse, Joey was already booked for surgery, and this was just the pre surgery check, his last ultrasound found no changes; but has that changed?

A half hour passed trying to keep Joey entertained, today we could have given him our cell phones to play a game on, but this was 1981 and there was no such thing. We were happy we had brought a few toys and story books with us to keep him occupied through the many long waits.

Finally,! Dr. Green returned with the technician and pulled up another chair to speak to us.

"Dave and Elaine, I don't understand but there has been a big change in Joey's ultrasound, so much so that I had to investigate and go over all his other tests. I am sorry it took so long."

Our eyes and facial expressions alarmed him to the point where he rushed on. "We can't find the hole in Joey's heart," he said somewhat shocked and confused. "I have looked at all his other tests, and the one we just did, in fact I asked three other cardiologists to also go over all the tests. They are in as much shock as I am. We cannot find Joey's defect in this ultrasound today. It was there three months ago, but not today. Are you sure Joey doesn't have a twin that you brought in instead?"

"Okay, okay," I needed a minute to digest what he was telling us, Dave was speechless.

"Okay, are you telling us that Joey no longer has an Atrial Septal Defect?" I asked.

"That is exactly what I am saying, there is no sign except for a small heart murmur to tell us it was there."

Dave took Joey into his arms, "this is a miracle Elaine, we got our miracle."

I sat in my chair holding my breath, was this really happening?

"Elaine," Dave said taking my hand tightly as if to wake me up from a confused, delightful dream, "we have our miracle."

"Tell me about this miracle?" Dr. Green asked.

I started to Praise God and told Dr. Green that we pray over Joey every night when we tuck him in asking God to heal Joey's heart. "We have our Church, Prayer Community, and many others also praying for a miracle. Dr. Green, it seems Jesus has heard and answered our prayers."

"I am a believer, a praying man myself Elaine, and we have proof, a great deal of proof that this large Atrial Septal Defect has been there since birth, was there three months ago, but now is gone."

I could tell that Dave wanted to jump up and down with me in sheer joy.

"Joey had a large hole, that needed surgery to repair, even if it did heal on its own it would have been a long process something that would have shown in all the other ultrasounds in measuring it. Yes, your son has had a miracle, and I want to see Joey again in three months, not because I don't believe, but because I do. This is one for the books."

As we left the room we were met with huge smiles as the other cardiologists had come into the hall.

Dave and I left that building walking on air, or was it wings that held us up. We told Joey he didn't have to have an operation, and he smiled, not knowing the extent of what we were telling him, but we knew and so would all the family and people who had been praying.

Our news was met with tears of joy, laughter, smiles, and of course in praising God loudly. We still had deep waters to travel through, ones that threatened to drown us with our daughter Mary's heart defect, but for now Joey's miracle would hold us in God's merciful grace, knowing His plans were not ours, knowing He was in control whatever the situation. What God has done stays done, Joey's following ultrasound three months later confirmed that the hole was indeed healed. Thank you, Jesus, thank you!

To God Be The Glory

Chapter Sixteen
Weight, and Wait!

Dave and I have five children, each pregnancy, each birth different, and each time the small still voice of God announced the sex of the baby.

My fourth pregnancy was an amazing, textbook pregnancy. I always lost weight while pregnant, no less then twenty-five pounds and no more than forty-six.

This fourth pregnancy was the forty-six-pound loss, despite my craving for Hot Fudge Sundaes.

It was a time of financial hardship for many in the form of a recession. It was widely considered to have been the most severe recession since World War II. A key event leading to the recession was the 1979 energy crisis, mostly caused by the Iranian Revolution, which caused a disruption to the global oil supply, causing prices to skyrocket. This made a ripple affect around the world and many suffered through the process of interest rates increasing and more contributing to many lay offs. It was a strange time, my husband and most of our neighbours were in the same situation, yet there were some who continued to work and collect pay checks weekly. We weren't as lucky; I wasn't working at the time, so I wasn't pulling in any money. We were blessed as Dave had unemployment pay along with added finances and benefits from the company he worked at. Reports were saying the lay offs wouldn't last long, so we didn't worry, we would be fine, or so we thought.

Dave worked at the Ford Motor Company, a coveted job to many due to the amount of pay and benefits that were given, which would probably last a year.

One year came to an end and the country was still in a recession. With Dave's layoff lasting well over three years our finances became nonexistent. Once unemployment pays and Ford benefits stopped Dave scrambled to find work. Being pregnant I was not employable.

Dave did anything he could, selling fruits and vegetables on a street corner working for a cousin who had an upholstery business. Dave's duties were delivering and receiving products all over Southern Ontario. The truck often broke down leaving Dave stranded, plus the embarrassment of having the cousin boldly say he was caring for two families, his and ours on more than one occasion. We appreciated his giving Dave the job, and believe me Dave was always a loyal, hard worker, never, ever calling in sick.

The pay was low but thanks to my cousin we were able to make it one month at a time.

My sister MaryAnn would come to our house often always supplying me with my deep craving for those Hot Fudge Sundaes, and yet I still lost weight.

I was always a heavy person; in fact, I was on my first diet at the tender age of eleven months old. I looked like the Michelin Man, whose body was made of tires, simulating what looked like rolls, only my rolls were made of baby fat, or what people called a pleasantly plump body. My doctor saw this as a potential problem that could be with me for life. Why I was heavy was unknown to my family, as mom always fed my siblings and I the same foods, and my siblings were not heavy by any means of the word.

God creates us in all different sizes, shapes, colours, personalities, abilities, disabilities and more. If we were created all alike, then we would be mere copies of each other. That would be boring, like a grey scaled world, no colour, everything shades of grey.

My first recollection that I was 'pleasantly plump' was when I was performing in my first and only ballet recital. My older sister MaryAnn was slender, born just eleven months apart, but we were as different as the sun and moon, or as Elizabeth Taylor compared to Spanky in the show Our Gang, viewed in the 1960's.

In the ballet recital we were all in a line and I was the last one on stage. I only remember stopping when everyone started laughing when I came on stage, my tutu flopped while my tummy shook like a bowl full of jelly. I was only five, but the memory of the laughter made me very aware of my body. I ran off the stage crying, my mom quickly ran to me and tried to convince me that the audience was laughing at how cute I looked. Even at that age I didn't believe it. They were laughing at me, and that day began my long road to low self confidence, shame, and body loathing.

Another memory happened in grade two, my teacher decided to hand out some Halloween candy she had left over. She went to each student and gave them one, including me, as she had more, she did another round, but when she returned to me, she said, "Elaine, you're too fat, you don't need another one." The classroom erupted into laughter. I was so embarrassed, but instead of crying I stood up and ran for the door. "I'm leaving and I'm going to tell the principle on you," as I stared at the teacher in anger. The teacher quickly stopped me, saying that the principle would be angry that I left the classroom and would give me the strap. After that day I was known as 'fatty, fatty two by four, can't get through the kitchen door.' I was bullied from that moment on. After that my life was centred around my being pleasantly plump and mom hurting for me tried her best to help me lose weight. It didn't help that our family doctor being a very large man himself who smoked cigarettes and fell asleep at his office desk in front of patients, told my mother, "Elaine is going to be well over 200 pounds before she is twenty." Okay, so the dice was rolled and my life, whole life would-be lived-in shame and hiding. I didn't know what it was like to eat a sandwich for lunch, I always had fruit and cottage cheese with lettuce. Easter brought me diabetic chocolate. I didn't know what it was like to eat without having my mom watch every mouthful. When I was about eleven a woman opened a candy store in her garage by our school. I watched as all the kids ran to buy her candy, chips, pop and everything that was denied me. One day, and I am horrified I did this, I stole twenty dollars out of my grandmother's purse hidden in her bedroom closet. Grandma, I called her Meme was living with us at the time, she was legally blind probably due to cataracts not an easy fix back then, she was also hard of hearing and had limited finances, and I stole from her.

I had come home from school for lunch, and Meme was out with my aunt. I quietly went into her room, knowing mom was busy cleaning up after lunch. I found Meme's purse and took the first dollar I saw which happened to be twenty dollars. Stuffing the money into my jacket pocket I kissed my mom goodbye and went back to school. Mom didn't question why I was leaving early as I often cleaned the dishes after my teacher, a nun finished her lunch. I ran from the house as fast as I could to get to the candy store to buy all the good things I had long wished for. I caught up to my sister who had left before me and told her I found some money, and did she want to go to the candy store with me.

"Where did you find the money?" my sister asked.

"It was in the bushes down there," I answered

We both ran to enjoy the fruits of my sin. After school as I went by my grandmother's room, she was telling my mom that she was sure she had twenty dollars in her purse. Mom told her as she looked for the money that she could be mistaken because of her eyesight, but grandma insisted she had that money. I went to my room and cried in my pillow, I knew I should confess, but I was scared to admit I was the family thief. I couldn't bring myself to tell anyone; to tell my Meme what I did, and I let her believe it was her mistake to the grave. I have long since asked forgiveness and prayed she heard me. I know God forgave me, but when the Lord takes me home, I will seek her out to do it in person. Candy never tasted the same after that. Being heavy didn't stop me from activities, especially sports. I was on a baseball team at school and pitched a no-hitter, twice. I was also on the basketball, volleyball, teams. I played Tennis in high school at lunch time instead of eating. I often rode my bike all over my city, or walked home from high school, which was quite far, and no I didn't walk home through piles of snow all uphill.

My mom I think was ashamed of my weight, some of my aunts spoke of my being fat and that my mother should do something about it. They didn't know I heard their hurtful conversation about me. But I held their words like a brick of shame in my heart.

I know my mom wanted me to be healthy and made many decisions for me. Not all heavy people are that way because of the food they eat, some are predestined to be that way due to genetics. I wasn't an overeater, and when I became older, I watched my own diet.

At age 13 I went on a milk diet, 3 glasses of 1% milk a day for three weeks, with mom's permission. At first it was difficult, but I was losing weight fast as I continued to starve myself while still playing sports and exercising. Mom was praising me for my commitment in my weight loss, little did she know I was well on my way to becoming anorexic. The longer I went without food, the more I didn't crave it, losing weight meant everything to me, as I connected it to my self-worth.

Although the so-called milk diet only lasted 17 days, my body started to betray. I continued to play sports, to exercise but it was getting much more difficult to do. My heart would beat so fast I thought it was going to come out of my chest, I became angry, dizzy, disorientated at times, along with constipation. With all that was going on in my body I didn't tell my mother, although I am sure she noticed the changes in my attitude but losing weight became my obsession, I wanted my mom to be proud of me.

Seventeen days in was when my body had, had enough. I became very ill with bloody bowel movements, although they were few and far apart. I couldn't get out of bed and collapsed when I tried. I thought I had the flu, but my parents knew it was much worse than that. They put me in the car and rushed me to emergency where my family doctor was waiting. After he examined me, and having my blood tests rushed, with the results, he asked my parents what was happening. "Elaine's blood tests are completely abnormal, dangerously abnormal."

My dad seemed to be in the dark as to my weight loss diet. But my mom told the doctor everything. Impressing on him that I had lost twenty-five pounds.

"Beatrice, you can't have realized how dangerous this was for Elaine. With the lack of food along with all her sports and activities, it could have killed her. We need to admit her, she is dehydrated, her heart is working too hard, and she needs to have an intravenous put in right away."

Even though I was exhausted and so sick, I was angry, I wanted to keep doing what I was doing until I lost all the extra weight on my body. Would I even know when to stop? I had lost twenty-five pounds; didn't that mean anything to my doctor? The next day Dr. McLister ordered a special diet with two milkshakes a day in between meals.

This was to build up my body, but I would have none of that. I wasn't monitored until my family doctor caught me dumping my milkshake in the toilet.

"Elaine, you are not getting better but worse, you need to eat and drink what I ordered for you. Your brain, heart, all your organs will start to shut down, fail you, and you could die if you continue this behaviour."

His words did frighten me and I decided I would rather be heavy than dead. Even though I promised to follow his instructions, he came to the hospital every time I had the milkshake to make sure I was drinking it. If he couldn't get there, he had a nurse monitor all my intake, food and protein shake. Eventually I gained that weight back and more.

As I grew older, I was so tired of family members trying to help me lose weight. Even though their hearts were in the right place it still hurt deeply, and I longed to go back to not eating, I even thought of making myself vomit after eating, but that would further harm my body.

My one, very close Aunt put a picture of this beautiful woman on our fridge saying, "This reminds me of what you will look like when you lose your weight." Really?

I went on diet pills where my heart almost flew out of my chest. My brother's friend said he would date me if I lost weight, I was so angry and spit out the words, "if and when I lose weight what makes you think I would want to date you." My biggest betrayal came from my mother when she asked my boyfriend, now husband of many years, if his car leaned to the right because of my weight.

My husband, Dave, from the time we met thought I was the most beautiful woman walking the earth and has made me feel that way every day of my adult life. I thank God for him for I am truly blessed with his unconditional love.

My mom had a big issue with weight, probably because of all the advice and remarks given to her about my weight. Why did they have to put me in a box? My sister looked like Elizabeth Taylor, I was the complete opposite, and I was on a continual diet, even to the point of developing a stomach ulcer. Today I am still pleasantly plump, well to be honest not too pleasant, and plump is a bit of an understatement.

I decided to write this chapter of my life because I want you, the reader, to understand my mother, and I, God Bless her, were not perfect. We both grew in our faith walk, and my mom would still mention my weight at times, but in the next minute would offer me a piece of home-made apple pie. I never held it against my mom, it saddened me to think that she was ashamed of my body, but my spirit, God's spirit lived in me, and her, and we grew to understand each other's issues with love and caring.

When I was first pregnant with my second baby, I was overweight as per my usual. At the time I was still quite young in my knowledge of all that Jesus could do. I took everything the Bible said word for word. As I was overweight, finding myself pregnant yet waiting for my first doctor's appointment to confirm the pregnancy, I didn't want to step on their weight scale, that nasty truth telling machine, I much rather live in my own belief of what I felt my weight was. I knew I was pregnant, and of course with our first born being just nine months old, the last thing I wanted was to be pregnant again so soon after Sean's birth. But as a young married couple, one night when love was in the air, so to speak, Dave and I lost control of our senses in the heat of the moment. When he was already inside me, I realized we forgot the condom, but it was too late, and we continued making sweet love, and a baby too.

I remember saying to Dave, "What if I get pregnant, it's too soon." But Dave being the logical man that he is said, "Well if it happens it happens, we can't do anything about that now except to leave it in God's hands. Would it be so terrible to have another baby, a close sibling to Sean? Remember you and your sister were born eleven months apart, and she is your best friend." Okay, he had a point, but he wasn't going to be the one carrying and giving birth, but I knew he was right.

As the time grew closer to my doctor's appointment, I had already known I was pregnant, I was nauseous, vomiting, my breasts were sore, yep, I was pregnant.

I began asking the Lord to give me a miracle, I prayed I would lose forty pounds before I had to step on the scale. In the two weeks I believed that the Lord would do this, I sought confirmation in the Bible. Believing I would receive this miracle I held firm to it, even to the night before, even to the moment I stepped on the scale.

The night before my appointment I told my family the amazing miracle God was going to do for me. I am sure many doubted. Was this the way God worked? Well,

I knew He could do it, and believed he would but what I forgot, everything had to happen in His perfect will. My brother Rick spent the night sleeping on our front room floor while my sister slept on the couch. When I woke up that morning I was no where near weighing forty pounds less, in fact I looked puffier. Dave, my brother and sister had to leave for work, and my mom came to care for Sean. Mom didn't say anything only that she loved me.

"You know mom, I am believing until I step on that scale that God will take the forty pounds off in that minute."

"Elaine, you have to accept the will of God, whatever happens."

Was I the only one believing until the end? Until proof was before me?

I didn't receive that miracle. Why? God could do anything, why not answer my believing prayer? I did what it says in the Bible, in

John 16:23, "…Amen, amen, I say to you,
if you ask the Father for anything in my name,
He will give it to you."

I was so disappointed that God didn't do what I asked, what I believed He would, could do. I went home upset and angry, and as soon as I walked in the door, I went to my bedroom throwing my purse and coat on my bed and stood there and cried.

Mom came to me holding me, "Elaine, we know God could do this, but you must remember that one statement in the Bible isn't the whole story. In short, was it God's will to follow your direction, or your will? When reading the Bible, you need to read the whole chapter, you need to ask the Holy Spirit for guidance. Did you? Our Lord loves you, but He isn't a genie in a bottle. Yes, He could have removed those forty pounds, but maybe there is a deeper meaning as to why He didn't, maybe to remind you that He is in control, not you."

Okay, she was right, my eyes sought what I wanted to read and although I believed God was guiding me to do this, I realized it was my desire for Him to unload forty pounds from my body. Now I had to face the people I had so positively told that I would be thinner the next time they saw me. Embarrassing? Yes, but only for me, everyone understood, as so many had done the same thing in different ways. God can and does answer prayers, but we must be in line with His will, not ours. I had to lose myself and rely on the one who knew what was best for me. It was a lesson that helped me to grow and grow I did.

My mother spoke from her heart and the leading of the Holy Spirit, she became my spiritual advisor, she was my shoulder to cry on when my daughter was diagnosed with a very rare heart defect. My mother, my weight issue aside, grew in her wisdom and was with me through all my trials, and I did the same for her. Love, pure love behaves that way.

As you read this you will come to understand the beauty of the Lord who holds us in His Loving Touch. He doesn't see my weight, He sees my spirit, He knows me, loves me and I am thankful He created me just as I am.

My mom and I weren't and aren't perfect, and we wrote many of these true stories from our lives in our imperfections, but in God's truth, and the truth of His actions in our family. I wrote about my weight because it is an ongoing issue and may come up in later stories.

Getting back to my fourth pregnancy, those Hot Fudge Sundaes were always very welcomed. Even though I was losing weight while eating all the wrong foods, cheap foods, as we couldn't afford the proper, healthier choices,

I found myself still very active, playing with my other three children, running up and down three flights of stairs carrying dirty clothes then clean clothes back and forth. I felt good, and I think my pre-natal vitamins helped me in that way.

All through my pregnancy God had been speaking to me through scripture. I didn't find time everyday to spend in prayer with the Lord, but each time I did, I would open the Bible to the exact same scripture. This would have been understandable if I used the same Bible each time, but we had many different Bibles, such as the King James Version, the New International version, the Jerusalem Bible, a Catholic version. Each the same yet different in their formats, but never straying from the truth.

Sometimes I would let the Bible fall to see if it would open to that particular scripture, it was a rookie move, and I wouldn't recommend you doing that, it was like I was testing God. I have long learned that putting God to the test was not the way to go. I have grown in my faith walk, and trusting in His Holy Spirit is a much wiser way to go.

The fact remains that when I was sitting praying and reading the Bible I was led to the same scripture when praying about my pregnancy, labour and delivery whatever Bible version I used.

The verse was in *Isaiah 66:7-10*

"Before she was in labor, she gave birth; before her pain came upon her, she delivered a son.[8] Who has heard such a thing? Who has seen such things? ...[9] Shall I bring to the point of birth and not cause to bring forth?" says the Lord; "shall I, who cause to bring forth, shut the womb? "Says your God.

[10] "Rejoice with Jerusalem, and be glad for her, all you who love her; rejoice with her in joy...

Although it says she delivers a son, the Lord had told me early on in my pregnancy that I was having a daughter. I would have to wait until she was born to verify that.

I believed that God was telling me I would have a quick, painless birth, and I clung to that word every day. Truly, how many women look forward to a painful labour and delivery? I knew the epidural was not an option and if what God was telling me would come to pass, I looked forward to it.

My baby was due March 17, St. Patrick's Day, but I was hoping for a week early as my baby bump grew very large, hindering my activity.

March 17 came and passed, days passed again and again. My hips were quite painful as I got out of bed, and thought I would put indented fingerprints in our wall as I pushed on it to steady myself. March 31st came and went, oh my goodness!

I called my doctor's office asking if I could be seen that day and was told to come right away. I wonder if my desperate pleas and crying helped me to get in.

Dave and I went right away and was taken to the examining room immediately. Possibly because they didn't want a very pregnant woman crying in the waiting room.

When Dr. Smeetin came into the room he took one look at me asking, "Feeling miserable Elaine?"

"Yes!" I exclaimed somewhat louder than I had hoped, my emotions getting the better of me. "Yes, yes, look at me! I am two weeks overdue, and no sign of labour, my hips are painful, walking is almost impossible, I feel like a beached whale fighting to get back into the water."

I heard Dave laugh but gave him an angry glance.

"Dr. Smeetin, I need you to get this baby out of me NOW! Please I am begging you."

Dr. Smeetin excused himself saying he would be right back.

I was still crying when he returned with the Obstetrician who had an office in the same building.

"You came back, I thought I scared you away."

"Elaine, you know I would never do that. I have had pregnant mothers do worse, much, much worse," he laughed.

"I am sorry Dr. Smeetin, I don't usually act like this. It's just I feel so desperate."

"I know Elaine, you are always a considerate, kind woman so I knew you must be in a great deal of pain, that's why I brought Dr. Grant with me, in hopes he could help you."

Dr. Grant shook mine and Dave's hand and asked if he could examine me, then proceeded to do just that. As he took my hand to help me back to a sitting position, he said he would like to do a stress test on the baby, along with an amniocentesis, a procedure used to take out a small sample of the amniotic fluid for testing. This is the fluid that surrounds the baby in the uterus, it can determine the age, and possible genetic problems.

We were booked the next day; the stress test was first. This determines if the baby can tolerate labour, measuring the heart and oxygen during a contraction. These contractions are called Braxton Hicks, or false labour, it is the uterus tightening, sort of a practice for true labour. The baby passed that test, now the amniocentesis, the test I was most nervous about.

Amniocentesis was everything I thought it was, only worse, the needle that would be placed in my baby bump was much bigger and longer, this needle would obtain some of the amniotic fluid. This helps to check for many problems, and in my case to determine the age of my unborn baby.

When the doctor pushed the needle into my abdomen with enough force to also enter the uterus, I felt as if I was stabbed. Dave was not with me for this test because it wasn't allowed, and plus Dave would have fainted at the sight of the needle. With no fluid result Dr. Grant tried again, I considered it a second stabbing and instead of fluid, blood gushed out.

Was my baby injured? Did he pierce her heart? Was she going to die? Where is the ultrasound that would help to guide you so you wouldn't stab my baby? All questions that rushed through my thoughts, thoughts I had unknowingly spoken out loud.

"Mrs. Vizard those are all valid questions, and I am going to ask your husband to join us."

When Dave entered his first words were, "Elaine are you okay?" The fact that the colour had drained from my face, and tears were flowing freely alarmed Dave.

Dr. Grant quickly answered, "We had a complication in trying to get the fluid, instead we withdrew blood. Mrs. Vizard needs to go home on bed rest, her blood pressure is high, and I am going to have to do a C-Section to birth your baby, as she is already very overdue. I will have my receptionist contact you as soon as I have booked it. If you see any bleeding at all you need to come to emergency immediately."

We did as Dr. Grant stated, and the next morning we received a call asking us to go to the hospital that afternoon to be admitted for surgery the next day. We had to quickly finalize the care of our other children, and having packed for the hospital stay we were soon on our way. It was always beyond my understanding that every time MaryAnn was needed, she either seemed to be laid off, or on time off from work. Whatever the reason God orchestrated my life around hers and vice versa. We have always been there for each other. Sisters and best friends, forever!

Before I went to the hospital, I decided I needed something to read as I would be in the hospital a little longer, so we stopped off at our favourite Christian Book store to buy some reading material. We didn't have much money, but my parents had donated to that cause. As I had the pregnancy walk, a penguin like waddle, along with being in pain, it was a slow process. Dave was able to park in front of the store, thank you Lord, so the walk was made much shorter. While in the store one of the leaders from our Prayer Community, came up to me, "How are you feeling Elaine?"

"Oh, hi Herman, I'm here looking for a good book to read while in the hospital. I was called a couple of hours ago to be admitted for a C-Section tomorrow. I wonder if this is God's plan when He kept leading me to Isaiah: 66?" Herman was familiar with the scripture God kept giving me, and we often prayed about it.

He then asked Dave and I to join him in prayer, in the middle of the store, the same store this baby I was carrying would years later embarrass me.

(Spoil Alert) This baby at age seventeen, although was brought up in the presence of the Lord would become stubborn in her belief. I believe it was her way of claiming her own power of choice. She denied attending church, or praying, although she was respectful, she stood her ground. It was her way or constant arguing, so Dave and I gave in. It was eventually her choice, we gave her all the teachings and encouragement, but she had to make the personal choice to accept Jesus as her Saviour, that was something we couldn't do for her.

We had dedicated her to the Lord, as we did with all our children on receiving the wonderful news that we were pregnant. I wondered how other people could raise strong Christian children into adulthood, I thought teaching them about His love as they grew would guarantee a strong Christian adult. But each child is different, all must make their own choices, all we can do as parents is to give our best in raising them, and leave the rest to our Loving and Merciful God, knowing He would honour and answer our prayers for them.

So, there I was with this child seventeen year later, in a Christian Book store I had decided to shop in on the spur of the moment. Why she came with me into the store remains a mystery to me, but there she was in all her stubbornness. As I walked around the crowded store, I suddenly heard her calling my name.

"Mom, mom," she called, "look at me," and there she was touching a bible, "mom, I'm melting, I'm melting."

I am sure I stood looking at her wide eyed with mouth open in shock at her behaviour. I was so embarrassed as I saw the other customers looking at her, but instead of being angry I eventually saw the humour in the situation. To her dismay I broke out in laughter, as did she, although I also wanted to slap her as I walked up to her, but all I could do was to stand with her in the middle of the store and laugh. I didn't look at anyone else as I only had eyes for her, and if possible, loved her more. I had chosen what I needed and we both walked up to the cashier's desk at the front entrance. The smile on the cashier's face said it all, but her comment was heart warming when she looked into my daughter's eyes saying, "thank you for the laugh, you made my day, and the day of many others shopping in the store." It seems my daughter's animated behaviour seemed to be more entertaining than shocking, and we walked out the door to the sound of thunder as a storm approached. "Maybe God didn't find it all so laughable," I teased her.

"Maybe not mom, maybe not, but I think He has a sense of humour," she said, "but maybe not," as the thunder roared again and we ran to the car laughing.

Going back seventeen years while Dave and I prayed with Herman, I became aware of other's praying with us. Herman looked up saying, "I don't believe you are going to have a C-section; God has other plans."

My first thought was, darn, I was looking forward to the C-section, no labour, no pain and more rest. I was hoping Herman couldn't read my mind as he hugged me, and I truly wondered when he said, "remember, God is more than able to answer that prayer of a quick, no pain labour and delivery without a C-section."

As I was being admitted my mind was filled with many emotional thoughts. Dave and I had decided that I would have a tubal ligation (a way of permanent birth control, also known as tying the tubes, fallopian tubes that is). As I thought on this and Herman's words, I took my Bible and re-read the scripture I had read several times a day for many months. However, this baby was born, I knew waiting for things to unfold would be the confirmation of all God had told me, or not.

We decided to name our daughter Jennifer, but God chose her middle name, Joy! "Because she will bring much joy into your lives."

Around two in the morning I began to feel like I needed to have a bowel movement, no cramps, no pain, just a pressure.

When I went to the bathroom, I found that I had a small amount of bleeding coming from my vagina. I called the nurse who then examined me.

"Mrs. Vizard you are seven centimeters dilated, are you in pain?"

"No, I answered, all I feel is a little pressure."

As this baby was my fourth the nurse quickly told me to call my husband while she called labour and delivery.

As I was dialing my home, another Nurse showed up and asked if I could wait while she examined me.

"How far was she dilated?" she asked the other nurse.

"Seven centimeters."

"Well, she is now eight and we need to get her to labour and delivery now. Mrs. Vizard, are you feeling any pain?"

"No," and I picked up the phone to call my husband again. As I was talking to Dave telling him to come quick as the baby was coming fast, I was un-ceremoniously put on a gurney and with the phone cord stretching to its maximum I dropped it, as I was rushed out the door.

"We might need to call my husband again, I'm not sure he was fully awake to understand," I said to the nurses who were practically running to get me to delivery.

I was assured that someone would call him right away when we got to the labour and delivery floor. It wasn't necessary as when he was called, he had already rushed out the door and was on his way. I prayed he would make it on time as we lived a thirty-minute drive away.

Dr. Smeetin was called and by the time I reached labour and delivery I was dilated to nine centimeters.

I was quickly brought to the delivery room, and asked not to push. Not pushing when your body is telling you to push with every fiber of your body takes a great deal of control, it is almost impossible. There are many reasons for being told not to push, in my case they didn't want the baby to be born before the doctor was ready to catch it.

Once prepped for delivery Dr. Smeetin and a Resident Doctor came to check on me. They were not dressed in their scrubs. I began to push as my body would not give me the choice any further. It was like a comedy as each time I pushed the doctors would rush back from leaving the room to check on me. Back and forth to a count of three times.

"Dr. Smeetin asked, "are you in pain."

"No, I just need to push."

"Try not to Elaine so we can get changed."

He had to be kidding, this was something I couldn't promise to do.

Finally, I heard Dave's voice, but he was stopped by a nurse as he too had to put on surgical scrubs. I began to laugh when Dave was at the delivery door fighting to put the hat on. Watching him struggle and on hearing the nurse call out, "Mr. Vizard that is for your feet, not your head," and she rushed to help him. That did it for me, I laughed so hard the baby made her appearance, just giving Dave enough time to be at my side, with the doctors ready to catch.

Jennifer Joy Vizard, weighing 8lbs 4oz arrived at 2:59 a.m.

"That was fast." Dr. Smeetin said.

"One minute short of an hour, from beginning to end, and she had no pain."

The waiting was over, and the labour and delivery was just as God had told me in Isaiah 66. A C-Section would have been convenient and an easy answer, but God had other plans, His word stood true, and Dave and I praised Him for His faithfulness.

The next day the Resident Doctor who had accompanied Dr. Smeetin at Jennifer's birth came to visit me. He thanked me for the honour of watching and assisting in Jennifer's birth. He told me it was his first

birth to assist, "It was a textbook birth, she did everything she was suppose to do, she turned at the right time. It was amazing Mrs. Vizard, I will remember this all my life. Thank you."

We continued to converse with each other and when he asked about my reason for Praising God when everything was happening and finished, I was able to tell him a little of what prayer was answered.

When he left, he had much to think on.

Our God is a God of love, miracles. He remains always faithful. If everything had not happened the way I felt He was telling me, would I have been upset? Possibly, but I have learned to thank God in every situation, and to know that if I feel God is saying something to me and it didn't happen, then I know it wasn't from God.

But it is easier to Praise and Thank Him when confirmation of the situation presents itself, and in my situation it did.

To God Be The Glory

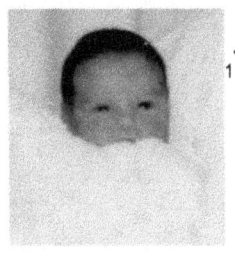
Jennifer
1 hour old

3 months old

2 years old

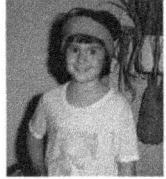
Age 5

3 year old
with me

Jenn with
her two dogs
Mya & Kaylee

A sassy teen

Jenn
so Beautiful

Chapter Seventeen
Daddy, You Forgot Me

A story of another birth? Another Miracle? Yes, to both. When Jennifer was four, I felt God was telling me He wanted me to have another baby. 'This baby will be a boy, you are to name him Adam Michael, and he will have the colours of the earth and curly hair.' Every time I went into prayer, I always had a pencil and paper with me to write down any insight, thoughts or messages I felt the Lord was saying to me, but this was the last thing I wanted to hear, and hoped I was hearing this message wrong. I did write it down and dated it. We had two children with congenital heart defects one that was miraculously healed, the other suffering, I worried over having another child, I knew if this message was from God, He would be in the control seat. I definitely needed to confirm this message so I went to my best friend's mother Evie, a strong Christian woman who I knew would fast and pray.

When I called Evie, after some small talk, I asked her if she would do me a favour.

"Of course, Elaine, anything for you."

"Well, you might want to know what it is Evie before you say yes."

Silence. I believed she was waiting for me to continue, so I forged ahead.

"God has been placing something on my heart, but I need confirmation before I follow through. I can't tell you what it's all about, but I know you will go into deep prayer. I need a confirmation Evie, and I believe He will tell you what it is if it is from Him."

"Oh, Elaine that is a big prayer request, of course I will do it but what if I don't' receive a confirmation or message?"

"First of all, Evie, if you are uncomfortable about this, please don't feel that you have to do this. I know how difficult this request is. I in no way want you to feel pressured, and if you don't receive a message or confirmation, then I accept that answer from our Lord."

"I will do it Elaine," I'm just somewhat nervous about it."

"I prayed on it Evie, and asked God to help me find the right person for this request, and your name immediately rushed into my thoughts."

With that Evie accepted my explanation of how I chose her, and I know my request un-nerved her, but she went forward into prayer and fasting. I too prayed and fasted until I would hear from her.

I hadn't told Dave about what I felt God was telling me, I needed it confirmed first.

Three days later Evie called me on the phone.

"Hi Elaine, well I did receive a message, but I don't think you are going to like it."

I laughed nervously, "that's okay Evie just tell me what you felt He was telling you."

"Last night in prayer I heard these words in my spirit: "tell Elaine I want her to have another baby, it will be a boy." And that was all I heard."

Evie was quiet after that, but started laughing when she heard my response, "Praise God Evie, that was exactly what He told me. Thank you so much, now all I have to do is let Dave know."

We both laughed Praising God together, and I thanked Evie for praying on this, we ended with a prayer.

When I found some quiet time, which was usually in our one and only bathroom, I began to pray hoping I wouldn't be disturbed. I was honest with God, "you know

Lord my fears and worries over having another baby. People will judge us, not understanding, especially Edna my mother-in-law. I know Dave doesn't want us to have another baby, neither did I, but now I need you to take your message to Dave. I am asking you Lord to tell Dave, I don't know how you will tell him, but I need you to take this off my shoulders and take control. I know Evie knew we didn't want another child, but you told her exactly what you told me, and now I am very excited over this. I just need you to break the news to Dave. It is in your name Lord Jesus I pray."

The next morning, I could tell something was bothering my husband.

"Dave, are you okay?"

"I don't know Elaine, I had a dream last night, it was so real, and I feel this dream was a message from God. I'm not sure how I feel about the dream, or how you're going to feel about it."

My heart skipped a beat. Had God already told Dave? but then I hadn't heard the dream, maybe it had nothing to do with having another baby.

"Do you want to talk about it Dave?"

"You might not be ready to hear this, it goes against everything we have talked about, and decided for our future. As it involves both of us you need to know my dream. In the dream there was a baby boy sitting alone on the ground, he had curly black hair, looked at me with outstretched arms saying "Daddy, you forgot me." It seemed so real like God was saying He had another baby for us to have. He looked like our others. I felt so sad when I looked at this baby, our baby to be, that we could forget him. What do you think about it Elaine?"

I smiled at Dave, my prayer was answered, and I went to get the paper I had written the message God had given me on it, with the date.

I then told Dave about Evie and the message God had given her about our having another baby, a son, and how I asked Him to tell you, as I didn't want to, it had to come from Him.

Dave just sat there trying to digest all the information.

"Well, you know Elaine, with that dream, and it feeling so real, and all that you told me, it looks like we're going to have another baby, another son named Adam. You want to start working on it now?" Dave hugged me smiling with a twinkle in his eye, that twinkle had to wait as it was the weekend and we had four children waiting to have breakfast.

That night Dave and I prayed accepting God's will for our lives. I was very specific in my prayer asking God for our baby to be full term, a healthy pregnancy, no birth defects and, not to weigh over seven pounds. I don't know why I was specific about the weight. My first two was five and four weeks early the biggest weighing six pounds eleven ounces, and our last two being full term the biggest weighed eight pounds eleven ounces. It would be a miracle if our new baby was born full term weighing seven pounds or under. These were my firm requests. Was I being bold? Would I hear thunder in requesting what I wanted? I don't think so as we should always go before the Lord with an honest and humble heart knowing He has the final say, His will be done.

A year later I found out I was pregnant. A whole year since God confirmed we were to have another child. Normally I became pregnant quickly, after our use of the condom was stopped. To be honest there were times I wondered if maybe in spite of all confirmation that we were wrong. I had to remind myself that God had a plan, a time chosen for me to have our son Adam. God used this time to help me to learn to be more patient, to grow in trust and faith. Often when I am going through a difficult time, I ask the Lord to show me what He is trying to teach me, and He does, through the Holy Spirit. So often it isn't until we look back that we see everything He had done to grow us and help us get through it. A great example of this was when our finances were so limited, and the burden of paying hospital bills and our monthly bills were so demanding we didn't think we would ever climb out of that hole. It wasn't until Dave, and I went with our daughter and her husband-to-be to see a newly built house they were thinking of buying, led us to the possibility that we too could buy a house. That took us by surprise when the bank confirmed the fact that our finances were good. What? When did that happen? We were so caught in the knowledge of that hole that we didn't see the ladder we had built to climb out of it.

When we looked back, we could see God's hand in it, and wondered why we were still in the dark, not seeing our financial growth. Praise God for the realtor we talked to that day bringing attention to our buying a house also. We did buy a house in the process of being built, but not in the same area as the kids, and we were able to put our own choices into it. To us, that was an amazing miracle.

Getting back to my pregnancy, our news was met with great joy with my family, I was more worried over Dave's mom's response. Edna however surprised me by not saying anything negative, that would come eventually. My mom already knew as she had been in prayer about God telling me about adding a new son to our family, mom knew that each baby was a miraculous gift.

During that time family doctors were only seeing pregnant women for the first trimester, and then the rest of the pregnancy was cared for by obstetricians. This made me very nervous; I disliked seeing different doctors because so many saw my weight first; many were rude, making me feel like I was a disgrace to womanhood.

One such doctor I was sent to was a urologist who specializes in treating kidneys and the urinary tract. At the time I was having many bladder infections and Dr. Smeetin wanted me to see this doctor.

To give this doctor a name would be giving him credit and this man did not deserve any form of positive descriptions.

I had heard of this doctor but nothing negative, until I went for my appointment.

I waited alone in the waiting room until the receptionist called me and led me to an examining room. The room was small messy with a dirty floor. The receptionist asked me to remove all my clothing, even my socks. I questioned why as I wasn't there for a physical, only a consult.

"Isn't there a nurse here," I asked, "She's busy," she answered abruptly.

I asked again, "why do I have to be naked?"

The receptionist replied without expression, "this is what the doctor wants," then limply handed me a thin blue paper cloth and left the room.

As a nurse I was taught that a doctor was always right and to never question them. These, mostly men, were not God but humans and made mistakes. I never agreed with the analogy of doctors being perfect. As my husband often said, "no one is perfect, the only perfect man who walked this earth was crucified and rose from the dead."

I removed all my clothing quickly, yes even my socks, and taking the thin paper cloth placed it over me as I lay on the examining table.

As I lay there waiting nervously the doctor walked in and shut the door behind him. He didn't introduce himself he just stood at the door staring at me, as if to show his dominance.

What felt like minutes was probably just one minute, but his intent was clear. He finally walked over to my side and stared at me with a venomous smile on his face.

"So, you have many bladder infections?" he asked not waiting for a reply, instead he grabbed the thin blue cloth and ripped it from my body, and then stared at me, moving his arrogant, disapproving eyes up and down my body.

By this time, I was so embarrassed I wanted to melt into the dirty floor.

I finally found my voice, "shouldn't your nurse be in here?"

Instead of a reply he walked closer to me and with his hands, he grabbed my breasts in a tight, painful squeeze that sought to dehumanize me. I was shocked, I couldn't breathe, I felt numb, I couldn't think, couldn't talk, I felt as if I was floating outside my body. In that moment my mind could not register what was happening, and if he did anything else I was not aware of it. As the minutes of his sickening evil behaviour passed, I eventually came to my senses, fighting the deep dense fog that sought to consume me, and found my voice.

My voice took me by surprise as my indignant voice was loud and clear.

"Where is your nurse? She needs to be in here! You need to call for her NOW!"

His hands finally let go at my raised voice.

"You are a fat ugly bitch," he snarled, "not someone a man could make love to," and he left.

I stood up quickly, shaking, crying and humiliated. I dressed as fast as my shaking body would let me and left the room to leave the office.

"Where are you going?" the receptionist asked, "the doctor said to book you for a cystoscopy."

"The day I let that man touch me will be a cold day in hell," I spat out as I left.

She had to have known what was going on or had at least a hint of what was happening. I am sure there were other women who had been abused by this so-called doctor.

I went to my car but couldn't drive due to my trembling body. I found it difficult to recall all that this man had done but his attack on my breasts left a throbbing memory of his abuse When I finally calmed down, I drove straight to Dr. Smeetin's office. The waiting room was full, but I decided to just walk into the door where the examining rooms were.

"Elaine, what are you doing here, you don't have an appointment. Are you okay?" my doctor's nurse asked.

"I need to talk to Dr. Smeetin."

"He is with a patient, can I help you, Elaine?" she whispered.

"Yes, please tell Dr. Smeetin to stop sending patients, especially women to the urologist I had an appointment with," and I left leaving her confused and upset for me, but not knowing the reason.

When I returned home the kids were watching television, I saw Dave and went to him and cried. Eventually that night I told him in detail what happened. My husband didn't like conflict of any kind, and it hurt me when he didn't jump to my defense, I needed him to become my hero, to be outraged, to take control; I needed him to go punch that doctor in the groin and face. I wanted to push him away as he held me, but it was his comforting presence and steady heartbeat that calmed my inner turmoil.

"Can't you report him, Elaine?" Dave whispered in my ear.

I concluded that it would be his word against mine. Even if I told my doctor would he have done anything? At that time doctors sided with each other, having each others backs, not sure if it is still that way today.

No, I would have to live like it never happened, although the black and blue bruising on my breasts told me otherwise. The bruises would disappear, but the hateful words and sexual abuse would stay with me, subconsciously holding me in their ugly grasp until something years later would renew the abuse I endured.

So now I had to go to another doctor for my pregnancy. Would he embarrass me about my weight? Would he try to understand? I had buried what is now known as sexual abuse so deep, yet it was a part of my every day life in hating my body even more than I did before.

I wanted to cancel my appointment with Dr. McLoud, something I often did with other doctors, but I needed to make sure my pregnancy was healthy so I went.

His waiting room was packed, and my nerves were calmed by all the other women waiting who began a conversation with me.

When my name was called, I began to shake, would I be asked to remove my clothing? Step on a scale? I could see my nemesis from where I sat, I couldn't see the numbers as its back was to me, but I knew those numbers I knew the hate I held for those stand-up weight scales. It was waiting for me, and it did not disappoint as I was asked to step on it before entering the examining room. It seems Dr. McLoud had his practice with two other obstetricians, so it was an extremely busy office.

When entering the examining room, the nurse did not mention my weight, she didn't ask me to remove my clothing. I was only asked to sit on a very comfortable couch. When the doctor entered the room, he smiled as he shook my hand congratulating me on my pregnancy. He then sat beside me and asked questions, conversing like we were friends.

He had all the information my family doctor had sent, but before he could embarrass me about my weight, I decided to bring it up first.

"Dr. McLoud, I know I am fat...," but he stopped me right there.

"Mrs. Vizard, we don't use that word here, I am here to make sure you get the best care possible for a very healthy pregnancy and baby. I am sure you know your weight, from what I have read you have been heavy all your life, so I don't need to tell you what you already know. I am not here to judge or disrespect you; I am here to care for you. Okay?

My shoulders relaxed as I nodded yes, and he continued with the questions.

"I read that with each pregnancy you have lost weight, but I don't want you to lose weight. You have had two babies born with congenital heart defects, and there has been new research of weight loss and its effect on pregnancy which can cause birth defects. So, no diets, just eat healthy, and we will monitor you every month. Does that sound good to you?"

"Yes, very much so," and this began a wonderful time in my life, being respected and accepted for who I was.

Our baby was due December 10th 1985, and dreading each appointment with Dr. McLovely, (a nickname many of his patients had given him, and to be very honest, he was) was no longer an issue for me.

Every month although eating normally with an added few treats I lost weight. The second visit the scale showed a loss of five pounds.

"Mrs. Vizard we can't have this happening, have you been dieting? Has nausea limited your food intake?"

No to both questions, "I am eating normally like you told me to."

"Okay then we have to add calories to your intake."

"Excuse me Dr. McLoud, but are you telling me to eat more calories?"

He laughed, "Yes, I am. You look surprised at that."

"Well, I am surprised because that's a first for me. Could you put it in writing, so I have proof that you have asked me to increase my calories? No one in my family will believe this, especially my mother."

This time he laughed louder and longer.

"If they have a hard time believing it just bring them to your next appointment."

Dr. McLoud was so kind and invited our other four children and my sister to my next appointment to hear the baby's heartbeat. Dave had heard it often.

I brought my mom to my October appointment. She had witnessed my eating the chocolate Halloween candy and often chastised me for doing so.

"Mom, I am not gaining weight, in fact I am still losing weight, and the doctor keeps upping my calories."

"Well, I just don't agree with that Elaine, it's hard for me to understand his concept."

I kept my mouth shut, I knew it wasn't logical, but I thought Dr. McLoud would better describe it to her, as I certainly wasn't getting through.

To my surprise, after eating all that chocolate I had gained a pound, only one pound.

The doctor introduced himself to my mother with a smile and a handshake. Then the time came to discuss my weight gain.

"Mrs. Vizard you gained a pound," he said smiling widely, "What did you do to gain the weight?"

"I did what I normally wouldn't do, I ate a great deal of Halloween candy, specifically chocolate, in fact I had to keep going to the store to buy more. I am weak and can't wait for Halloween to get here."

He then started to write it in my chart, "No, no, no, please don't add that in my chart. It's embarrassing that I kept eating the candy and then had to replace it again and again."

He laughed, "I am charting you gained a pound, but not saying how."

My mother asked why he wanted me to gain weight as I was already heavy. I was so happy she asked him because maybe then she would believe. Dr. McLoud explained why women shouldn't lose weight in pregnancy, and that weight loss could contribute to birth defects.

Mom was comforted in the answer, but I could tell she was still hesitant in my gaining weight.

Dr. McLoud then asked mom if she would like to hear the baby's heartbeat. Mom was thrilled at hearing her new grandchild's heart beating so beautifully. I think mom was walking on clouds after hearing it, in fact she talked about it at every opportunity.

The doctor checked the growth of my baby bump, and said the baby was growing well, he felt the baby weighed at least seven pounds with six more weeks left to grow.

"Seven pounds," I almost cried. I wasn't sure God was going to answer my prayer for this baby to weigh no more than seven pounds. I looked at my mom as she knew the history of my prayer.

"In fact," the doctor continued, "this will be at least a ten-pound baby or more. I think you should come every week so I can carefully monitor you. I also want you to have another diabetes test."

"I already had one Dr. McLoud."

"I know Mrs. Vizard, but considering this baby's weight with having six more weeks to grow, I want to monitor you closely. You have only gained one pound, so that means you are continuing to lose more weight then previously thought."

At that he said he would see me next week, said his goodbyes to my mom and left the room.

My mom hugged me, "don't stop believing Elaine. We know God is more than able to answer your prayer, it will happen if it's His will. Just keep believing."

Ultrasounds were still not widely used, so all we could go on was the expertise and experience Dr. McLoud had.

I must admit Dr. McLoud's words kept ringing in my thoughts and heart, overpowering my belief that God's will coincided with mine.

What if my prayer wasn't His desire for me? What if I was meant to have a very large baby? What if the answer to my prayer request was no? I continued to feel in my spirit as I prayed that God's answer was yes, and my mom's words to believe regardless of what others were saying. Yes, I would have a baby that would weigh seven pound or less.

Only a few people knew about my prayer, my mom, dad, sister, Evie, Mae, a good friend, and Sister Rosalie, a nun who ministered to our church family. They continued to pray but ultimately it was God's decision and His will needed to be my will.

Dr. Mcloud contacted me with the results of my latest test to detect diabetes, but that and all other blood tests came back normal.

On my next visit Dr. McLoud's nurse checked my baby bump and thought that the baby was at least seven and a half pounds. When the doctor checked me, he agreed with his nurse's estimation.

"This isn't making sense; you lost that pound you gained plus three more. Maybe you need to see an endocrinologist, he might be able to make sense of this. My thought on this is that your metabolism is extremely heightened during pregnancy, and slow when you aren't pregnant."

"That does make sense Dr. McLoud, because as soon as I have my babies, I begin to gain weight again even though I am careful on what and how much I eat. No one believes me that I am not an overeater."

Dr. McLoud referred me to see the endocrinologist Dr. Mezzo. almost immediately. Dave came with me because I was still very nervous meeting a new doctor, that feeling has never left me to this very day.

Dr. Mezzo agreed with Dr. McLoud, however he wanted to meet with me again when I was recovered from giving birth, which would be six months or more. Until then I continued to follow Dr. McLoud's advice to increase my calories. I had a difficult time with this as my brain was wired to constantly try to lose weight. Don't get me wrong, I loved enjoying the freedom of eating more calories instead of always starving myself; however, I often found myself in the ever diet mode and Dave would have to remind me I needed to eat more.

Dave always told people our dog ate more than I did but was this believable when looking at me standing there overweight, well, actually fat? I would have a hard time believing that fact even though it was about me, myself and I.

This pregnancy was very different, I was never off balance with any other pregnancy, but this one had me toppling over often.

One time I was bringing groceries into the house when suddenly my balance was thrown off and I fell. I was so embarrassed I told my kids to hurry up and close the door when I get in. Of course, they were worried that I had been hurt, or the baby, but all I could think of was that someone could possibly see me.

Another time I was tying my shoes, one foot was on a kitchen chair, as I brought my foot down to join the other, both feet on the floor, I toppled over like a tree being chopped down; I fell like a rock, straight and on my back. My mom was with me and after seeing her look of shock I began to laugh.

"Elaine, that is not funny, are you hurt?"

"No mom, this happens all too often. I am fine."

My sister MaryAnn sent me an early Christmas gift of having my house cleaned, Mom and I were going out for lunch during the cleaning time. The two women cleaning came running when they heard the loud sound of my body making contact with the floor. They were all so upset which for some reason made me laugh longer and harder.

Everyone reached toward me to help me up, but I stopped them as I didn't want anyone to hurt themselves. I asked the one woman to put a kitchen chair in front of me, and little by little I crawled up to eventually sit in it.

"I am fine, really," I tried to comfort them, "this has happened before, I just for some reason lose my balance and down I go. I am sorry for laughing as I know you're upset, but I think it was either laugh or cry, and laughter was a better choice for me."

With that mom and I left so the ladies could clean, without our interrupting them. I laughed about that fall for days as I pictured someone yelling timber…and down I went.

Time was quickly passing, Christmas presents were bought, wrapped and put under the tree, except for the one's Santa would bring, as Jennifer at six years old still believed in that magical man on a sleigh.

Now all we had to do was wait for labour to begin. Every time I went for my weekly visit with Dr. McLoud the baby's weight continued to grow, eight, nine pounds, then just before labour eleven pounds. Of course, these were all estimates, that said I began to think of how many nurses, and doctors held the same estimates, and maybe, just maybe my prayer of a seven-pound baby or less would not be answered.

I am a person who worries, a person with anxiety, and as easy as I say I am trusting God, well it isn't easy at all.

Trusting God takes growth, it doesn't come easy. All through the Bible we are told to trust God, and that information always came with examples.

Jesus himself was overwhelmed when facing His death.

Jesus said to His apostles **in Mark 14: 34-36…**

"My soul is overwhelmed with sorrow to the point of death," He said to them. "Stay here and keep watch."

Going a little farther, He fell to the ground and prayed that, if possible, the hour might pass from Him. "Abba, Father," He said, "everything is possible for You. Take this cup from Me. Yet not what I will, but what You will."

Jesus is the Son of God along with being human. Jesus was fully God and fully human, He didn't have to subject himself to what lay before Him, He could have just said the word and it would have all disappeared. But even as He asked God the Father to take this cup (suffering, torture, hatred, humiliation death …) away from Him, He knew that His Father's will must be done.

I often ask the Holy Spirit to help me, yes, I believe, but help me in my unbelief.

God is trustworthy and good, and trusting Him comes with growth, when studying the Bible and plainly getting to know Him in the peaceful moments of just listening.

I had a set time for prayer, and listening to God, or just spending time in His presence helped me to grow.

I honestly believed that God could make this miracle happen. When all around me gave their expert opinion, I continued to trust Jesus would answer my prayer request.

I knew He could say yes, but I also knew He might say no, and I had to trust in Him no matter what.

I didn't want to give birth to a large baby, or possibly have a C-Section. I remembered Joey's birth and his shoulders getting caught on my pelvis. This could be life threatening, but in most cases mom and baby usually come through the ordeal happy and healthy.

I had hoped this baby would come a little early, but that didn't happen.

On December 9th 1985 I went into labour, but because we lived thirty minutes away from the hospital my mom and sister talked me in to coming to their place so I would be closer to the hospital.

"Elaine, you don't want to give birth on the side of the road, remember Jennifer's birth, if you hadn't been in the hospital, you would have either had her at home or in the car," my sister made sure she emphasized every word, and Dave quickly agreed, took the phone from me telling my sister, "Okay, after we pack the kids' clothes, and everything else we need we will come there. I will pick the kids up from school on the way there."

Were my parents ready to have their four grandchildren, Dave and myself crowding into their two-bedroom apartment. My sister was excited about it, as was my mom, but my dad looked hesitant not sure if he wanted his quiet space turned upside down.

As we all settled down, I was blessed to have the most comfortable chair to sit in. Sitting there watching a good movie with the kids or so I thought, as I looked around, each face was staring at me, I was their entertainment. My sister held a watch ready to time my contractions, her attention solely on my face and baby bump.

"How's Thumper doing, "she asked.

I don't remember when we started calling our baby Thumper, but the reasoning for the name was because he loved to jump, kick and move. "Let's call him Thumper," Jennifer squealed in delight as she felt his many kicks.

We all agreed that Thumper was a great name, a name he would live up to.

I looked at my sister, "MaryAnn there is no change from the last time you asked, three minutes ago."

I was the center of attention, except for my dad who was playing solitaire on the kitchen table.

My contractions were slow in coming and very irregular. I wanted to go home and rest in my bed, but because my water had ruptured, I wasn't going anywhere; not yet.

The minutes and hours passed slowly; I was uncomfortable but not in pain. Everyone lost interest in watching me, thank goodness, I was beginning to feel like a bug under the microscope.

We kept things simple; we ordered take out, played quiet games, put puzzles together until bed time. MaryAnn had already made sleeping arrangements for the kids by placing sleeping bags and blankets all around her bedroom. Of course, they couldn't settle, they were waiting for their baby brother to arrive, and I wasn't doing it fast enough according to Jennifer. "Hurry up mommy."

Eventually everyone went to bed. Dave fell asleep on the couch, and I remained seated in the comfortable chair, a chair made more uncomfortable with each contraction.

It was midnight when I thought we should go to the hospital. I went to the labour and delivery floor, where, I was weighed, a very unpleasant routine that I completely hated. The last thing I wanted to see before me were those high numbers reaching for the stars.

"Are you sure you have lost weight Mrs. Vizard?" asked the admitting nurse.

"Yes, I have lost ten pounds, the lowest amount of all my pregnancies. Dr. McLoud didn't want me losing any weight."

"A woman of your size would probably gain thirty pounds, so losing ten pounds, and not gaining, it's like you lost forty pounds and possibly more," the nurse commented.

"Can I get off the scale please?"

"Of course, but you must realize your weight makes you a high risk."

"And yet I have made it through without any complications. I might be overweight, but I am healthy," I tried hard not to spit those words out.

"You don't have diabetes?" she asked as a statement of doubt.

"No, I don't."

"That's odd a woman of your size and pregnant would almost be guaranteed a diagnosis of diabetes. I am sure you will be later when in your fifties."

Honestly, I wanted to smack that nurse, she was making me feel uncomfortable, like an oddity of mass proportions. I jumped at hearing my doctor's voice behind me.

"How about taking Mrs. Vizard to her room," Dr. McLoud said rather annoyed. "I think Mrs. Vizard's weight is not an issue to comment on. Let's concentrate on admitting her and leave the topic of her weight to me and her."

Dr. McLoud had stood behind us during the nurse's rude intent, and he was not having it. My hero came to rescue me, and I was so happy when he gave that nurse another patient to care for, one who was not overweight.

My baby bump was measured, "Oh my, you are having a big baby," nurse Judy said, "probably ten pounds if not eleven pounds."

I quickly said, "epidural please."

Judy laughed but I wanted to cry.

Judy asked me if I would allow an instructor with her nursing students to help care for me. I wanted to say no, but how are they going to learn, so I reluctantly said yes.

As the instructor entered the room with her students, she seemed nice.

My blood pressure was checked and was high. "Oh my, you're obese and it is probably adding to your high blood pressure. Are you on any medication for high blood pressure?' asked the instructor who could easily be mistaken for a Disney villain.

There was that word, obese, one of many words used to describe my weight.

I had, had enough and did not hold back.

"I know or at least hope you are not meaning to be insulting or unkind, but it feels like you are. I have been overweight all my life, but it never stopped me from being athletic, playing many sports, your attitude isn't professional, it is demeaning to me. You should get to know me first before you assume my weight is the main reason for all my issues. I allowed you to be my nurse along with your students, and you are not giving them a good example on how a patient should be treated. Especially a patient who has been kind. Now please stop insulting me, I am in labour, and I might not be able to hold back on what I truly want to say.

With that she mumbled a quick apology, and decided to check my baby bump, asking all her students to do the same.

"How much did your biggest baby weigh," she asked quickly.

"Eight pounds, eleven ounces."

As her students checked my baby bump, she asked them "how much do you they think this baby weighs". They all stated that the baby was a large baby.

"Actually," the instructor said, "this is a very large baby, I believe it to be around eleven pounds."

There was that fear and doubt again creeping into the answered prayer of no. Every nurse, every resident doctor agreed with her, "eleven pounds seems right."

It is difficult to be in active labour with so many nurses hovering over you. What was worse was the internal checking of my cervix, by every student nurse, and Resident doctor.

When Dr. McLoud entered my room, he found me to be very emotional, to say the least.

Dave answered quickly, "Dr. McLoud my wife is in active labour and having so many nurses check her is painful and exhausting. Could you please stop them from coming in, and just allow her nurse to take care of her? The instructor has been rude in my opinion, Elaine needs to be cared for by someone who is professional and kind."

If I wasn't in a full bloom contraction I would have jumped up and kissed my Knight in shining armour husband.

"I will take care of that right away, although I do need to check you first Elaine. Is that okay?" I nodded yes.

I took a few minutes to tell Dr. McLoud what I was praying for. "I know everyone is saying the baby is big, but I believe in miracles, and still hope and pray, in spite of all the evidence telling me otherwise, that this baby will be no bigger than seven pounds." I waited for his response at my outrageous hope and belief. I could tell he was wrestling to say the right words. I am sure he thought I was one of those crazy, religious zealots.

"Well Mrs. Vizard, I know you have great faith, and you have a heart for God. Like you said if it's His will, we will know soon."

Dr. McLoud had gentle hands and was always considerate of my feelings and level of pain.

First, he checked my baby bump, and I asked that dreaded question, "what do you think the baby weighs?"

"I don't think you want to hear my answer Mrs. Vizard. It won't be long before you know if God answered your prayer, let's just say the baby is probably big. He then checked my cervix.

I had asked to be told when I was eight centimeters so Dave could call and have our other four children brought to the hospital. Dr. McLoud had already made arrangements for this to happen. He was a firm believer in having family members supporting and waiting for the good news, allowing them to see the baby before they left.

"Please tell me when I am eight centimeters," I asked him.

He looked at my husband and smiled, "Mr. Vizard it is time to call the family in, your wife is at nine centimeters, almost time to have the baby."

Because the baby was allegedly large, I was brought to the operating room in case I needed an emergency C-Section. I would be able to try a vaginal birth, and God Bless Dr. McCloud when he ordered an epidural to be administered. Dave wasn't present for that due to the needle, we didn't need him fainting, again.

Epidurals are a gift from God and science, my last thirty minutes of labour were spent without pain, 'oh what a feeling, or should I say, oh what is not a feeling.' I thanked the anesthetist at least five times, probably the most thanked person on the obstetrics floor

Dave entered the operating room in full gear and walked to the left side of my head. Dr. McLoud was in the receiving position, a nurse at his side, and one at my side.

"Okay, you are having a contraction time to push."

I pushed as hard as I could. I couldn't think, couldn't pray, the prayers had been said. As the baby's head came down the birth canal, I heard a gasp escape from Dr. McLoud.

One more push, and this time Dr. McLoud told me to look at the baby. I wanted to say, "I'm kind of busy here…" but his words implored me to look, and I did.

"Look at the size of the baby's head, this is not a large baby; are you watching?" I am embarrassed to admit that with the news that the baby's head was not big I thought of a deformity. However; as our son slipped into his new home on earth, and into the loving arms of his family and our devoted friends, he was definitely not a big baby.

Dr. McLoud handed the baby to the nurse saying, "I'm going back in to see if there's a twin?"

Dave and I both were stunned at the prospect of having two babies.

"No, no twin, and it seems Mrs. Vizard that God answered your prayer." With that answer came a sigh of relief from Dave and I.

Adam Michael Vizard was born at 5:31 a.m. on December 10, 1985, weighing six pounds fifteen ounces, one ounce short of seven pounds, and perfectly healthy.

How could this be? Everyone was amazed, they were all sure Adam was a large baby, and yet here he was at a weight no one could deny, and no one could understand.

For Dave and me, our family and friends it was the miracle I had prayed for, we had prayed for.

It's difficult to imagine the feeling and thoughts of all the medical staff who physically knew Adam was a large baby. I didn't question it or them, I believed but had to wait for Adam's birth for confirmation. That morning, we experienced the miracle we prayed for, the miracle that seemed impossible at the estimates of all the professionals. That morning Dave and I experienced the miracle of God's love in a six-pound fifteen-ounce answered prayer.

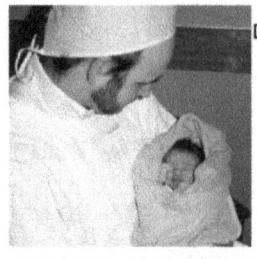
Dave holding one hour old Adam

Me holding one day old Adam

Adam on Christmas Day, a beautiful gift.

Evie holding Adam, she made his Christening gown and the cake.

Adam's Christening day with our other children and Father Sam who Christened Adam.

Adam age 3 with my sister

Adult Adam

Chapter Eighteen
I Will Pay the Price

There are times when miracles are taught through lessons learned. As we grow in Christ we are often tested. Will hardship destroy that growth, or will it remain a growth in our lives?

When I first started going to the prayer meetings life couldn't be better, I was in love, happily married, and expecting our first child, but like all good things there is the bad.

In the New Testament I often read in **Matthew 5: 45** where Jesus tells His disciples the depth of God's love, and that was to love everyone as God the Father loves everyone. He has no favourites.

"…He causes His sun to rise on the evil and the good, and, sends rain on the righteous and the unrighteous…"

I thought in my simple faith that loving Him was an open door to a wonderful life; but I couldn't have been more wrong. I guess I was putting God in a box, in a genie's lamp, He was my make a wish God.

But I learned quickly that God has no favourites, and as His children we are all loved completely, yes even the bad. Every person was created in the image of God, and I needed to remember that, especially when the bad came rushing at me like a freight train.

It began when I went to visit my mother before my afternoon shift at the hospital.

I found mom sitting on her couch looking exhausted and scared. Her heart was beating irregularly again, but more so. Was it her thyroid, stress or both?

Mom said the doctor told her the irregularity was not dangerous to her health, and to go about her regular activities of living. She continued to use her mother's little helper to calm her body, Valium, which was often used for anxiety and other health issues. Today, doctors do not easily give this out as it can become very addictive. However, my mom was level-headed and took it sparingly, but that didn't mean she was exempt from becoming addicted to the drug.

I felt so horrible for my mom, I had never had an irregular heartbeat, and mom looked so uncomfortable, and stressed.

Two days later after a six-day schedule I began my two days off. Dave was working the afternoon shift and as I waited for him to come home, I sat on my couch having some much-needed prayer time in the quiet presence of my Lord and Saviour. I asked God to heal my mother, but that felt hollow, just not enough, I needed to do something in return. As I was still a baby Christian, I learned a valuable lesson about paying the price for Jesus to heal my mom.

Could I have learned this lesson in a simpler way? Probably, but it wouldn't have had the same effect of a lesson learned to pass on to others. If I could have changed my request in knowing what I know now, I would, but God has His ways, and His way showed me the right way.

I decided to kneel to ask Jesus for this gift, and then I just spoke simply from my heart. 'Please Lord heal my mom, I am younger and will take on her symptoms in thanks for healing her.'

What was I thinking? There should have been a neon sign placed in front of me blinking 'Danger, Danger Elaine Vizard, Danger!'

We need to remember that growth comes from mistakes, if we choose growth. We also need to remember that God and, His Angels are real, I have had much growth in this knowledge. My greatest growth in the power of the name of Jesus came from experiences with the devil, and he was right there just waiting to pounce on me when I said that prayer.

When Dave arrived home from work, we each had a small glass of wine and chatted over the happenings of the day. When I told him about my prayer, he thought it was a good prayer, and right to pray for my mom. As we crawled into bed, both tired and desiring to sleep, it started.

What was that? It did it again, my heart didn't have a normal rhythm.

This did not feel good, and I knew at that moment what my mother was feeling and going through. I didn't sleep that night, but like a child on Christmas morning I couldn't wait to call my mother to ask if she was feeling better.

"How are you feeling mom?"

"About the same Elaine."

"Are your heart palpitations gone?"

"No and your dad is taking me to the doctor's again."

"Okay, call me when you get home," I didn't mention my 'great sacrifice' and my ensuing palpitations.

She said she would and our conversation ended. My irregular heart beat was getting worse, and mom wasn't healed.

Why didn't God heal my mom knowing I took her symptoms on myself. This didn't make sense; I willingly paid the price for mom's healing by taking on her symptoms; and that's where the lesson was taught, and learned through time and my suffering.

Mom called me when she returned from her doctor's appointment. He didn't say anything different except that it will probably end as suddenly as it began.

Thinking my situation would be the same, and everything would be as it was before I made the request. When I went to bed that night the palpitations worsened.

I became frightened when my heart seemed to skip every other beat. As a nurse I wasn't educated in the mechanism of the heart. I was taught the basics but not to any great extent.

All night long as I lay in my husband's arms my heart rocked his and my body with its hard irregular all consuming scary beat.

"Elaine, I think you need to go to emergency to get your heart checked," Dave said at six in the morning. "We aren't going to get any sleep with your heart doing that."

I continued to think it would correct itself so I decided to wait, until one hour later we rushed to the hospital, not because of my heart, but because I started bleeding, and I was worried for our unborn baby.

In the emergency room I was seen almost immediately, and my anxiety grew as I was hooked up too many monitors, which made the monitors alarms sound their warning of a rapid heart rate, and palpitations reaching the highest limit.

The emergency doctor decided to admit me for observation, and it was with great shock when sitting in the wheelchair I saw the sign, Intensive Care on the thick glass doors. I thought my heart was fast, but it was nothing compared to what it was doing at seeing that sign. Dave couldn't follow me into the Intensive Care Unit, they had very strict visiting hours and rules. I needed him, I needed my mom, I needed God.

While being admitted and hooked up to more monitors Dave called our parents.

A Cardiologist, an Internist and an Obstetrician (it sounds like the beginnings of a joke, but far from it). These doctors were called in to be the medical team caring for me and my unborn baby.

I was so frightened by my surroundings, an Intensive Care Unit cared for the very ill, those patients whose medical conditions could not be met on a regular hospital floor.

Dave was finally allowed to visit me later that afternoon, but only for thirty minutes. Back then they were very strict, not so much today in 2021, hours are often flexible depending on the illness and condition of the patient.

Dave prayed with me, telling me everyone was calling different prayer chains, (people who dedicate their time in prayer for a specific person, or situation.) Although this should have given me some comfort in knowing hundreds of people were now praying for me, the person I needed most was my mother. Mom was my spiritual support in Jesus, her support was Aunt Nellie, they were amazing women who loved and learned through their experiences in growing with God.

I wondered how mom's heart was doing with getting the news of my admission, I prayed for her that she was feeling better and not worse over worrying about me.

The Intensive Care Unit was a noisy place as I listened to all the monitors and activities within the unit, I grew more frightened. I learned that when I moved my monitors would sound their alarm as my heart rate and palpitations increased. I decided after that first time I would try to remain quiet and still. I tried, but that was impossible as my body needed to move, and using a bed pan to pee and poop in were not the most comfortable and sanitary.

One time when I decided to change my position the alarms sounded, and the nurses came running. As I watched them rush toward me, I asked them if I was dead?"

That was a silly question, I was obviously alive. I started to laugh at how that sounded, and the nurses joined in, some stress being released from their facial expressions.

When my mom and dad were finally able to visit me two days later, they prayed with me, and mom handed me a book titled The Healing Light by Agnes Sanford. Some people have described her as a modern mystic, I guess if you read her works in a nonspiritual way, you would miss the point. I dislike the words mystic and spiritual because its meaning has far reaching concepts. I couldn't care less what Christian religion you are, Catholic, Anglican, Pentecostal and so forth; although there are some who would rather cause dissension and wrong thinking, leading to hateful actions. I learned to see which church followed Jesus, the true birth of the Christian faith, you know the truth of someone if they walk the walk and talk the talk. I have also learned to rely on the Holy Spirit to guide me in my walk receiving the insight needed to understand healings and miracles. I was not perfect then, not perfect today, we are always learning, growing through our mistakes. We are human, we don't always get it right but if our hearts are in the right place, we can trust that the Holy Spirit will guide us.

    I often wrestled with the three persons in one God concept. My cousin Ivy put it into perspective for me saying, "How wonderful is God. We have God the Father, God the Son, and God the Holy Spirit, at any time when we need a Father He is there, when we need a Saviour, He is there, and when we need guidance and insight, God the Holy Spirit is there."

I often have dreams, dreams that teach me, dreams I know are from God.

One such dream was when I stood before the throne of God, and there sat The Father with Jesus on His right sitting on thrones. Their faces were not clear, although that would have been nice. As I stood before them, I noticed a person standing to my far left. His clothes were mismatched purple plaid shirt, yellow checkered pants, red socks, and tattered blue shoes. He was almost translucent.

"Elaine," came a soft loving voice from the throne, the voice seemed to penetrate my very soul, two voices but heard as one. "Elaine, go stand behind that person."

I did as the voice asked me, once behind him the voice told me to step into the person.

"Step into the person, like just step into him?"

I knew what the voice was saying I guess even in my dream I was needing confirmation of the direction. It didn't make sense to me, but then again, I was before the throne of God, who was I to question His direction?

I hesitated for a second then stepped into the translucent person not knowing what was going to happen.

I stood very still after I stepped into whoever that person was. I slowly began to look at myself, and realized I was now wearing the unmatched clothing, down to the red socks and tattered blue shoes.

"Elaine," the voice returned, "when you received Jesus as your Saviour you also received the gift of the Holy Spirit. He is Jesus living in you. The Holy Spirit is not in step with the world, He is who He has always been, comforter, guide, advocate to name a few. You have stepped into the Holy Spirit and are now out of step with the world. You have taken on a different life. The Holy Spirit does not conform to you; you conform to Him. Take the necessary step to walk out of the worlds definition of living and follow our heart," and the dream ended. The voice didn't say 'follow our hearts,' it was heart, and to my understanding God was saying the Trinity were one, together, one heart.

At first, I thought it was just a dream until I remembered the message and details. Wow I was before the throne of God, presented as it was for my human understanding. I remember thinking "now I get it, well almost get it, I get the concept of the three persons in one God, I get the beauty of having a Triune God. I also understand that in receiving Jesus as my Saviour He lives in me as the Holy Spirit, the third person in the Trinity, the God of action, teaching and guiding us, a continuation of Christ's forever light, forever presence after His death and resurrection.

The Healing Light, the book mom gave to me, became a learning tool that taught me more about the Trinity and, healing touch of God.

As I read the book, I started to put what I was learning into practice. There was a little girl who was constantly crying even with her mother at her side. I learned through hearing the conversations that she was in kidney failure, had a high fever with much pain. I asked the Holy Spirit to guide me as I prayed for this precious child.

I began to concentrate on her, to pray for Jesus to bless her by embracing her with His Healing Light. I asked that He take away her fever, her pain and heal her kidneys. That whole day I prayed seeing this child healthy and strong. I heard they had to put her on a cooling blanket as the medications weren't working to bring her fever down. Now remember I was twenty-one at the time and I had much growing to do in the Lord, and what Jesus did was a large steppingstone in my faith walk. Now I knew many people were praying for this child, I had mom put her on many prayer chains, we aren't the healers, Jesus is, and I'm sure the voices of praise and worship reached His heart as we rejoiced in the knowledge that this little girl went home two days later, healthy and whole. How wonderful is our Saviour? So Wonderful!

I was learning how to pray, how to seek the wisdom of the Holy Spirit, how to put others first before myself, how to cope when the answer to my prayer was No!

I prayed for those around me, the elderly man who had fallen down a flight of stairs and was in a coma; another man who went into cardiac arrest, and the woman in her forties who accidently swallowed a chicken bone, ripping her esophagus, all were prayed for, all died. I wasn't in charge of who lived and who died, Jesus was, my part was to lift them up in prayer. I also prayed for the nurses and doctors as they cared for and fought to save lives.

There were many prayers said, some were answered with a resounding Yes, others, sadly No!

I had also kept my prayers and focus on my baby as I prayed for others.

If I had one comment about the book, The Healing Light, it would be how it taught me to pray focusing on God's healing light, and the power of the Holy Spirit. I don't accept everything I read as the reality, I pray on the guidance of the Holy Spirit for wisdom and insight, something I hope you will do as you read this book.

Having been in the ICU for seven days it came as a surprise to me when my prayer was answered when my heart's rhythm returned to normal.

As for my baby, the bleeding had stopped and I believed that this was a sign of God's intervention on holding my baby in His tender care.

I soon found myself transferred to another floor, which was exciting as I could now walk to the bathroom in my semi-private room. I could now have visitors, especially Dave at regular visiting hours. My biggest fear was to be alone at night, I found myself wishing, praying for a roommate.

I became more anxious after visiting hours, after everyone left due to the sheer fact that if something happened I had now no monitors connected to me, monitors that would sound the alarm if anything was wrong. Although the monitors were a deep fear in the beginning, they were now my life line; but now, alone in a room, the absence of the monitors frightened me. Help would not come at the sound of a beep. I had nothing to keep my mind off my fear, no television that could softly lull me to sleep. The only sound was that of the wall unit that hummed its constant air flow in keeping me comfortable.

After the night nurse brought me my pills and said goodnight, she left, and I was alone.

I have always fought fear, whether real or imagined, fear has been my constant companion; something I would need to overcome as I grew in trusting God.

It is an emotion that I would much rather do without, I needed to be brave, run into it's roar instead of cowering under its emotional presence.

Fear is a good thing, it alarms us to danger, pain, threat and so much more. Fear can be a normal reaction, but it can also become a phobia, like in the fear of spiders, heights, and your own imagination.

When I was around twelve years of age my parents were going out to a party, and my sixteen-year-old brother Rick was left in charge. Before mom left, she had asked me to hang up some clothes to dry on the basement clothesline. After my parents left, I stood up to go downstairs, but my brother said I could do that later enticing me with a television movie and popcorn. My sister MaryAnn was with us and thought Rick had a great idea, so we all sat on the couch and began to watch the movie. Now, the movie was not exactly entertaining, definitely not a movie for a twelve-year-old with a great imagination. It was about three strange men breaking into a house and threatening a family if they didn't get what they wanted. The details fail me however, there was much shooting, and killing. Bodies everywhere covered with blankets. I was so frightened, and the thought of going downstairs to hang clothes scared me to the point of not doing it.

As the dreaded movie continued, we heard a noise at the side door as if someone was trying to get in.

"Someone is trying to break into our house," Rick said but instead of checking the situation ran into his room and returned with a very large BB Gun.

"We need to call mom and dad so they can come home," I said.

"Why? I'm here with my gun, I can protect us," Rick said with a sly smile.

MaryAnn was deeply upset and wanted to call mom and dad too, but Rick insisted we would be fine.

My brother Rick had a mean streak at times, especially in scaring others, as an adult he's now the complete opposite, and we are not just siblings, but good friends with a common denominator, Jesus.

Rick told us to sit down and watch the show, we did as he asked mostly because we were afraid of him.

Another noise, another twisting of the knob, we were being threatened, so Rick grabbed his gun and ran to the side door, opened it and ran outside to face the culprit.

We heard fighting and his gun being shot, MaryAnn ran to the phone and called the number Mom had left in case they were needed.

MaryAnn and I were terrified. Was Rick killed? Would we be next?

We were too frightened to go check, in fact my legs could only move in the direction of my bedroom, and MaryAnn and I took refuge in our closet.

I can't remember how long we stayed in the closet, fearing for my brother's life, shaking, crying, but needing to be as quiet as possible. I could just see the closet door opening and a man with a gun shooting us dead.

Finally, after what seemed like an eternity MaryAnn, and I screamed as the closet door was forcibly opened. Our eyes were shut tight; I mean who wanted to see the gun that would kill you.

"What is going on here?" dad's voice strong yet calm.

"Daddy?" MaryAnn and I asked in unison. "Is Rick, okay?"

"Yes, Rick is fine. I hear you have had a scare, come out of the closet."

Mom was just behind dad, and we were guided to the couch and told to sit down. Our legs were still shaking.

"Rick, why would you scare your sisters like this? Mom asked. If there was any time for mom to yell, now was the time. Mom was soft spoken, even when she was upset, and I for one wanted to hear her yell at my brother. Nope, not even when her daughters were in danger of being shot dead, well, almost shot dead, well not really, but in MaryAnn's and my mind we were going to be shot dead.

"We all wanted to watch the movie mom," Rick lied, "and when we heard someone trying to break in, I needed to protect them."

"With this BB gun?" dad asked.

"Probably not a smart idea," Rick answered.

Mom then told us we should go to bed and the conversation would continue the next day, As I stood up mom asked me if I had hung the clothes up.

"No mom, I was afraid to go downstairs."

I thought my mom was angry with me, but she was more upset about what went on, taking my hand she led me to the stairs telling me she would help me.

I didn't want to go downstairs, the big coal furnace always looked like a monster ready to pounce on an unsuspecting victim. I hated that thing, especially at night.

Going down to the basement I flipped every light switch I could find. As we hung the wet clothes on the clothesline that reached from one end of the room to the other, mom asked me questions as to what happened. As I told her she started to laugh but soon her laughter turned into a sigh.

"I think your brother had it all planned, his friend Ray who was outside waiting to join in, they pretended to get into a fight with the movie being the background to make it all seem real. When Rick brought his BB Gun from his room, it made for the perfect prank to scare you and MaryAnn. Dad is giving them a talking to right now."

As we hung up the clothes, I looked in the direction of the menacing monster that pretended to heat the house. My eyes calmly rested on something that was too horrible for me to speak. I tried to call mom, but my attempt was muffled at best. Again, I tried to call mom, but only a fearful noise escaped.

Mom looked at me as I stood frozen in place, she didn't know what was happening, but she told me my face was as white as the sheet she was hanging. I couldn't move, so she grabbed my hand and pulled me out of the room and up the stairs. She didn't dare look back, my face said it all. Something horrible was behind me.

Calling for my dad as we climbed the stairs, he met us at the top with my brother and his friend.

"What's wrong Bea?"

Dad looked at me not waiting for my mother to answer, but before he could grab me Rick shook my shoulders telling me to calm down, "Elaine, stop, you're going crazy."

Dad grabbed me from Rick's hold and quickly brought me into the front room, holding me tightly he sat at my side on the couch.

"What happened Bea?

"I don't know Joe, I heard Elaine make a scary noise, and when I looked at her, she was as white as a sheet, and not able to move. I grabbed her hand running with her up the stairs. I didn't dare look behind her, the fear on her face told me everything I needed to know. Run!"

Once I began to calm down dad asked me what I saw. With my whole family and Rick's friend all staring at me, I cried out my answer.

"I saw a dead person laying on the floor by the furnace with a blanket on him."

Rick and Ray jumped up followed by my dad to investigate. When they returned dad said there was no one there.

"Maybe the movie spooked you Elaine," Rick said.

"Spooked her Rick, your prank more than spooked her," mom said sharply, and there it was, mom yelling in a much stronger angrier voice, I knew she could do it.

"Mom, she's hallucinating, look at her, there is no one there. Right dad?"

My dad had to agree but the look he gave Rick and Ray was a look that meant we will discuss this later. At least my brother had the decency to hang his head.

"I'm not going crazy, I saw a dead person under a blanket," I said with body shaking and tears streaming down my face. Mary Ann came to my side hugging me.

Mom got up and took my hand saying MaryAnn and I needed to get to bed. Since we were already in our pajamas we sat on our beds, and mom asked MaryAnn, to stay by my side while she went to get something.

While mom was doing this dad, Rick and Ray went to search the entire house, inside and outside.

Mom returned to my side and gave me a little pill to take saying it would help me calm down, and it did. Of course I would not advise any parent to do that, it could have undesirable reactions.

Dad came into our bedroom telling mom they looked everywhere but couldn't find anything, except for my Uncle Wilfred, who lived in the kitchen side of the large basement.

"So, I am going crazy," I said.

"No Elaine, you're not. I have an idea, Joe, come downstairs with me, I think we need to speak to a certain someone."

Mom and dad returned to my bedroom about twenty minutes later, with smiles on their faces.

"We know what happened. What you saw was not a dead man, or a ghost. It was your Uncle Wilfred."

Uncle Wilfred was an alcoholic, we all knew his drinking was his attempt to forget June 6th, 1944, D-Day when his troop landed by crafts on Juno Beach. Today his condition would have been diagnosed as Post Traumatic Stress Disorder. Uncle Wilfred was never the same after WWII.

He was staying with us for a little while. He could never stay in one place for very long. He was a short order cook and traveled to many different restaurant jobs. It seems Uncle Wilfred was the first intruder to enter the house. Rick, knowing it wasn't part of the prank went for his gun to protect us. The second intruder was his friend Ray who was part of the prank.

When Uncle Wilfred clumsily opened the door with his key, he quickly (as quickly as a drunk person is able) slipped downstairs to his bed. Finding it to warm he decided to go into the furnace room and lay on the floor in front of it.

That's where the sighting of the dead body comes in. Seeing the body under the blanket I reacted as did mom. Uncle Wilfred said there was too much commotion and after we left, he went quietly back to his bed on the other side. The reason no body could be found after the sighting.

"So, you see Elaine, it wasn't a dead body, it was Uncle Wilfred trying to find a cool place to sleep. It was all very innocent, except for the prank your brother and Ray had planned out."

That prank grew my fear, and it has been difficult to overcome, as much as I pray to be released from fear, I know release comes when I need it most, Jesus alone is my deliverer.

So, there I was alone in my hospital room, afraid to be by myself, not connected to any monitor, fearful of what could happen, yet the answer to my fear was given to me through all that I had learned in the Intensive Care Unit.

God is and will always be faithful, it is up to Him how my prayers were answered, yes, or no. God knows our hearts; He knows our inner souls. Jesus was and is my safe harbour, my saving grace and protector. I had been through a life changing blessing of wisdom and insight. I was still quite young in my faith walk, but all my experiences that were behind me, and in front of me will continue to grow me into the person I was meant to be in Christ. It's a good thing that we do not learn spiritual wisdom all at once, because that would overwhelm us, and possibly turn us away from the truth. Life in following God would become a heavy burden, too strenuous to cope with. Each experience brings us closer to knowing God more, whether good, or bad, there are lessons that only life can teach us in the wisdom of the Holy Spirit.

I had a restless night, it was too quiet, too empty, yet I took all that I had learned and put it into practice. I was not alone, God was with me, in the noise, in the quiet, in my soul. As I rested in the tender care of His presence, I finally fell asleep, and woke up to a sunny, warm new day.

I was surprised when I was discharged that very day, the doctor's felt I was healthy as was my unborn baby, there was no reason to keep me from going home.

Dave, still on the afternoon shift couldn't stay home from work so he made arrangements for my sister to stay with me, which she often did.

I rested as the doctor had suggested I do, but MaryAnn and I played card games, watched television, ordered take out, enjoying each other's company.

It was around seven in the evening when in the bathroom I had a cramp and gush of blood. I called for my sister, and she led me to my bed instead of the couch.

"What do you want to do Elaine?"

"I think we just need to wait as it might have been just a one-time thing."

It wasn't as the cramping continued and the bleeding increased. I was in labour, although only three months along the pain was very uncomfortable.

I asked MaryAnn to call Dave at work before she called an ambulance. While in the ambulance MaryAnn had a long conversation with the attendant, no it wasn't about me, it was about everything else when they realized they both went to the same high school.

There I was, suffering on the stretcher possibly losing my baby, and there they were talking and laughing as if I wasn't in distress.

I became upset about that, how could they possibly forget about what I was going through, acting as if everything was normal. How dare they make light of the emergency I was in.

I became my own therapist, acknowledging my own selfish thoughts.

What did I want them to do? Were they supposed to be attending to my every want and need? Were they supposed to be kneeling at my side praying through the whole journey?

No, they were doing what was normal, trying to keep my attention off what was happening while listening to their conversation; although I was not listening and couldn't for the life of me say what they were talking about. I was lost in my own self pity. I had just returned home after being in the ICU for a week, now having been discharged that day I was in an ambulance rushing back to the hospital.

Dave had made it to the hospital before we did and was at my side the moment the wheeled stretcher touched the pavement.

At that moment I started shaking, and as I was brought to a cubicle in the emergency room, a nurse was placing a warmed blanket over me.

When I was finally examined by the emergency doctor, I asked him if I was losing my baby.

"Mrs. Vizard I am going to admit you, I don't believe you have lost your baby and I am ordering that you stay on bed rest. However, this is your first pregnancy, and it is actually common to miscarry. You win some, you lose some," and with those last words spoken, cold and unfeeling, I was brought to a four-bed unit where I stayed three weeks as my baby fought to live.

Why was this happening? Why did God allow all this to attack me?

While I lay on my back, using the bed pan for both bodily functions, I felt sorry for my nurses as they cared for me. Bed pans were awful, I always worried I would either fill the pan or soil the bed. As a nurse I knew that part of the job was not pleasant, I had asked to have bathroom privileges but that was denied.

In the room with me were three other women, each with their own medical problems.

One had a hysterectomy, another had bladder surgery, and another who had gone through surgery for cancer.

When visiting hours were over the four of us would talk into the night. One conversation began with a question from the woman suffering with cancer.

"What is the most disgusting and funny thing that ever happened to you?"

Each had their stories, but I won the title of the most disgusting and funniest story.

"When I was a student nurse, I was caring for a woman on bed rest. Like me she had to use the bed pan for everything. I now know what that feels like, and how embarrassing it can be. There is a bed pan cleaner called a hopper. I don't know why it was called hopper, but it did live up to its name. As I took the bed pan from this lady, which was filled with both urine and poop, I covered it with a towel and took it to the room where the hopper lived, called the dirty utility room. The hopper is opened by touching a lever at the bottom with your foot, much like a garbage can, only the hopper opened from the front. Once opened you place the bed pan in the compartment made just for it, and close it, then you flush it away where it is cleaned and sanitized. There were many complaints about this hopper. There were three in the room the others were in use, so I had no choice but to use the not so dependent one. Well, as I flushed it the hopper decided to fail and the door that held everything in flew open spreading all its content over the room and on me. The ladies were in fits of laughter as they pictured the devastating onslaught of poop and urine. I remember standing there in shock, I had poop in my hair, a poop splattered uniform and shoes, I was a proper poopy mess. Another nurse came rushing in when she heard my scream, she told me to stay where I was, then left to get housekeeping. In the halls I could hear laughter, and then the door to the hopper room opened and shut as more staff witnessed my unfortunate happening.

The head nurse opened the door but kept her distance, trying hard to mask her huge smile that threatened to turn into a laugh.

"Elaine, you need to get home to take a shower and possibly throw your uniform in the garbage. Do you have a car?"

"No, I take the bus." That laugh that she fought to keep from escaping, escaped, and I didn't find that humorous at all.

It was a Friday, and my dad and boyfriend, now my husband Dave were working, they couldn't pick me up and no one offered to bring me home, I guess the smell and thought of getting poop in their car held them back from offering.

There were no extra uniforms to put on. I guess I could have showered at the hospital, but I had no clothes to put on after, just a sheet. I decided to go home, I could walk, but then the poop would bake in the sun. After some of the nurses helped me to make myself more decent, I left the hospital, stepped into a bus and swallowed my pride. There were yellowish-brown stains all over my clothes, and shoes. I was thankful the bus was almost empty as it was the middle of the day. I had made the decision to bring a sheet with me and laid it on the seat before I sat. The bus driver was polite and did not say anything about the stench that emanated from me. I thanked God I didn't have to transfer to another bus, and soon found my stop and walked the rest of the way home.

I had called my mom from the hospital and was relieved she didn't laugh. I told her not to come near me but to place a garbage bag at the back door where I would take it downstairs, strip throwing shoes, clothes, cap everything I wore in the garbage bag. I then ran up the two flights of stairs naked and right into the shower, as I washed my hair, I thought it would have been more sterile if I were wearing a wig and could throw it in the garbage too. I scrubbed my body and hair multiple times until all the hot water turned to cold. I then stepped out of the shower and sanitized the tub. I was thankful that all this happened on a Friday and had the weekend to recover, and it took two days for everyone to come close to me, even my boyfriend. I don't think I smelled of poop but just the thought of it kept people at arms length. Dave loved my long hair, but that weekend he couldn't bring himself to run his fingers through it.

When it came to laughing my mother, the traitor who told the story to everyone, laughed loudest and longest. My boyfriend Dave didn't dare smile in front of me, until I too found the humour in my poopy experience.

When I returned to the hospital I was met with many smiles, at least they had the decency not to laugh out loud.

The head nurse met me leading me to the room of horror to show me the naughty hopper had been replaced with a shiny new one.

"You had quite an experience and we thought for your bravery we would exempt you from emptying bedpans for the week." That was good news indeed, she also placed a custom button that she had made on the weekend in my hand, saying 'Shit Happens.' It was rather crass but truthful, and I was told not to wear it, just keep it and look at it on the poopy kind of days you will have. I thanked her with a smile on my lips and went to work.

My hospital roommates laughed until they coughed. Some of the nurses came to make sure we were okay, and we were, the laughing was good for the soul and the lungs.

One at a time my roommates left only to be replaced with another patient. Those three weeks brought laughter, tears, and much prayer, for everyone.

As the third week of my stay ended, I again began to have pain, and while laying on the bedpan I miscarried. I remember the look on the nurse's face as she took the bedpan with my baby's remains in it.

I was told a week later at my doctor's appointment that the baby didn't form properly causing the miscarriage.

Losing our baby was difficult, but I knew I would meet him one day when I was called to my eternal home. I look forward to meeting this beautiful soul I fought so hard to keep. At the same time, I felt relief that this long ordeal was over. I was assured I would have other healthy pregnancies, and I did. Having a miscarriage brings about many different emotions, especially the feeling of losing a child; whether in the first trimester or later, the fact remains your baby died along with all your hopes and dreams for this precious gift. At that time there were no therapists to help you through this transition. No suggestions on how to grieve this deep loss. Today there is much help, in fact years later after having my second miscarriage it was suggested I name both babies, and I did. Corey and Frances, names that could be masculine or feminine. I so look forward to meeting them one day when God calls me home.

God knows who He created, He knows everything about our lives, and the questions that swirl around us like gender, transgender and all the differences that make us; us. We are all created in His likeness, and although we struggle to understand all the differences of who we are, one thing is sure, God calls us to love each other. He lives in us, and there is no room for prejudice of any kind. Love others as He loves us, it is not our place to judge, our place is to love, and as long as you do that you are counted as a blessing to all you love and meet.

The lesson I learned through this chapter was to leave the healing to God. I didn't have to take on my mother's heart problem, Jesus paid that price through His death and Resurrection. I could pray but not ask Jesus to give me the illness in return for healing my mom. I learned that the devil is truly a roaring lion always looking to devour someone. My willingness to take on my mother's heart condition was an open invitation for the devil to pounce on me and make it happen. I have never, ever said a prayer like that again, and I tell everyone the lesson I learned through it. We have a Lord and Saviour who paid the price, He can heal and keep us protected at the same time. So, sometimes healings and miracles come in the form of learning, and with that lesson taught, God can and often does swoop in as our Hero. Let Him carry your burdens, fears and hopes, but also remember that we are also called to pick up our cross and carry it, trusting God through it all. Mom had bouts of irregular heart beats all her life, until she died at the age of eighty-seven of cancer. What was so amazing mom never complained about pain, we had prayed He would keep her from that form of suffering, He did as do she, until the last two days before her death.

I have grown in my walk of trusting God; He will always be there in the calling of His name. I am comforted like a small child knowing the trust I place in Him is forever steadfast. He is the rock on which I stand, He is the healer and miracle giver, and I trust in His will whatever may come, He is Jesus!

Uncle Wilfred

A year before I decided
to pay the price for mom's heart ailment.

Scared in Intensive Care

Scared out of Intensive Care
and on my own, without
the assurance of monitors,
they were my lifeline, or so
I thought, but Jesus was
so much more.

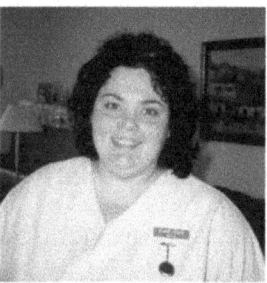
Actively Working as a Nurse

Life after a miscarraige
and blessed with 4
more children.

Chapter Nineteen
Choices Made

Have you ever prayed for your adult child to make the right choices in their life? Have you interfered with their choices pointing out their mistakes? I believe every parent does, some more than others. As their parent we know the pain that comes from living with the wrong choices, why? Because that is how we learned.

My parents, Joe and Bea trusted me, they had no reason to interfere with my adult choices, in fact if they needed to say something it was always through loving suggestions, and advice, but never forced on me. I imagined my parents prayed a great deal for all their children and grandchildren.

A parent's job is to first love, second to respect, and third to allow your child to live their life without ridicule or condemnation. It is certain we will make mistakes, as our parents did before us, and theirs before them.

One of my big mistakes was in blurting out the word stupid when my child did something they shouldn't have. I wasn't calling my child stupid, but it always came out wrong when I tried to say what they did was stupid. I know there were many other ways to convey how I felt about their actions, but no, that word stupid flew out of my mouth before I could shut it. I always apologized, but I couldn't remove my word from their mind and heart. We change our children with our words and actions, and although I can do and say so many positive things, the fact remains that the negative is remembered more.

In James 3: 9-10 the Bible states,

"9) With the tongue we bless our Lord and Father, and with it we curse men, who have been made in God's likeness.

10) Out of the same mouth come blessing and cursing. My friends, this should not be!"

An example of this was when I was in grade eight, at age thirteen. My friend Frances and I decided to walk home together after school. We decided to make a detour to go through the new houses that were being built.

I knew my dad would not be happy about this detour as the men working on the houses were young and charming. We were curious and although our conscious told us something different, we decided its warning was not loud enough.

As we went through one of the houses two men approached us, I immediately regretted my decision.

One of the men came up behind me, turned me around and pinned me to the wall, telling me in English how beautiful I was.

I heard Frances's yell to the man to leave me alone, but he only laughed and started to touch my breast. I yelled at him to stop that and pushed him away as hard as I could. He stumbled backward and laughed loudly yelling as I ran away, saying in broken English, "Ahh, little girl, isn't this what you wanted, why you came here," as I ran away from him and out of the house.

Frances came from an Italian family and spoke Italian and English. I being of Italian and French background only spoke English.

As we ran from the houses on to the main road to our homes Frances told me to yell, vorrei che fossi morto e anche la tua famiglia!

I didn't understand what I would be yelling but I yelled it at the top of my lungs, and the men's laughter flowed loudly from the houses.

Frances laughed at my attempt in speaking Italian.

"What did I just yell, Frances?"

"You said, "I wish you were dead, and your family too."

I was horrified, I would never say something like that to anyone. Frances quickly comforted me by saying they were just words and not to worry about it.

"Was that like a curse?" I asked with a very shaky voice.

"Yes, but not a real curse."

I wondered what a real curse consisted of, as that sentence felt like a curse to me. I wished I had asked her what I would be saying before I said it.

We soon arrived at our homes and my mom walked up to me and placed her hand gently to my face. "Did anything happen on the way home Elaine? Your face is red and warm, and you are later then usual?"

I couldn't help it, I started crying, and as my mom held me, I told her what happened. It wasn't the men that bothered me most, it was the words I had yelled.

Of course, I received the lecture I knew mom would give, but what she said next surprised me.

"Elaine, don't tell your dad what happened, I will tell him tonight when he gets home."

I was happy about that as my dad can be very loud when upset and would probably rush out to those houses to do some damage to the man who dared touch his daughter.

That night my dad arrived home after I had gone to bed. I heard them talking, and I am sure my mother was soothing dad's inner anger. My mom was a soft-spoken woman, my dad, not so much, in fact he lived up to the definition of an Italian man, loud and passionate, or so they say. I still don't know who they are.

The next morning as I ate my breakfast dad came to the table. I hung my head down knowing I would not escape his worry and disappointment of my actions. Dad said exactly what I thought he would say and the words, dangerous, foolish, disobedient, careless and the typical never do that again. As for the curse, which was what you said, always check before you say something you don't understand, okay? "Yes daddy." and went to get ready for school.

That went well I thought, my dad didn't yell at me and that was saying something, I never worried that he would spank or hurt me, his loud yelling was the thing I expected, and he didn't disappoint, as goes the saying, 'his bark was worse than his bite,' not that he ever bit me.

When I arrived at school Frances wasn't there, I was told she was home sick. Walking home I heard my name being called, "Elaine, Elaine wait for me."

I stopped waiting for Francese's sister to catch up to me.

"How is Frances feeling Anna?"

"She's not sick, but very upset with the news."

"Did your family get bad news?" I asked.

"Well we didn't know them well, only from church, don't get upset Elaine but Frances told me about what happened yesterday, and what she told you to yell."

"Who didn't you know well?" I asked Anna.

"The family that died in the car accident last night."

My stomach lurched, my head became fuzzy, I fell to the ground with my arms holding my body tightly; somehow I knew what Anna was going to tell me. I sat like a stone statue, not daring to move, yet wanting to run away. I needed to know about that family that died in the car accident. As I struggled with the courage to ask Anna, I whispered my question.

"What? Elaine, I can't hear you," and she came to sit beside me.

I whispered the question again, only slightly louder.

"Anna, the family that died, were the men from the houses we went into part of that family?"

She nodded yes, and I felt like I had killed them. I murdered them with my words. I cursed them with death, and they died. I killed a family.

I stood up and started to run home as fast as I could. Like a moving text banner the words scrolled in my mind over and over again. 'Family Killer,'

Mom always watched for us to return home, and that day was no different. Through tears and hysteria I told her that I killed that family. Of course, mom told me that what I thought wasn't true. "You didn't know what you were saying Elaine, their accident wasn't your fault."

Her words did not soothe me, nor did my dad's when he came home. No words could make me feel less guilty and stressed. I should have asked Frances what I was saying before I said it.

That incident stayed with me for a very long time, I dreamt about it, thought about it, it was a nightmare that wouldn't go away. It wasn't until I reached adulthood growing in my faith that I felt relief from the constant nightmare. I reached out to God and was released from that venomous burden. I asked the Lord to forgive me, and left it at His feet. I knew I was forgiven, and when He called me to enter into His Kingdom I hoped I would meet this family and ask their forgiveness.

As adults we grow in understanding, our experiences bring us blessings if we search for and learn by them. Everyone lives with their own choices, wrong or right, and the greatest gift of our experiences is in how, if we let them help us to become the person God created us to be; or, we could let them destroy us.

My son Sean, our oldest seemed lost in his life. He had no real goals, he never settled into a job that could satisfy him. Each job found little contentment, and I prayed and prayed that God would lead him in the direction that would make him happy.

During this restless time in his life he had girlfriends, and Sean was always searching for what would complete him.

When Sean was a child he readily acknowledged Jesus as his Saviour; but as he grew he put Jesus on a shelf with all his other childish beliefs. I knew what Sean was seeking, even if he didn't, he needed the Lord in his life. It is in God's presence where we become more aware of not being content. Sean was restless in his life, still is in many ways. I am sure Sean has low self esteem, and his teen years did not help that situation as he was often bullied. Some people can rise above their feelings of negativity, but Sean couldn't seem to pull himself out of the hole he and others had dug for him to fall in to, especially anxiety.

My heart ached for my son, I wanted so much to hold him, and whisper into his soul that the one thing he was denying, the one thing he had come to know, that one thing he no longer seemed to believe in, Jesus, and that Jesus could help him. I am not fond of every answer to every problem is Jesus, because we have to do our own work to help improve ourselves, but Jesus can help us see where we need growth, healing and recovery through the wisdom and insight of the Holy Spirit.

Jesus is the one who can soothe our souls, our bodies, our minds. He can bring wisdom and insight into our lives, and I have seen Jesus deliver people from the earthly things that hold us hostage. It all comes down to choice. You can lead a child into knowing Jesus, but you can't choose for them, as accepting Jesus as their Saviour must come from the soul, it doesn't have to make sense, it just is, it is a matter of stepping into faith.

For some it is easier to believe that aliens have the power, than to believe Jesus was born of a Virgin, was the Son of God, the Saviour to all who call on His name, and the Creator who loves us most. That knowledge cannot come without having a personal relationship with Jesus, and not everyone finds Him in a church of cement and brick. Many of us find Him on our knees in our houses, in nature, through trials and tribulations, through calling out to Him in desperation.

As a Christian mother I had prayed for my son from the first day I knew of his existence in my womb, growing under and in my heart. My deepest prayer was in hoping he would follow the path that God had laid out for him, but that would happen in Sean's timing and choice, it is not my decision to make, it is his and his alone.

What do you do when your adult child chooses to date and love a woman you know your child will be unhappy with.

Well, you don't confront them, you never tell them you disagree, you love both of them, accepting them, until things happen and you can't be silent any more, and always with calmness, love and respect.

I can't remember where Sean met Kris, but they quickly became a couple. Now my son is an intelligent man, a good, loyal man, a man of integrity with a soft heart. I didn't know Kris but knew the beauty of what my son saw in her would eventually reveal itself to me.

Before Kris there were other girlfriends, one while he was in grade twelve in highschool. Sean became good friends, really good friends with his sister's friend. My husband and I had signed a consent paper that Sean could leave the school at lunch time to go by some food. Now the high school Sean attended was a fair distance from any fast food place, so Sean could only leave school if he drove my car on my day off from work.

I had complete trust in Sean until I received a phone call from the school.

"Mrs. Vizard, this is Ms.Connely from your son Sean's school."

"Yes, is he okay?"

"Oh yes, I probably should have led with that so you wouldn't worry, but we do have a situation."

"A situation? What kind of situation?" I asked.

Her answer seemed to catch in her throat, and I thought oh my this is not going to be good.

Mrs. Connely finally cleared her throat and nervously told me the situation.

I realized why Mrs. Connely was nervous, there was much publicity about our one daughter and her rare heart condition. In fact most people in our community knew us from all the publicity, having our faces, stories printed in newspapers.

"I know you gave Sean consent to leave the school at lunch time, and he has many times. However a certain young lady does the same, and they have been meeting in the parking lot and leaving together. The problem is Mrs. Vizard, they do not return for afternoon classes."

I was shocked at this news and asked who the young lady was, actually I said the girls name so she wouldn't have to give out that information.

I could almost see Mrs. Connely nodding her head when she answered, yes. "How do you know her name?"

"She is a friend of Mary's and Sean has been mentioning her name quite a bit. I just put one and one together."

"Well Sean is going to have two weeks of detentions, and the Vice Principal asked me to call you to give you this information."

I felt bad for Mrs. Connely as this should have been the Vice Principal's job.

"Mrs. Connely please inform the Vice Principal that I will take care of Sean's punishment. I want him to suspend Sean for two weeks, take away that consent form of allowing him to leave school and, to send Sean's school work home with his sister and or brother."

I know she thought the punishment was a little harsh, but Sean being the oldest and example to his brother's and sisters, this needed to be something the kids would not forget, especially Sean.

I then called my husband at work, and informed him of what was happening and how I handled it. Dave thought it was a good plan, especially when I told him I was going to get Sean to clean all the walls of our house. He is going to make this house shine, as in the movie Annie, "like the top of the Chrysler building"...my son was going to have a "hard knock life" for two weeks.

Now it was time to call this girls home, where I knew they would be, and I was sure the meaning of the song

'Afternoon Delight,' was being played every time they were together.

Sean was not brought up this way, and his actions were definitely going to have a reaction.

The phone rang and Sally answered, and as soon as she heard my voice she handed the phone to Sean.

"Sean, I know what you have been doing and you are to come home immediately. You have been suspended from school for two weeks, and you will not enjoy it."

On thing I have to say about Sean was that he was never defiant, never disrespectful in a mean way, he was disrespectful in not following our rules, and stood his ground even though he knew he was wrong.

I can't remember if I yelled at him, but I know I drove the message into his very soul.

I have to say Sean took his punishment with grace and respect. However, my son showed me a different side of him, and I didn't like it. My heart sank each time Sean would describe himself as the 'black sheep of the family,' he was not, nor ever would be. God chose him to be our first child, I don't believe Sean understood what that meant. Yes with the first comes growing pains for the parents, and with a small or large family the oldest has much more responsibility than his younger siblings.

Sean was nineteen when he met Kris, it was a time in his life he needed someone to boost his self esteem and Kris seemed to do that for him.

I liked Kris, but knew she wasn't right for Sean. Kris was very naive, simple really in the way she looked at life. She was the kind of girl who would not stop at anything to get what she wanted, and what she wanted was my son.

I knew if I spoke to Sean about it, it would just push him more toward her.

Sean's behaviour was so beyond how he was brought up. He insisted on Kris being in his bedroom with the door shut, and that was against house rules. We found him on the couch with a blanket over both of them, while his siblings were close by. Every time I saw his bedroom door shut with Kris in it I opened it always to his surprise and loud protests in declaring he was an adult. If so he wasn't acting like one.

As time went on I decided I needed reinforcements in asking God to help out. Kris tempted Sean at every opportunity, and being of the same age she too felt she was above parental rules .Yes Sean was old enough to live on his own, but while living at home there were rules to follow.

I truly believed Kris was not the person for a long term relationship with Sean. "Please Lord, Sean will never leave her, he is loyal and for them to split Kris will have to break up with him."

So, I began praying and fasting, and asking my friends, my prayer warriors to pray also. They readily told me they were in, and most of them added fasting to their prayers.

It looked as if we were losing ground when Sean asked Kris to marry him and put that diamond ring on her finger.

All I could do, all anyone could do was to continue to fast and pray. I so desperately wanted to say something but held my tongue. Our other children didn't like her, probably for the fact that she didn't encourage Sean to follow the house rules. Sean was intelligent, and needed someone who would challenge him, Kris was not capable in doing this. Not wanting to seem harsh, I just feel you should know that we were also praying for Kris, and that God would bless her, just not with my son.

Everything came to a head on New Years Eve, when we had a little house party. When midnidght arrived we all circled and prayed the New Year in, then resumed to playing our games.

Sean and his brother Joe left the room to help get more snacks, leaving Kris with the rest of the family. This is when it happened, Kris watched the boys leave and without thinking, (or was she thinking this all along,) when they were out of reach she said, "Joe is really cute, in fact if I wasn't engaged to your son Sean, I would totally go for him, I really have a crush on Joe."

What! Was she kidding? No she wasn't, and the rest of those within hearing distance gave a little gasp at her words.

What to do? Do we tell Sean that Kris had a crush on Joe? The next day while Sean left to go to Kris' family's New Year celebration, our family opened up, they couldn't believe what Kris had said. Joe was now in the know of Kris' crush on him.

This was getting out of control, but I asked Sean's siblings to keep this to themselves, and to pray

"Mom, aren't you going to tell Sean?" asked Mary.

"No, I am not sure he will believe it, he will probably say she was joking. No, God is in control and He will answer our prayers." But to make sure I decided to fast and pray even more. I also called in the heavy prayer warriors, our parish priests and nuns.

I can't remember if Kris and Sean had been in the planning of their wedding, but one afternoon Sean came up to me crying.

"Sean, what's wrong?"

"Kris broke up with me, and gave me my ring back."

I held my son as he cried, telling him how sorry I was, but that was a lie, it took every part of my being to not jump up and down yelling Praise the Lord, Thank you Jesus!

We all gave Sean our sympathy but behind his back we would smile with a thumbs up.

God answered our prayers, making what seemed impossible possible. There was nothing to hold Sean in keeping Kris in his life. I eventually told him what Kris said on that New Years Eve night, he didn't answer to that, but I prayed he had realized he had dodged a lifetime of heartache.

Sean eventually started dating a young woman from his past, his sixteen year old sweetheart. They had broken up to live their lives which eventually brought them back together, and they married and have two children. Their life experiences grew them to commit to each other. To this date Sean continues to struggle with the knowledge of God in his life. I need to say one thing, Sean wasn't so strong in his disbelief until he went to University, studying psychology, in fact I believe his university education grew the gap between him and God farther apart.

I see Kris breaking up with Sean as a miracle, and now I wait for the Holy Spirit to reveal the truth of who Jesus is to Sean. I believe he will have a greater sense of who he is, and the importance and self awareness of the special person God created in him. I pray Sean becomes strong in his self esteem, calm in his soul, and hopes in a life of self worth. This is a choice he has to make for himself. I just want him to know that God loves him for who he is, not for the grandeur he hoped to be. We all need to follow the reality of who we are, accept the strength of our capabilities, whatever who that is or will be. Don't expect more or less of who you were meant to be, settle in the peaceful knowledge of who you are and let the Holy Spirit guide you in your growth. Always remember whoever and wherever you are in your life, God loves you just the way you are. Allow that knowledge to flow over you with the serenity and beauty of who you are. You are a miracle, own that, remember that, you are a miracle.

To God Be The Glory

Am I Christian or Catholic? or Both

As of the chapter before this, I thought I was finished this book and celebrated the thought that this book which was years in the making, was now ready to publish. However, when I was in prayer God put it on my heart to write this now last chapter. I hope. In my thoughts I needed to be finished this one to begin writing my next, 'A Fragrance So Rare.' I am on God's time, not mine, and as this is His book, He has the last say. Thus, this chapter.

I always thought it was a done deal, my religion being Catholic meant being a Christian. Some people don't see it that way. If I say I am Catholic some people back away as if the devil himself burned them. What is the problem? Is it the Catholic history that bothers them? Or is it the Pedophile Priests and the way the church dealt with it for so long? I understand how that would destroy some peoples views on the Catholic Church, it upsets me, but we must move on, and remember that this happens in every religion, every church. I am not trying to minimize the horror because the reality is the Catholic church has many things to own up to, many sins they have swept under the rug and need to be dealt with.

As of this writing the implications centered around the federal government of Canada and the Catholic church along with other Christian churches have come under fire due to the finding of many large graves on the grounds of residential schools; finding many skeletons of children some as young a three.

To make it simple, if that can be done, the government started and funded these schools one hundred and twenty years ago, making it their responsibility to assimilate the Indian, Indigenous population to their way of living.

The Catholic church was asked to run these schools not just for education of the mind, but also their health and spiritual growth. Actually, the government was telling this population that they needed to be changed for the better, but the main goal was to boost the nations progress.

In recent decades, the human costs of the Indian residential school system have come to light, even if they are not yet fully understood. While many former students and staff have spoken positively of their experiences at specific schools, many others tell of more painful experiences. Here the children were forbidden their Aboriginal languages and cultural practices as well as being emotionally, physically and in some cases sexually abused. This is an ongoing investigation, and a time to heal the deep wounds along with understanding and respecting our differences, if only all people could understand this.

I am better than you has long been a factor of violence, growing more intolerance and injustice in most countries. Healing begins when we push aside the indignities that kill the very nature of our existence. That needs to be changed, but that means people, all people need to realize the creator of all life lives in each and everyone of us; we are one in navigating life.

In some small way I learned this as a child, the, we are better than you mind set.

We use to live next door to a family where the father actually hated Catholics, in fact he wouldn't allow his children to come near us. I remember being very confused and frightened as he would yell if he found his children playing with us, telling them to get away from "those heathens."

I remember crying, not understanding why he hated us. Mom would explain that some people just didn't like other people who believed different from them, not that this man and his family went to church, or had a religion. Mom would just tell us to pray for him, because he didn't understand, and was taught differently. "Always be good Elaine, don't say anything to hurt him as God loves him as much as he loves us; be kind."

My siblings and I went to a Catholic school, and our neighbour's children went to a Public school. The dad didn't realize that when he went to work in the morning we all walked together as our schools were just a block apart. I was always afraid he would see us together walking to our schools. As children we didn't see our differences, we only saw friends.

Eventually he came around, I think my mom influenced him as she respected his choices, and never defended her faith, nor did she argue with him. Mom walked her walk and talked her talk by her actions. She was a bridge in which many people crossed over to seek the God she worshiped. Actually mom was just doing what Jesus said in the Bible,

Mark 9:39 "... for whoever is not against us is for us."

also in John 10:16 "... I have other sheep that are not of this sheep pen..."

you probably should read the whole chapters, but what Jesus is saying is that there are many different Christian Faiths who believe in the same Saviour. There is not one church that is perfect, we all have a history and fall short of how we follow Him, most important is that you know Him so as not to be fooled by those who pull you away from the truth, and many have been fooled joining cults which led to abuse, sexual assaults, and so much more. These leaders were not Christlike, they did not follow the truths and led many to their deaths. Jonestown comes to my mind. Google it, this is just one example. Although the Catholic Religion teaches us about Jesus, it is a personal decision to accept Him as your personal Saviour. Catholics are led to the Saviour, but cannot make anyone believe in Him. That is personal and needs to be respected whatever they choose in their faith walk.

I remember as a little girl going to church and never understanding the mass as it was always said in Latin and the Priest always had his back to the congregation. One day that all changed, and to my knowledge it was during Lent in 1964 when the Mass was now said in English with the Priest facing the congregation. It went from boring to not so boring in my little girl mind. When and why did it change?

It is my understanding that Pope John XXIII announced the creation of the Second Vatican Council (also known as Vatican II) in 1959 and it, as described by some, "shocked the world." This was an Ecumenical Council consisting of Roman Catholic religious leaders who assembled to settle doctrinal issues. This was the biggest change in one hundred years. Since the mid eighteen hundreds the Pope was believed to be infallible, meaning he didn't make mistakes, now Pope John XXIII (23) changed that and assembled a Council for the purpose of helping to pray on making decisions for the Church. Some thought it should stay the way it was, others felt the wind of the Holy Spirit refreshing the Church. I think one of the better things to come out of this much later, was when the air of secrecy was lifted and Priests and other members of the Church were brought to attention and charged for their crimes of sexual assaults;

of course the Church was thrust into this decision by those who had been victimized.

I have known many priests and they were and are of the purest heart. The one thing I know is that the Church is alive and living in a better light, walking the walk, talking the talk, it isn't perfect, but no church is. Our present day Pope Francis in my opinion is bringing a new light of understanding to the Church.

At age eleven I made the personal choice to choose Jesus as my Saviour, and I have sought Him out every day since. My walk has strengthened, grown, and has become the power source of my life. Jesus isn't a genie in a bottle, He doesn't give us what we want or at least not all the time, but He will always give us what we need, spiritually and physically according to His will.

As a child I made my First Communion. I was taught about the breaking of bread at the Last Supper, and what Jesus did for me. Being able to receive Communion (Holy Eucharist) was a very important part of my life, because as a Catholic I believe when I receive the little round wafer, what is know as the Host, that Jesus lives within the Eucharist, other churches believe it represents Jesus. To me it is both.

The Host had its birth a little over a hundred years ago created by Sister Mary Agnes of the Benedictine community. She was asked to make an altar bread and created the host; and to this day that small thin wafer has represented Jesus and continues to do so.

Not to be disrespectful but I remember my first time receiving the Eucharistic Host on my First Communion Day. This special day was celebrated with my whole second grade classroom. We were prepared and told we couldn't touch the host, or chew it. When we reached the Priest we were to stick out our tongue and let the Priest put it there, and then make the sign of the cross and go back to our seats. I was not told that the host would cause a problem when it met the roof of my mouth. There it was stuck like glue. Would wiggling it with my tongue be considered touching it? It was an awkward feeling, I had to loosen it, get it back on my tongue. But how? I decided my tongue used as a tool would not be considered touching it. So I wiggled it, tried to get my tongue under it all to no avail. My jaw became tired and sore so I did what I had to do, I put my finger in my mouth and pulled at it until it became loose, then I respectfully laid it back on my tongue and chewed it softly. I didn't want to hurt

Jesus, and I didn't want to get caught, but I was going to go to hell, because I touched and chewed Jesus, that I was sure of.

It took a couple of days before I told my mom and dad I would not be joining them in Heaven. "I'm going to hell." Mom and dad laughed and told me they too had the same problem when they were young but, "Jesus was not hurt because you chewed the host". What a relief! Wait! Was my mom and dad going to hell?

As I grew older I felt very strongly that receiving Communion should be a decision most children should make when older. If my thoughts were of going to hell at chewing the Host, then I was missing the point. Some children are young and ready to receive Communion. My one granddaughter Nadia desired it to the point of asking the priest if she could make her first communion; she made it at age eight, and we celebrated as a family.

There is so much to be said about my Catholic religion, most importantly that it isn't an occult, it isn't a pagan ritual, it is the celebration of Jesus. I don't understand how people can believe that catholics are not christians. Some pastors and ministers speak openly against the catholic church, causing much damage to their congregation, in my opinion they are teaching hatred, I am sure Jesus isn't a fan of that.

I have throughout my life visited many different Christian Churches, and one day I hope to go to a Jewish Synagogue service. God is our denominator, the pillar of many faiths, and I know miracles and healings are not just a catholic happening. We have a supernatural God, a Saviour who walked this earth, fully human, fully God.

Miracles and healings happen every day, a simple prayer answered, a request to find an object you lost is found, a bad case of the hiccups disappears after a quick plea to God to make them stop; and they do. And like at the beginning of this book, a pair of socks ordered but delayed or lost are delivered the day you asked God to somehow find and deliver them, so you can gift them to your grandson that day on his birthday.

What is important to you, with good intent, is important to God. He listens when you pray, which is just a conversation with your creator, and Saviour.

Sometimes the most major of prayers are unanswered, and the simplest of prayers are. God knows, His plan isn't ours, He sees the whole picture, we see glimpses of what could be. Anger at unanswered prayer is often a useless pile of blocks interfering with His will. Learning to trust Him in every answered or unanswered prayer brings about understanding. Whatever the answer accept it, and trust in His will for your life and the life of those you love.

If a person you are praying for is not healed and dies, remember that death is not a punsihment, it is a glorious renewal of life. Death is not the end, it is the beginning, and sometimes death is the answered prayer, the ultimate healing, the forever miracle.

We were born to die, to be united for eternity in our heavenly, beautiful intended home with God. For me Jesus is the highway on which to travel toward the right way to live, the right way to die, the right way of reaching eternal life.

I know that many will find this hard to understand, I think one of the greatest prayers we can pray is to ask God to help you believe through your unbelief. He will if your heart is truly open and sincere.

Don't test God and give up if He didn't answer your prayer, remember He alone knows your true self, your true heart, your true reasoning.

Life is filled with many roads and detours, and often we forget to ask God to help us navigate them.

In my life I choose to respect the beliefs of others, I choose to love and not condemn something I don't understand, I pray on it. Also it is not a church that makes you a Christian, being a Christian is a choice. You can sit in a church, kneel and pray in a church, receive communion, drink the wine, tell everyone you're a Christian, but if you aren't sincere in your walk, then you aren't a Christian. Being a Christian is walking the walk, talking the talk in truth with a heart that is faithful, a heart that grows, a heart that hears the teachings of Jesus through the Holy Spirit, and follows them. Reading the Bible helps you in that walk as does having prayer time, being in the presence of God, being sincere and honest with yourself. Being a Christian is doing what's right, and allowing your righteousness to flow fully from your heart. You can be a member of any church that follows Christ but that doesn't make you a Christian, your choice to accept Him as your Saviour, your choice to live and walk with Jesus, be the example of Him on this earth, that makes you a Christian, along with the choice to constantly grow and delight in His presence, being a example to others.

God is good, and if you happen to get the host stuck to the roof of your mouth, it's now okay to chew it. Jesus isn't hurt, and when you get to Heaven one day when He calls you Home, He will not be showing you teeth marks. Just saying!

Epilogue

Miracles and healings are a daily occurence. Not all miracles and healings are followed by fireworks, some are as soft and gentle as a rose petal made of the softest velvet.

I pray this book helps you to see God's love for you, for all. He has no favourites, He loves each and everyone of us the same. He longs for you to know Him, to seek Him and feel His Loving Touch in whatever your life's situation is.

There are other miracles and healings to tell, especially in the life of my daughter Mary. Her's is a story of life and death, pain and suffering, with many moments of happiness and sorrow. It is titled A FRAGRANCE SO RARE, that book is in progress.

As my mother Beatrice Frenette Balestrini was a deep part of this book I want to leave you with this.

Mom couldn't write a poem if her life depended on it; but when in prayer the Lord would bless her with one or two. This is one of the little poems mom received from God while in prayer.

May you walk with one another
As I walk My child with you
May you touch their hearts my child
And love them as I love you.
Oh, walk with me all through your life
And bring others with you too
That I might love them all
My child, as I love you.

Thank you so very much for reading this book I pray it blesses you as it has blessed my mother and I in writing it. May His love bless your lives as He touches your spirits, and may you find miracles within your day to day living; they are all around us.

To God Be The Glory

www.ingramcontent.com/pod-product-compliance
Lightning Source LLC
Chambersburg PA
CBHW070524090426
42735CB00013B/2859